INVENTING THE MOVIES

Hollywood's Epic Battle Between
Innovation and the Status Quo,
from Thomas Edison to Steve Jobs

BY SCOTT KIRSNER

First Edition
© 2008 Scott Kirsner / CinemaTech Books

Cover design by Lisa Foulger. Images: Edison's Kinetoscope, upgraded with audio (courtesy of the U.S. Department of the Interior); Gone with the Wind, in triumphant Technicolor (used with permission from Corbis); Apple chief executive Steve Jobs brandishing a new video iPod (used with permission from Reuters).

Printed and bound in the United States of America

10 9 8 7 6 5 4 3 2 1

Contents

Introduction

Whenever you buy a ticket to see a movie on a Saturday night, the secret technological history of Hollywood is included free with the purchase price.

When you walk the downward-sloping aisle to pick out a good seat, you're doing something that Thomas Edison was convinced would never happen; although Edison was among the first to capture motion on film, he was sure it'd be more profitable to charge individual viewers to watch movies at personal viewing stations, rather than projecting images on a screen for a large audience.

The movie has sound because the Warner brothers, despite several failed attempts to improve the silent film experience by adding a soundtrack, tried one more time, and happened to hire an ebullient vaudeville performer named Al Jolson to star in one of their first talkies. Unless you're a classic film buff, the movie you're seeing is likely in color, and that wouldn't be the case were it not for a chance meeting at the Saratoga Race Track between Herb Kalmus, the founder of Technicolor, and Jock Whitney, a wealthy playboy who wanted to make movies. That encounter kept Technicolor from running out of money, and led to the making of *Gone With the Wind*, the 1939 blockbuster that finally convinced Hollywood to switch over to color.

Even if you decide to stay in on Saturday night and watch a movie, that's a choice that's linked to Hollywood's hidden technological history, too. Walt Disney and William Boyd (who played Hopalong Cassidy, the righteous cowboy) were among the first people in Hollywood to understand that television might actually represent a new business opportunity, rather than just a threat to ticket sales. Recorded movies on tape and DVD exist thanks to the patronage of Bing Crosby, who paid a team of engineers in the 1950s to develop the first prototype video recorder.

[2]   INVENTING THE MOVIES

The story of how new technologies enabled Hollywood to become America's dominant culture factory, and remain in that role for more than a century, hasn't been told before. It's a story that's relevant not only to avid movie-goers and industry insiders, but to businesspeople, artists, and inventors working in any field who are interested in the relationship between innovation and the status quo. How does innovation ever prevail when just about everyone working in a given field would prefer that things remain the same?

Innovators rarely win on the merits of their idea alone, or on personal charisma – despite the wonderful fables recounted endlessly in business magazines and books. New ideas always encounter stiff headwinds. Some succeed, while others flicker and fade.

Hollywood is one of the best examples of an established industry (and the movies an established art form) that, like every established industry, relies on innovation for its survival, but resists innovation at every turn. That makes it an ideal place to explore the obstacles that innovators face, and the persistence, luck, and cleverness required to vault past them. It also offers insight into the mindset of those who fervently defend the status quo.

How did I stumble down this particular rabbit hole? After writing a few magazine articles about cinema and technology, and briefly working as a newspaper movie critic, in 2005 I was lucky enough to be invited to a gathering that the director George Lucas was organizing at his secluded Skywalker Ranch, in the emerald hills of Marin County. It was a one-day conference to explore the latest wave of technologies that were changing the way movies are made and experienced.

As I drove through the gates to Lucas' 4,700-acre homestead on a brilliantly sunny Saturday in late April, I wasn't sure who else would be there, but I'd been told that for the first conference Lucas had organized, two years earlier, Steven Spielberg, Martin Scorcese, and Francis Ford Coppola had all made the trip. I was nervous, and I had no idea about the dress code ("Auteur casual"?)

This time around, the cast of characters sipping iced tea in the library of the ranch's Victorian-style main house included Ed Catmull and John Lasseter, two of the founders of the pioneering computer animation company Pixar; Robert Zemeckis, the director who'd overseen the "Back to the Future" trilogy and won an Oscar for *Forrest Gump*; Robert Rodriguez, the fiercely independent director, cameraman, composer, and editor from Texas who'd totally abandoned film cameras for digital cameras with movies like *Sin City* and *Once Upon a Time in Mexico*; and James Cameron, director of the top-earning movie of all time, *Titanic*.

Standing toward the back of the library, seemingly rooted in place, was Lucas himself, wearing jeans and one of his trademark plaid shirts, sleeves rolled up to the forearms.

Like everyone else in the room, Lucas was a die-hard innovator. In the three-and-a-half decades since his making first feature film, *THX 1138*, he'd poured his energy and resources into developing new technologies to solve the creative problems he encountered, and allow him to put images on the screen that hadn't been seen before. Lucas had guided (and personally bankrolled) research-and-development projects to advance special effects, sound and picture editing, and cinematography; at almost every speech he gave, or every lunch meeting with a studio head, he harangued the rest of Hollywood to follow along.

Some of Lucas' efforts had been successful – Industrial Light & Magic, his special effects firm, had grown into Hollywood's leader in computer-generated visuals, with more than 1000 employees, a shelf-full of Oscars, and over $1 billion in estimated annual revenues – but others had left him feeling frustrated with the pace of change, like his push to persuade theaters to switch over to digital projection. He was a pioneer who'd learned through hard experience what it takes to make new ideas truly permeate an industry. And most of the other people at the conference came with similar war stories.

After lunch, the filmmakers and technologists walked over to a nearby building, and filed into the Stag Theatre, a sleek, Art Deco-style screening room. Like students hoping to avoid being called on by the teacher, the attendees occupied the back eight rows of seats, and left the rows in front empty. Lucas ambled to the front of the auditorium, and kicked things off by observing that Hollywood was still cool to the concepts of digital movie-making and digital projection. "The last time we had this gathering, I said that the next time, this theatre will be full of people who've accepted digital," Lucas said. Gesturing to the empty rows, he continued dryly, "As you can see, digital has been accepted wildly."

The afternoon was filled with show-and-tell presentations. Lucas talked about replacing hand-drawn storyboards, used for planning an action sequence, with digitally-crafted animations called "pre-viz," which offered a better sense of space, speed, and movement. Zemeckis and Cameron made the case that digital 3-D projection could help cinemas compete with the latest wave of high-tech, high-definition entertainment equipment that consumers were installing in their homes. Lasseter, who'd once worked for Lucas, showed a stunningly-clear digital clip from *The Incredibles* on the big screen, and compared it with a scratched-up film print that had just come back from a suburban multiplex. Rodriguez talked about blending live-action footage with virtual sets, built by expert programmers rather than master carpenters, in *Sin City*. "I don't think I'll ever shoot on a real set again," he said. With virtual sets, he continued, "You can get it to look the way it looks in your mind."

All of the A-list directors who had converged at the ranch shared the same restless energy: like cinematic innovators stretching back to Thomas Edison and the Lumière brothers, they were eager to experiment with new tools and technologies that could stretch the bounds of what was possible on the screen, and deepen the immersive experience of entering a movie theater. But they needed others to buy into their vision and support them. One theme that kept surfacing was how difficult it could be to persuade others in their industry – whether equipment suppliers, studios, financiers, or cinema-owners – that a given innovation was worth the risk and investment it inevitably required.

"We all have bloody foreheads from beating our heads against the wall," Lucas said. "You've got to be patient. Keep beating your head against the wall, and eventually it will fall over."

Lucas was expressing the frustration that innovators feel in any industry when they try to introduce a new idea. Instead of being thrown a ticker-tape parade, they're often met with hostility or indifference. Sometimes, the status quo defeats the innovative concept, or at least delays its introduction.

In the course of my later conversations with Lucas, Cameron, Rodriguez, Catmull, and other Hollywood innovators (and in my interviews with people trying to make change in other industries), it became increasingly clear that successful innovators spend a lot of their time honing their ideas and products – but they spend even more time chiseling away at resistance. Yet most coverage of Hollywood and the wider business world succumbs to the "better mousetrap" mythology: if you invent something that makes someone's job easier, or creates new opportunities, they'll welcome it.

But the savviest innovators acknowledge that not everyone loves change. In their minds, the world can be divided into three groups:

- Innovators

- Preservationists, and

- Sideline-sitters.

Innovators and preservationists couldn't see the world more differently.

Innovators view change and new technologies as an opportunity. Preservationists view change as a threat. Innovators are willing to take risks that could lead them in new directions, creating new artistic possibilities, new businesses, or new revenue streams. Preservationists want to protect the way they do things today, the traditions they've grown up with, the skills they've learned, and the businesses they've already built. (For more on innovators and preservationists, see Appendices A and B.)

Between the innovators and the preservationists are the sideline-sitters: they aren't interested in having to learn something new or change the way they work right now (even though they know they may have to eventually), and they don't have the time to experiment with a new technology. They aren't active nay-sayers; they're simply content to wait to see how things pan out.

(In the movie industry, of course, the term "preservationist" also can refer to someone who works to make sure that important films are preserved for future generations; I'm using it here in a different way, to refer to individuals who seek to preserve the status quo.)

These three groups – innovators, preservationists, and sideline-sitters – exist in every business, and every art form. All change is the story of how innovators combine new ideas and new tools to create something spectacular and compelling, overcoming the resistance (whether active or passive) of the other two groups. In the end, the preservationists and sideline-sitters are often forced to acknowledge that those annoying, persistent innovators haven't destroyed the art form or damaged the business, but rather taken it someplace new, strengthened the bond with the audience (or the customers), and expanded the opportunities for turning a profit.

The weekend gathering at Skywalker Ranch – Lucas dubbed it simply the "Digital Conference" – was an invitation-only conclave of innovators. But in Hollywood, as in all other industries, the innovators are out-numbered. I encountered plenty of preservationists and sideline-sitters while researching this book, and writing articles for two of Hollywood's venerable trade papers, *Variety* and *The Hollywood Reporter*. Even in 2006 and 2007, they still weren't sold on the merits of shooting movies with digital cameras, distributing them to theaters via satellite instead of in battered metal canisters, or selling them directly to consumers over the Internet.

If I'd been working a hundred years earlier, I might've spoken to Edison about his opposition to the idea of projecting movies on screens; written about how Louis B. Mayer, the imperious head of MGM, stubbornly refused to attend a talkie; or interviewed Bette Davis about her reluctance to star in a Technicolor movie.

Although it may have a slightly higher glam factor than, say, the insurance business, Hollywood is a perfect case study for the way that any big, successful, well-established industry responds to new ideas. Over more than a hundred years of technological progress, as cinema has changed as an art form and matured as a business, there have been constant battles between the forces of innovation and the forces of preservation.

This book is a chronicle of those battles, and how innovations ultimately helped the industry survive and maintain its powerful connection with audiences. But it's also a parable for innovators, whether they are free agents, employees of small start-ups, or part of a big organization.

By traveling from the days when silent films were accompanied by the noisy whirr of a projector and the plink-plink-plink of a live pianist, to the era of the $100 million computer-generated spectacle made by Lucas, Cameron, or Pixar, projected digitally and accompanied by booming surround sound, we'll develop a better understanding of the brilliance, tenacity, and luck required of innovators – and the unpredictable obstacles they must overcome.

So, as the red velvet curtains part to reveal a blank silver screen, this is the story of Hollywood's battles between innovation and the status quo.

1: Inventing the Movies

T he first people who ever paid money to watch a movie were Manhattanites who just happened to be strolling down Broadway on a Saturday afternoon.

The entertainment industry in 1894 was dominated by live performances. That year, the 1,100-seat Herald Square Theatre opened to the public with a production of "Arms and the Man" by George Bernard Shaw, which turned into the playwright's first major hit. The author Mark Twain spent several months in New York, giving lectures and readings. Ethel Barrymore made her first stage appearance, in a play called "The Rivals."

If anyone had tried to estimate the market potential for a new form of entertainment — visually-recorded performances which, unlike the live shows they competed with, were shown in black-and-white and had no sound — it would have been a zero-billion-dollar industry for the foreseeable future.

But two entrepreneurial siblings, George and Andrew Holland, were convinced that New Yorkers simply didn't know yet that it was their destiny to be cinephiles. The Holland brothers had rented a former shoe store at 1155 Broadway, just a few blocks south of where the Empire State Building now stands, and turned it into the world's first Kinetoscope Parlor. On the weekend of April 14, 1894, pedestrians lingered in front of the storefront in curious clots; no one had the slightest idea what a Kinetoscope was. The Holland brothers hadn't planned to open for business until Monday, but the early interest convinced them to unlock the doors two days early.

Greeting patrons at the entrance was a plaster bust of Thomas Edison, the Kinetoscope's inventor, painted to look like it had been cast out of bronze, and perched atop a Greek column to give the place an air of class. Edison was already famous as the inventor of the incandescent light bulb and the phonograph, and for the past six years, he and his team of engineers in Menlo Park, New Jersey had been working on technology to capture reality on film and then play it back.

Inside, customers encountered two rows of chest-high wooden cabinets: Kinetoscopes. Leaning against a brass rail that ran in front of the Kinetoscopes, a customer would look through a peephole at the top of the cabinet. Inside was a continuous loop of 35-millimeter film, threaded around a series of spools like a cat's cradle. The viewer looked into the Kinetoscope through a magnifying glass, literally examining individual frames of the film, lit from behind by one of Edison's miraculous light bulbs. A revolving shutter allowed each frame to be illuminated only briefly, the staccato flashes of light ensuring that one frame would seem to be replaced by the next, creating the illusion of motion. After each twenty-second long movie had finished, the machine stopped automatically, and the customer proceeded to the next Kinetoscope. Customers paid 25 cents to gain entry, which entitled them to watch all ten movies.

The novelty of life and motion stored inside a box and triggered on command – the startling realism of those flickery, black-and-white scenes – was what drew in customers, not the films being exhibited. Among the movies shown at the Holland brothers' Kinetoscope Parlor were the aptly-titled "Roosters," "Trapeze," "Wrestling," and "Barber Shop." A few of the films on display featured celebrities of the day: the strongman Eugene Sandow, a German who was touted by Florenz Ziegfeld as "the modern Hercules," and a contortionist known as Madame Bertholdi.

By the close of the first day of business, nearly five hundred people had watched Edison's movies, and the Holland brothers had raked in $120. By May 1894, a second Kinetoscope parlor opened on State Street in Chicago, and in June, a third popped up in San Francisco. "Kinetoscope parlors were now the rage, and opened up across the country as fast as the Edison Manufacturing Company...could supply machines," wrote film historian David Robinson. Before the year was out, London had its first Kinetoscope parlor, too.

Edison's Kinetoscope films were shot in a large wooden shed in West Orange, New Jersey. Vaudeville performers and dancers made the journey across the Hudson River, as did Buffalo Bill Cody and the sharpshooter Annie Oakley. The camera filmed cockfights, and a dentist named Dr. Colton extracting a tooth.

Another set of siblings who'd visited the Holland brothers' Kinetoscope parlor, Otway and Grey Latham, were inspired by the technology. They imagined that they could attract an even bigger audience if, instead of capturing barbers and dentists at work, they used the Kinetoscope to show boxing matches. (At the time, boxing was illegal in most states, including New York.) So the Lathams founded the Kinetoscope Exhibition Company with a friend of theirs from the University of West Virginia. The trio persuaded the Edison Company to make some small changes to the original Kinetoscope, building a new model that could hold films as long as 150 feet, and slowing down the speed at which the film ran, so that the machines could show longer films. Their plan was to stage a boxing match between two prizefighters, with six rounds lasting a minute each.

When the Lathams' Kinetoscope films were put on display in August 1894, in a new Kinetoscope parlor in lower Manhattan, customers paid 10 cents to watch each round. (Some customers, short on cash or just impatient, skipped straight to the final round, and that film wore out most often.) Boxing on film was an instant phenomenon; the crowds spilled out onto the sidewalk. A later fight, between "Gentleman Jim" Corbett, the world heavyweight champion, and Peter Courtney, earned Gentleman Jim a royalty totaling more than $20,000.

After their success with the boxing movies, the Lathams became convinced that the next logical step for their business was to be able to show motion pictures to a group of viewers simultaneously. The Lathams set up a new company, called Lambda, to develop the technology they'd need.

But Edison wasn't interested. Incremental changes to the thing he'd already invented weren't a problem, but designing a projector would require a bigger financial commitment. It would upend his burgeoning business of selling Kinetoscopes to penny arcades. And Edison didn't think that the market for projectors would be anywhere near as large as the market for his high-tech wooden Kinetoscopes.

"We are making these peep show machines and selling a lot of them at a good profit," Edison said. "If we put out a screen machine there will be a use for maybe about ten of them in the whole United States. With that many screen machines, you could show the pictures to everyone in the country – and then it would be done. Let's not kill the goose that lays the golden egg."

At the time, Edison was not just an inventor, but also a manufacturer, selling Kinetoscopes, and a studio head, producing movies for them. Like the studio chiefs who'd succeed him decades later, Edison seemed to be hoping that technological progress would hold off, so it didn't pinch his profits. And he was assuming that no new technology could ever vault past the existing technology's revenue-generating abilities. (Sometimes, innovators can behave like preservationists.)

Unfortunately for Edison, progress didn't pause. One of his former employees went to work for the Lathams, and on the side, one of Edison's chief technical lieutenants, who'd received some stock in Lambda, offered them important advice. (The cranky and self-aggrandizing Edison wasn't very good at sharing credit for "his" inventions with the rest of the Menlo Park team, which didn't help employee retention or loyalty.) There was no way to be certain that people would prefer a communal movie experience, with a bigger screen, to the Kinetoscope's private viewing experience – or to be sure that the goal was even feasible. The Lathams simply believed that it was, and started slogging toward it.

On April 21, 1895, almost exactly a year after the first Kinetoscope Parlor had opened, the Lathams demonstrated their new projector for the first time to the press. By May, they'd opened a storefront theater on Lower Broadway to show an eight-minute boxing film. (They'd also petitioned the governor of New York to film an execution at Sing Sing, but were turned down.) The image on the screen was dim and fuzzy. *Photographic Times* wrote, "There is considerable room for improvement and many drawbacks have yet to be overcome," before adding, "Quite a crowd of people visit the store ... making their exit wondering how it's done." A headline that summer in a Chicago newspaper tweaked the Wizard of Menlo Park: "Edison Not In It! Kenetoscope (sic) Outclassed by Prof. Latham's Newest."

In France, August and Louis Lumière had seen Edison's Kinetoscope, and they also decided to develop a way to project images on a screen. Before the year was out, they'd held their first public demonstration, in the basement of Le Grand Café in Paris, charging one franc for admission. The movies shown included slice-of-life snippets like *Men and Women Employees Leaving the Lumière Factory* and *The Sprinkler Sprinkled*. Within a week, police were called in to control the crowds forming outside the café.

Edison eventually realized that preserving the dominance of the Kinetoscope wasn't viable, and as the sales of Kinetoscopes began to slow, his company licensed a technology for film projection that had been developed by two inventors, Thomas Armat and C. Francis Jenkins, who'd met while studying at the cutting-edge Bliss School of Electricity in Washington, D.C.

In April 1896, their projector, now re-branded as "Edison's Vitascope," was demonstrated at Koster and Bial's Music Hall in Herald Square, and trumpeted as "Edison's Latest Marvel." (Koster and Bial's was eventually replaced by a retail establishment founded by R.H. Macy.) Armat personally ran the projectors for that first show. There were clips of dance routines that had been hand-tinted with color, and a film called *Rough Sea at Dover*. The New York *Times* wrote, "The waves tumbled in furiously and the foam of the breakers flew high in the air. So enthusiastic was the appreciation of the crowd long before this extraordinary exhibition was finished that vociferous cheering was heard." Through a smart licensing deal with Armat and Jenkins, Edison had managed to play technological catch-up.

The brothers Lumière brought their projector to New York in June 1896, and other projectors followed. Before long, vaudeville shows, circuses, amusement parks and magic lantern shows all began featuring moving pictures as a novelty. The Lumières provided a "complete package" to touring vaudeville outfits, including films, a projector, and a technician to oversee everything. At the Paris Exhibition of 1900, they set up a screen 80 feet high and 100 feet wide – larger than the biggest IMAX screen that would be in use a century later.

In Pittsburgh, the first nickelodeon – a small room in the back of a penny arcade – opened in 1905, showing movies continuously for a five-cent admission fee. Patrons could stay as long as they liked. Within two years,

> **1902: The 200-seat Electric Theater, considered the first venue in the U.S. specifically built for the purpose of showing films, opens in Los Angeles. Admission is a dime.**
>
> **But the novelty wears off quickly, and after just six months the proprietor converts the space into a vaudeville theater.**

the proprietor had opened up fifteen others. By 1914, the number of nickelodeons exploded, to about 14,000. Singers entertained the audience while the reels were being changed. In the projection booth, an employee cranked the projector by hand; it was a dangerous job, since the nitrate film stock was highly flammable, and if it was exposed to too much heat from the projector bulb, it would ignite.

"In cosmopolitan city districts the foreigners attend in larger proportion than the English-speakers," observed Joseph Medill Patterson, a writer for the *Saturday Evening Post*. "This is doubtless because the foreigners, shut out as they are by their alien tongues from much of the life about them, can yet perfectly understand the pantomime of the moving pictures."

That fact didn't escape a group of scrappy entrepreneurs, many of whom were recent immigrants themselves. William Fox, born in Hungary, began his career in the movies at age 25, buying a Brooklyn nickelodeon that was on the verge of closing. His business would eventually grow into 20th Century Fox. Among the others who got their start in the nickelodeon era were Carl Laemmle (founder of the Independent Motion Picture Company, which evolved into Universal Pictures), Marcus Loew (founder of Metro-Goldwyn-Mayer), Louis B. Mayer (MGM), Adolph Zukor (Famous Players, which later became Paramount Pictures), and the Warner brothers.

But almost from the very start, this cadre of entrepreneurs ran into roadblocks – especially if they wanted to be more creative in selecting the movies shown at their theaters, or even make their own product. By 1909, Edison and Armat, along with Biograph and Vitagraph, two other pioneers of the industry, formed the Motion Picture Patents Company to pool their patents on cameras and projectors, collect royalty payments, and "standardize" the industry. Producers would make a fixed number of movies, and release them on certain days of the week. The Trust, as the MPPC became known, made a deal with the Eastman Kodak Company so that Kodak wouldn't supply raw film to any producer not in league with the Trust. The Trust also bought up most of the companies that rented movies to theater owners in the U.S., which enabled the Trust to set prices and force theaters to take a specified package of films each week, whether the movies were any good or not.

The Trust didn't totally squelch outside activity; theater owners like Fox, Laemmle, and Zukor ignored the Trust's demands, making their own movies using cameras and film obtained on the black market, and creating underground distribution operations to supply their movies to theaters. They began making longer movies, adopted more sophisticated editing techniques, and built up the reputations of sexy stars like Theda Bara. ("The Vamp," as Bara was known, was especially popular for her skimpy costumes.)

While the Trust fixed the salary that could be paid to a talented director, the independents, as they came to be known, could dangle better pay. One of the most prolific directors churning out movies for Biograph (a member of the Trust) was a stage actor from Kentucky named D.W. Griffith. Over a four-year period, he made more than 400 short films for Biograph, before setting off on his own and taking his entire troupe of actors with him, in part because his employer didn't think that longer, feature-length movies were financially viable. (The actress Lillian Gish, who starred in many of Griffith's movies, added that Biograph executives "thought that a movie that long would hurt [the audience's] eyes.")

Trust members were serious businesspeople, focused on wringing the most revenue possible from the fast-growing movie industry, using technologies and filmmaking processes they'd already developed. Like all successful companies, they hoped for stability and steady growth, and that led them to presume that conditions in the market would stay the same, or change incrementally and predictably. They were skeptical that audiences would ever want to watch movies longer than about a dozen minutes; in contrast, the independents were willing to experiment, making movies that lasted twice as long, stretching over two reels of film instead of just one. Pretty quickly, they found that theaters showing them could raise their admission price from a dime to fifteen cents by marketing the longer movies as "first-class" pictures, which returned more money to the independents.

Carl Laemmle was the independent who seemed to most enjoy tweaking the Trust. He hired an unknown-but-popular actress from one of the Trust's studios, who'd been known to audiences only as "Little Mary," and promoted her as Mary Pickford, one of the first movie stars. The possibility of fan worship hadn't occurred to the established powers; they dismissed the audience's affection for individual performers as a fad that would run its course.

"The real rulers of the [Trust] were not in touch with the consumers of their product. They never had been exhibitors, nor did they make any effort to discover what the public might happen to want," wrote historian Benjamin Hampton. (In the movie industry, theater owners have long been referred to as exhibitors.)

Edison had distributed the first true blockbuster movie, *The Great Train Robbery*, a 12-minute long Western. (It ended with a scene of a bandit firing a gun straight into the camera, a shot to which Martin Scorsese would later pay homage in *Goodfellas* and *The Departed*.) But the industry's second blockbuster, *Birth of a Nation*, came from an independent, Epoch, and was directed by D.W. Griffith, the ex-Biograph employee. With a budget of $110,000, and a running time of more than three hours, it earned more than $10 million at the box office. (And there were no complaints of eye fatigue from audience members.)

Now that they were making serious money, the independents could afford attorneys to battle the Trust. William Fox led the charge, launching a lawsuit alleging that the MPPC was in violation of the Sherman Anti-Trust Act; the suit (and the Trust members' reluctance to innovate) eventually eviscerated the Trust, and it was the independents, now ensconced in Hollywood, who achieved dominance in the motion picture industry. (Hollywood, they'd discovered, had better weather, cheaper land, and lower labor costs than the Northeast.)

But just as Edison and the other Trust members had grown resistant to new ideas once their business of making movies and selling equipment and film stock was established, some of the independents would eventually follow that same pattern when cinema shook off its silence.

•   •   •

As the movies gained in popularity in the first decade of the 20th century, inventors tried many different approaches to add sound, usually by forging a Rube Goldberg link between the projector and a record player. Inadequate amplification was one problem; skipping needles were another. The Cameraphone, Photophone, Synchroscope, and Chronophone all came and went quickly.

Edison, the proud inventor of the phonograph, had been interested in talking pictures from the moment he began work on the Kinetoscope; at his Menlo Park labs, there had even been some rudimentary experiments in the late 1880s. But synchronizing the image with a soundtrack was vexing, and an upgraded version of the Kinetoscope that included a record player in its wooden cabinet didn't even attempt it; the music was merely an accompaniment, heard through tubes that a customer inserted in his ears. (This can be thought of as the great-great-grandfather of Apple's video iPod.)

In 1913, abetted by his Barnum-esque promotional skills, Edison introduced the Kinetophone. "Talking Pictures. A Fact! A Reality!" the advertisements blared. "Thos. A. Edison startles the civilized world and revolutionizes the picture business with his latest and greatest invention..." The Kinetophone relied on wax cylinders for its soundtrack, and a taut pulley that connected the phonograph to the projector. While it worked fine in carefully-controlled demonstrations, in theaters it was booed by audiences when the sound diverged from the action on screen. Film historian Scott Eyman has compared the audio quality of Kinetophone recordings to "a static-filled radio broadcast." Only 45 Kinetophones were ever sold, and *Variety* dubbed it "the sensation that failed."

Inventor Lee De Forest took a leap forward when he developed a method to record sound onto the same strip of film that held a movie's images, ensuring that the sound and picture wouldn't drift out of sync. De Forest's Phonofilm process used a device he called a "light valve" to convert the sounds captured by a microphone into varying densities of black and gray, which were printed onto the film alongside the picture. (His approach was called sound-on-film, or optical sound.) When played back on a projector, a light cell would interpret the shades of gray that were encoded on the film, and convert them back into sound.

Thirty-four theaters were converted to sound in the early 1920s using the Phonofilm system, and Calvin "Silent Cal" Coolidge became the first American president to speak in front of a movie camera. But no studio was willing to make movies using the system; the only movies ever made in Phonofilm were the shorts that De Forest and his partners produced. Their films lacked stars, and they lacked the studios' promotional abilities. The public still wasn't swayed, despite De Forest's technical advances.

Throughout the 1920s, movies were accompanied by pianists and the sound of audience members reading the words on the title cards to one another. Rival chains poached one another's best organists. In the nicer theaters, there were complete orchestras. While inventors were still striving to solve the problem of synchronization, many people had grown convinced that films were meant to stay silent. "We talk of the worth, the service, the entertaining power, the community value, the recreative force, the educational influence, the civilizing and commercial possibilities of the motion picture," wrote James Quirk, editor of the magazine *Photoplay*, in 1921. "And everyone has, singularly enough, neglected to mention its rarest and subtlest beauty: 'Silence.'"

Market research wouldn't have supported any effort to change the status quo. Exhibitors told MGM that if the studio made pictures with sound, they wouldn't book them. No one saw the audience as dissatisfied with the current product. Edison, after the failure of the Kinetophone, concluded that "Americans require a restful quiet in the motion picture theater, and for them talking from the lips of the figures on the screen destroys the illusion…"

"I wouldn't give a dime for all the possibilities of [motion pictures with sound]," declared Kodak founder George Eastman. "The public will never accept it."

2: 'Who the Hell Wants to Hear Actors Talk?'

By the mid-1920s, motion pictures, restful and quiet, had grown into a giant global business. Hollywood employed 42,000 people and produced 82 percent of the world's movies. Box office receipts totaled about $1 billion per year (adjusted for inflation.) In Manhattan, a 6,200-seat "cathedral of the motion picture," the Roxy, opened to the public in 1927, built at a cost of $10 million. Movies at the Roxy were preceded by live ballets, chorale performances, and a trio of organists that ascended from the orchestra pit, illuminated by rose-colored spotlights.

But at the same time, Americans were bringing a new technology into their homes that allowed them to listen to their favorite entertainers. The first radio station in the U.S. went on the air in 1920, and by 1923, half a million radios were being sold annually; coin-operated radios started appearing in public places, offering five minutes of listening for a nickel. Radio stations broadcast church services, political conventions, boxing matches, the musings of the cowboy humorist Will Rogers, and Nashville's Grand Ol' Opry. (Smaller stations without the money to pay performers simply played phonograph records over the air.)

The movie industry was facing its first big external threat: a new technology that, though expensive at first, could do things movies could not, and came to audiences in their homes. (Home radio sets at first cost $100 or more, but quickly dropped in price: the first mass-market model was introduced in 1923, for just $9. And the programming, of course, was free.) Radio prepped the movie industry for change in two important ways. Its development helped improve the equipment available for recording, reproducing, and amplifying sound – all advances that would be necessary to marry moving pictures with audio. And it supplied a sense of urgency.

Even staunch preservationists, when they face a serious threat from outside their industry, begin to give change some consideration. As *Photoplay* editor James Quirk observed, "The motion picture theater owners are lying awake nights worrying about the effect of radio on box office receipts."

The Warner brothers were among the few theater owners who hadn't been losing sleep. Harry, Albert, Sam, and Jack Warner were the offspring of Polish immigrants who had gotten their start in the movies, legend has it, by convincing their father to pawn a gold watch and a horse. With the money, they bought a projector and an old print of *The Great Train Robbery*, which they took on tour through Ohio and Pennsylvania. They used the profits they earned to set up a small theater in New Castle, Pennsylvania.

By 1925, the Warner brothers had bootstrapped their way to success. They'd built a studio – though not one of the top-tier Hollywood operations – and were cranking out movies like the "Rin-Tin-Tin" series, starring the noble German shepherd, and *Beau Brummel*, starring John Barrymore. (John was Ethel's younger brother, and a notorious ladies' man.). Seeing potential in the new medium of radio where others simply saw competition, the Warner brothers decided to buy the equipment of a Los Angeles radio station that had gone bankrupt, and set up a station called KFWB to help publicize their movies. (The station's call letters stood for "Four Warner Brothers," and the youngest of the brothers, Jack, made occasional appearances as a crooner on KFWB, using the stage name Leon Zuardo.)

Coincidentally, the engineer who was in charge of setting up KFWB, Benjamin Levinson, became friendly with Sam Warner, tutoring him on the electronics gear that made the station run. Levinson worked for Western Electric, an arm of AT&T, and during a visit to New York, Levinson checked in with AT&T's research group, Bell Labs, and happened to see a demonstration of a new system that synchronized sound with film.

When he returned to Los Angeles, Levinson couldn't wait to tell Sam Warner. "I'm bringing you hot news," he gushed. "I just saw in our New York Laboratories the most wonderful thing I ever looked at in my life. A moving picture that talks!"

Like everyone else in Hollywood, Sam had followed the earlier attempts at talkies, and after all the disasters, he wasn't enthusiastic. "Benny, haven't you been around the show world long enough now to know that a picture that talks is something to run away from?" he asked. Already, Louis B. Mayer, MGM's chief, and Adolph Zukor at Famous Players-Lasky (a predecessor to Paramount) had dismissed AT&T's system as "a toy" and "just a gimmick."

Levinson tried to explain that Bell Labs had developed a talkie that relied on a new generation of radio technology – like condenser microphones that allowed for higher-quality audio recording, and vacuum tubes that provided clearer amplification in the theater – and he managed to extract a promise from Sam Warner that he would see the demonstration the next time he was in New York.

Visiting New York to finalize Warner Bros.' acquisition of another studio, Vitagraph, Sam saw the demo – and was even more impressed than Levinson. But the oldest sibling, Harry, was vehemently *not* interested in talking pictures. Sam snookered Harry into seeing the demo. "I am positive if [they] had said talking pictures I would not [have] gone," Harry said later.

But the demo Harry saw, fortuitously, included a short movie of a twelve-piece orchestra playing, which sounded so good to Harry that he checked behind the screen to see whether Bell Labs had secretly stashed live musicians there. Harry became convinced that the biggest benefit of adding sound to film would be in capturing musical performances – singers, jazz bands, and symphonies – not talking actors. "Who the hell wants to hear actors talk?" he asked.

The Warner brothers decided to pour their energy, as well as some new financing they'd raised, into talkies. AT&T and its Western Electric subsidiary weren't particularly excited about going into business with the Warners. But there were no better offers. The Warners put down $100,000 in earnest money, and promised to give Western Electric eight percent of the box office revenues from all their sound releases. They dubbed the new technology Vitaphone.

The Warners began putting together their first all-sound program of shorts and a feature. The feature would be a version of *Don Juan* starring John Barrymore; though there was no spoken dialogue in it, there was an original orchestral score. That'd let them test the technology in a low-risk way, without running into the synchronization problems that had torpedoed earlier attempts at talkies.

Though some aspects of Vitaphone had improved over earlier sound systems, it still relied on records that could warp or become scratched. Anticipating problems, Warners decided it would send out an extra set of soundtrack discs with each print, in case the main set was defective. A

Vitaphone disc could only be played 24 times before it had accumulated too many scratches and pops, and had to be pulled from service. So a replacement set of discs was shipped about once a week. It was far from a streamlined system.

To get the projector and record player in sync, the projectionist would thread the film through the projector, until a frame marked "Start" was centered in the projector's gate (a mechanism for steadying the film, located just behind the lens). An arrow on the disc marked exactly where the needle should be placed in the first groove. The record player and projector were both powered by the same driveshaft, so if they were synced up at the beginning, they would run at the same speed.

Don Juan premiered on Friday, August 6, 1926, at the Warner Theater in midtown Manhattan. It was preceded by operatic interludes on film. One woman found the performances so realistic that she stood outside the stage door, waiting for the tenor Giovanni Martinelli to emerge. The New York *Times* labeled it an "amazing triumph." *Musical Courier*, a music journal, said that "with closed eyes one could easily believe that the actual orchestra was playing," though by some accounts the sound was muffled.

Don Juan ran at the Warner Theater for nine months. When the movie premiered at Grauman's Egyptian Theater in Los Angeles, the sold-out crowd of 1,780 included Charlie Chaplin, Samuel Goldwyn, Cecil B. DeMille, Buster Keaton, Fay Wray, Greta Garbo, Roscoe "Fatty" Arbuckle, and John Barrymore himself.

Jack Warner telegraphed Harry from Los Angeles: "We are spellbound – all other openings like kindergarten in comparison with tonight," adding later, "No use trying to tell you how it went over; multiply your wildest imagination by one thousand – that's it." Warner Bros. quickly made the decision to add music to all of its features from that point forward.

After everyone in the industry (including several of the Warner brothers) had determined that sound would play no part in movies, that the art form didn't need it, that the audience didn't want it, and that the technology wasn't good enough, the Warners' risk-taking was being rewarded.

The only other studio pursuing talkies was Fox. The studio's founder, William Fox, was "the most avaricious individual in the history of the motion picture industry, a man who was singularly shrewd, devious, demonically energetic, and incapable of trusting anyone but his family," according to historian Scott Eyman. Fox wasn't convinced there would be much of a market for feature-length talkies, but he did think people might prefer newsreels with sound over silent ones. (For a time before television, newsreels capturing world events were shown as part of the program before feature films, and there were also specialized theaters in big cities that showed only newsreels.)

Fox paid to license several different technologies for imprinting sound information on film – one of them from an inventor who'd earlier worked with Lee De Forest – and merged them into a system he dubbed Movietone. The advantage was that the picture and the sound would never diverge. In April 1927, Fox presented his first newsreels with sound. The following month, he had a newsreel crew on the scene when Charles Lindbergh took off for Paris, and the film, complete with the buzzing sound of the *Spirit of St. Louis*' engine, was in theaters the day after the event.

Only six months after the debut of Warner Bros.' *Don Juan*, the more established studios – including Paramount, MGM, and Universal – decided to join together to assess the Vitaphone and Movietone sound systems, and decide which one to use. "They were undoubtedly hoping that, by referring the situation to a committee…the sound fad would fade away long before they ever had to make a decision," Eyman wrote. The committee eventually decided not to decide, and ratified both systems, forcing theaters to choose one over the other, or spend more for equipment that could play both Vitaphone and Movietone. (This would be the first of many format clashes in the movie industry.)

It was difficult to discern whether talkies represented a new direction for the industry, or a fleeting trend. But demand from theater owners for the Vitaphone equipment – which cost anywhere from $16,000 to $25,000, depending on the size of the theater – was outstripping Warner Bros.' ability to satisfy it. Western Electric was training new installation engineers in just two-and-a-half weeks, and still couldn't keep up. Soundtracks helped ensure that Fox's Movietone newsreels were booked into more theaters than all of the other newsreel producers combined.

The Jazz Singer, which debuted at the Warner Theater in New York on October 4, 1927, will always be remembered as Hollywood's first talkie, although aside from Al Jolson's six musical numbers, there was only a smattering of dialogue. The movie still relied heavily on title cards flashed on the screen to explain what was happening during the silent sequences.

Showing *The Jazz Singer*, like *Don Juan* before it, was a complicated proposition – and the smallest flub could've resulted in a total wash-out for Warner Bros. Though the film was just 89 minutes long, there were fifteen reels of film and discs to change, and the projectionist had to be incredibly dextrous in cueing up each disc and threading each reel of film. Miraculously, nothing went wrong during that first show. The audience clapped at the conclusion of each musical number, and Jolson's famous line – "Wait a minute, wait a minute, you ain't heard nothin' yet" – sparked shouts and more applause from the audience.

The Jazz Singer, about a cantor's son who feels driven to sing pop songs in nightclubs rather than Jewish prayers in the synagogue, was a triumph for Warner Bros.: the reviews were glowing, and the line outside the box office never seemed to shrink. The movie cost $422,000 to make, and eventually earned $2.6 million at the box office. But in a tragic twist, Sam Warner, who'd helped persuade the other brothers to commit to Vitaphone, died of pneumonia the night before *The Jazz Singer* opened in Manhattan.

> "...[T]he panicky rush into talkies is just going to set our dear little picture business back about two years...[and] the helluva rush to beat the other fellow in getting talking pictures out is going to mean lousy pictures – no two ways about that..."
>
> – *American Cinematographer,* August 1928

In Hollywood, few people expected talkies to render silent films obsolete. (Preservationists usually hope that change will come slowly and smoothly, and that can color their judgment.)

Riding home from the Hollywood premiere of *The Jazz Singer* at the end of December 1927, MGM executive Irving Thalberg told his wife, the actress Norma Shearer, that "sound is a passing fancy. It won't last." MGM head Louis B. Mayer eventually would be shown a demonstration of talkies against his will, after several days of nagging by his lieutenants.

Universal had been enjoying a run of profitable years in the mid-1920s, with silent horror films like *The Phantom of the Opera.* Founder Carl Laemmle thought silent movies were simply too popular to fade away. Sidney Kent, the head of distribution for Famous Players-Lasky, agreed: "I believe the time will never come when the outstanding silent pictures will be out of the market. We are trying to work out the best possible combination of sound and silent." Even Fox executives said that they expected to continue releasing a mix of sound pictures and talkies. It was impossible to envision Hollywood's primary product, which audiences loved so much, becoming obsolete.

Innovators like the Warner brothers (and the Holland brothers and Latham brothers before them) tend to let intuition lead them, since there isn't yet reliable data from the market that would support moving in a new direction. Who could've proven that audiences would respond so powerfully once someone got sound technology working well enough? Preservationists and sideline sitters, in contrast, wait for others to move first, and for evidence to accumulate.

By 1928, when Warner Bros. released *The Lights of New York*, the first all-talking movie, the American public's preference for sound was becoming hard to ignore. The movie, about two barbers who are conned into serving as frontmen for gangsters, wasn't a great artistic achievement. But ticket-buyers didn't care, and the film ended up earning $1.2 million (with a budget of just $23,000). Daryl Zanuck, then a writer for Warner Bros., saw *Lights* as the movie that "turned the whole goddam tide," and Will Rogers agreed. He predicted, "In four or five years you will look back and laugh at yourself for ever having sit [*sic*] for hours and just looked at Pictures with no voice òr no sound..." (Rogers had a vested interest in the success of talkies: he'd signed on with Fox to make four talking pictures, for which he was paid the stratospheric salary of $150,000 apiece.)

> "The talking picture – how often so absurd...They drag the infernal microphone around, and there is such an infinity of difficulty and labor that the entertainment is squeezed out."
>
> – H.G. Wells, 1931

Jolson's next picture for Warner Bros., *The Singing Fool*, had more dialogue than *The Jazz Singer*, and it was an even bigger hit. *Variety* estimated that talkies had improved business at some theaters by 15 or 20 percent, pulling customers from theaters that were still playing solely silent films.

Other studios started to invest in talkies, but not without hesitation.

The director Frank Capra (who would go on to make the classic *It's a Wonderful Life*) recalled that Columbia Pictures chief Harry Cohn "was afraid of nothing, absolutely nothing. ...But sound panicked him!" Cohn asked Capra for help, and Capra, who'd earned an engineering degree, did his best to explain how the technology worked, and the shift that talkies had sparked.

In May 1928, Paramount, Loew's/MGM, and United Artists signed up to convert the theaters they owned to sound. Aside from the cost of installing a Vitaphone system, there was also a charge of 10 cents per seat every week, and a royalty on every foot of sound film that was shown, payable to Warner Bros.' Vitaphone Company. By early 1929, theaters were being converted to sound at the rate of 250 a month. Eventually, about $400 million would be spent wiring theaters for sound. (Converting to sound did produce some savings: theater owners typically stopped booking live stage acts and musicians to perform before and during the feature, and started showing short films instead to round out the program.)

Studios were also forced to invest in new "soundstages." In the silent era, movie sets were often built outdoors, to take advantage of the abundant natural light of southern California, and one set might've been in use right next to another that was still under construction. The sound of sawing and hammering was only a minor distraction in a time before microphones. Now, on the door of Warner Bros. soundstages, signs warned, "Do Not Enter While Red Lights Are On – Vitaphoning." MGM flew a large balloon over its studio lot in Culver City, warning noisy airplanes to stay away. *Variety* estimated that between June 1928 and February 1929, the studios spent $24 million investing in sound recording gear.

They didn't always rush to use it. United Artists spent $250,000 installing both disc and sound-on-film recording equipment on one soundstage. (The studio ended up releasing its talkies using the sound-on-film process.) But neither Mary Pickford nor Douglas Fairbanks, two of the studio's founders, nor producer Samuel Goldwyn, were vying to use the stage. Rather, "they were trying to avoid getting onto it," remembered soundman Edward Bernds. (The careers of Pickford and Fairbanks, along with many other silent stars, faded in the early 1930s as talkies took over.)

Recording sound on the set bogged down the production process, introduced new costs, and spawned power struggles. Cameramen and soundmen would fight over the positioning of microphones. Directors wanted actors to move freely around the set, and soundmen wanted them to stay in place so their voices could be captured evenly by the microphones. Cameramen had to make sure mics weren't visible in the shot, and for years they and their cameras were locked into stifling hot "iceboxes," tiny, soundproof sheds that prevented the whirring sound of the camera from being captured by the mics. (They got their name not because they were cool inside, but because they resembled an oversized icebox.) After most takes, members of the crew would rush into a playback room to check the dialogue they'd just recorded.

Accommodations made for the new sound equipment were occasionally comical, as when a hunchback walked in front of two actors in *Mamba*. A microphone had been hidden inside the hump, and the hunchback was instructed to swing his protuberance from one actor to the other as they spoke their lines.

As the transition from silent films to talkies gained steam, many Hollywood stars were being forced to submit to nerve-wracking "voice auditions," which would determine if they could continue working in talkies. Gary Cooper made a deal with two friends that if it one of them was deemed unemployable in talkies, the others would share their salaries with him. Actor Ronald Colman flatly refused to sign a rider to his contract with United Artists that would cover talking pictures. "...I am not sympathetic to this 'sound business,'" he said. "I feel, as many do, that this is a mechanical resource, that it is a retrogressive and temporary digression insofar as it affects the art of motion picture acting – in short, that it does not properly belong to my particular work (of which naturally I must be the best judge)."

> In 1929, the first year that the Academy Awards were handed out, the Best Picture winner was MGM's first musical: *Broadway Melody*.
>
> The only silent film ever to win the Oscar for Best Picture was Paramount's *Wings*, about two young men in love with the same woman (Clara Bow) who become fighter pilots in World War I. It won in 1930.

Colman eventually was persuaded to sign, and audiences felt that his British accent fit perfectly with the sophisticated personality he'd already established in his silent pictures. Colman's first talkie, *Bulldog Drummond*, was a hit.

Sending movies to foreign countries became an expensive headache for the studios. In the silent era, it was only the title cards that needed to be translated into a local language; now, every line of dialogue had to be translated. (The technology for dubbing a new dialogue track in the local language didn't yet work well.) Studios experimented with subtitles, and also tried remaking the entire movie in various languages. MGM chose French, Spanish, and German. For a time, Laurel and Hardy – the comic duo who'd smoothly negotiated the transition from silent films to talkies – made their movies in those three languages, plus Italian, doing four successive takes of each scene, wrapping their tongues around utterly unfamiliar words.

Preservationists had dozens of perfectly rational reasons to object to the changes sweeping through their business: they added cost and time, they created all sorts of hassles, and they rearranged a power structure that already worked perfectly well.

Despite their resistance, though, the conversion to sound helped expand the motion picture business, and once it started, it gained momentum fast. By March 1929, Fox announced that it would no longer make silent films; Columbia followed soon after. MGM released its last silent film, *The Kiss*, starring Greta Garbo, in November 1929.

Warner Bros., the company that moved first and most definitively, benefited the most from the transition to sound. The studio's net profit leapt from $2 million in 1928 to $17 million in 1929, the year that the studio received a special award at the very first Academy Awards ceremony for helping to introduce talkies. The value of Warner Bros.' assets increased 4600 percent in five years, and as a result, Harry Warner, the studio's chief financial officer, was able to buy the First National studio in Burbank, where Warner Bros. is still headquartered today. Fox's net profits nearly doubled from 1928 to 1929. Thanks to sound, Warner Bros. and Fox had created a place for themselves in the upper echelon of Hollywood studios.

But while Warner Bros. had been first with sound, it was also the last company to abandon the disc-based Vitaphone system. The sound-on-film technology had improved more quickly than Vitaphone, and its use surpassed Vitaphone in the marketplace. Warner Bros. made the switch in 1932. (Sound-on-film endures today, in various analog and digital formats.)

> Charlie Chaplin, master of the silent film genre, made his first talkie, *The Great Dictator*, in 1940. But his previous film, *Modern Times*, included sound effects and voices – although there was no synchronized dialogue.

The coming of sound helped the movie business become a truly mass medium. Weekly attendance at the movies rose from 50 million in 1926 to 65 million in 1928, and 90 million in 1930. Profits from talkies also allowed studios to expand their theater chains. (Smaller theater chains, unable to afford the transition to sound, had no choice but to sell out.)

The success of talkies helped Hollywood respond to the growing popularity of radio, but it couldn't help Hollywood defy the gravity of the Great Depression. Movie attendance began to drop in the 1930s. Paramount filed for bankruptcy, and Warner Bros. and MGM cut salaries. By 1932, the majority of cinemas in the U.S. had switched to sound. But more than 4,000 theaters that hadn't converted to sound went out of business. And nearly 2,000 theaters closed despite having converted to sound, mostly in the northern U.S., which had been hit hardest by the Depression.

The last silent film produced in Hollywood was *Legong: Dance of the Virgins*, filmed in Bali with an all-native (and mostly nude) cast, and released by Paramount. Though there was no dialogue, the cockfighting and dancing in *Legong* were accompanied by a musical score.

But while *Legong* marked the end of the silent era, it represented the start of another. It was part of the first wave of films to employ a new kind of color movie camera made by a small Boston start-up company called Technicolor.

3: How Television Led to Smell-O-Vision

William Coolidge was a corporate attorney, and he had money to burn – the kind of investor every entrepreneur dreams of meeting. In 1912, Coolidge approached the founders of a freshly-formed consulting firm in Boston and asked them to evaluate the potential of a new invention. Coolidge's plan was to put a million dollars into a new kind of movie projector that would reduce flickering on the screen, but the consultants told him the technology wasn't viable.

The project – along with their connection to the deep-pocketed Coolidge – got the consultants interested in motion pictures. Two of them, Herbert Kalmus and Daniel Comstock, had attended MIT together, and the third, W. Burton Wescott, had skipped college but was a self-taught mechanical whiz. They started working on a movie camera that would be able to capture color imagery. When they showed Coolidge a working prototype, he agreed to supply $10,000 to fund further development. In November 1915, the consulting firm metamorphosed into the Technicolor Motion Picture Corporation.

Technicolor's three founders were too naïve and too confident to be dissuaded by the conventional wisdom about color. "Throughout the industry, the 'it can't be done' atmosphere was general," observed Comstock. If anyone could succeed in bringing color to the movies, the widely-held belief was that it would be a big company capable of investing large sums of money in the project over many years, not a start-up like Technicolor, with $10,000 in the bank.

The trio knew that putting realistic color up on the screen was an ambitious mission, and they broke it up into what they called "progressive steps," each of which would require a reasonable amount of time and money. And they intended, at the completion of each step, to have results they could show on the screen.

Innovators had been trying different techniques to add color to film since the 1890s. First, they tinted each individual frame of film by hand. *Annabell's Butterfly Dance*, shown at the Holland Brothers' Kinetoscope Parlor in 1894, took this tack, and in the late 1890s, the French filmmaker George Melies set up an assembly line of workers to add color to individual frames of movies such as *A Trip to the Moon* and *The Flower Fairy*. In 1905, Charles Pathé in France developed a way to apply color using stencils, which sped up the process a bit.

But it wasn't until 1908, when a system called Kinemacolor was demonstrated in London, that movies began trying to capture the colors the camera saw. Kinemacolor involved running film through the camera at twice the normal speed (at the time, 32 frames per second), and exposing the first frame through a red filter, the second through a green filter, and then back to the red filter. When the film was projected, the red frames were shown through a red filter, and the green frames through a green filter. The technology could reproduce an impressive range of colors – except for pure white and blue.

Kinemacolor projectors were installed in about 300 theaters in London, and many of the films made using the process captured important news events of the day, like the coronation of George V. Kinemacolor was demonstrated at Madison Square Garden in 1909, and an American affiliate was set up.

But Kinemacolor was expensive: it used four times the film of a black-and-white movie (twice as much in the camera and twice as much in the projector), and required installing its own projector apparatus – a rotating disc that held the red and green filters – and making sure the film stayed in sync with the disc. There was also the problem of "color fringing." When objects moved quickly on the screen, their edges blurred, since the red and green frames hadn't been exposed at exactly the same moment. Then, in 1914, a British court ruled that the patent at the foundation of Kinemacolor was insufficiently detailed, and thus invalid.

Other color systems came and went, including Kromoscope, Biocolour, and Cinechrome. The Hollywood studio that Kinemacolor had set up on Sunset Boulevard was eventually taken over by D.W. Griffith, who also adopted a movie project that Kinemacolor had begun to develop. It became *Birth of a Nation*.

•   •   •

Technicolor's first offices were set up in a charcoal black railroad car that doubled as a mobile film processing lab. Built into the car were an electrical generator, a darkroom, a fireproof safe, a photochemical lab, and an office with several simple oak desks. Outside, along the top, the words Technicolor Motion Picture Corporation were painted in proud white capital letters.

The Technicolor founders had attacked one of Kinemacolor's biggest problems – the distracting color "fringes" that surrounded fast-moving objects on the screen. Kinemacolor had tried to capture a single frame's worth of motion by exposing it twice in succession, once in red and once in green. But when objects were moving, the red frame and the green frame didn't match perfectly. Technicolor's process inserted a prism into the camera, took a single frame's worth of motion, and "split" it onto two adjacent frames of film, eliminating the fringing – in theory.

In early 1917, Technicolor hitched its headquarters to a train heading south. The founders' plan was to produce a feature film to show what their system could do. Skepticism about what Technicolor was trying to achieve was pervasive, and, according to Comstock, it "even extended to the actors who appeared in our first picture. Their attitude was, 'This picture will never reach the screen.'"

Made in Jacksonville to take advantage of the sunny skies, *The Gulf Between* was a love story about a girl raised by a sea captain who falls for a boy above her station. The snafus started as soon as film began running through the camera. Comstock had stayed behind in Boston to work on the new projector that'd be required to show the movie, but he was summoned by telegram to hurry down to Florida and help the crew figure out how to coax usable footage from the camera. The production finally wrapped in the summer.

When *The Gulf Between* debuted in New York on September 21st, 1917, the audience burst into applause several times, and *Motion Picture World* wrote that "the final shot, showing the sun setting over the water, is beautiful – mindful of a Japanese painting." The magazine pronounced Technicolor "vastly superior to any of its predecessors."

Kalmus was a stickler, though, legendary for his long work hours and his ability to motivate his employees through intimidation. (Around the office, he was known as "The Doctor.") He wasn't satisfied with the color in *The Gulf Between*, since fringing could still be a problem if a prism attached to the projector wasn't adjusted carefully. There were other limitations, too: interior scenes were nearly impossible to shoot because of the amount of light Technicolor required, and it was hard to see the expression on an actor's face in anything other than a close-up. Technicolor kept working to improve its color process. But by 1920, William Coolidge and other early investors had poured $400,000 into Technicolor without seeing a return. The Doctor was forced to find other backers.

Despite new funding, several technological steps forward, and a handful of other movies made using Technicolor, no one was convinced that the public wanted to see movies in color. Douglas Fairbanks, a co-founder of United Artists and marquee star, was one of the few filmmakers interested in using Technicolor, for an adventure called *The Black Pirate*. Fairbanks was deep into his swashbuckling period, having just made *Robin Hood*, *The Three Musketeers*, and *The Mark of Zorro*. He summed up the arguments against color:

> Not only has the process of color motion picture photography never been perfected, but there has been a grave doubt whether, even if properly developed, it could be applied without detracting more than it added.... The argument has been that it would tire and distract the eye, take attention from acting and facial expression, blur and confuse the action. In short it has been felt that it would militate against the simplicity and directness which motion pictures derive from the unobtrusive black and white.

Talkies hadn't yet arrived when Fairbanks was planning his pirate epic, but the case against color was almost identical to the case some would make against sound: movies were meant to be in black and white, just as they were meant to be silent. And there was no discernable demand for color from the ticket-buying public.

Fairbanks' attorneys warned him that the production, if done in color, would cost a million dollars. Fairbanks pushed ahead, shooting the movie in the waters surrounding Catalina Island and on the United Artists lot. At the time, there were just seven Technicolor cameras in existence. *The Black Pirate* commandeered four of them.

The movie, released in 1926 (the same year as Warner Bros. musically-enhanced *Don Juan*) was a triumph for Fairbanks at the box office, and a catastrophe for Technicolor. Technicolor's process now involved printing the red frames onto one strip of film, and the green frames onto another, and then gluing the two strips together back-to-back. That meant the film no longer required a special projector. But since the film had emulsion on both sides, when it ran through a projector, it scratched twice as easily as a normal black-and-white print. Also, the side of the print that faced the hot projector lamp tended to warp and veer out of focus. Technicolor had to organize an army of employees to produce and deliver replacement prints of *The Black Pirate* to cinemas.

Studio chiefs concluded that the hassles weren't worth it. Sidney Kent, the top distribution executive at Famous Players-Lasky (who felt that talkies and silent films would coexist in the market), concluded that the additional $146,000 he paid for prints for one Technicolor release simply was "out of all proportion to its added value to us."

In the industry, Kent wasn't alone in his dismissal of color. Fairbanks thought the night scenes in *Pirate* were too dark, and he didn't expect to make another Technicolor movie. Others had heard the scuttlebutt – most of it true, but exaggerated – that Technicolor required more light, more shooting time, and a different approach to costumes, make-up, and sets.

Kalmus pitched a crazy, last-ditch idea to Technicolor's board of directors: he argued that the only way for the company to convince more studios to adopt its process was to fund more of its own movies. If Technicolor could succeed at making color movies and attracting ticket-buyers, he figured, then studios would have to follow. He hoped to convince the studios "that black and white cameramen could easily be trained to light for Technicolor cameras, that talented art directors could readily begin to think in terms of color, that rush prints could be delivered promptly, and generally that the job could be done efficiently and economically..."

Amazingly, the board gave Kalmus the go-ahead. Technicolor made a series of shorts and a feature, *The Viking*, which were distributed by MGM. (By now, the company had developed a process that printed the red and green images onto the same strip of film, which solved many of the focus and warping problems that had plagued *The Black Pirate*, but the range of colors that could be reproduced was still limited.) By sharing information about how much it had cost to make the movies – and how long – "we dissipated most of the prevailing misinformation" about filming in Technicolor, Kalmus wrote. (Kalmus realized the importance of directly addressing the doubts of preservationists and sideline-sitters.)

The arrival of sound also gave Technicolor a boost; prior to that, Kalmus felt, "studio executives were loathe to permit any change whatsoever in their established method of photography and production. But with the adoption of sound, many radical changes became necessary."

The studio that was first to make a big commitment to Technicolor production was Warner Bros., flush with money from the success of its talkies. Jack Warner signed up with Technicolor to do a series of twenty features, including *On With the Show*, the first all-talking feature made in Technicolor. 1929 and 1930 were banner years for Technicolor: simply to book a spot on the company's production schedule required a deposit of $25,000. Technicolor ballooned to 1200 employees, and spent more than $3 million expanding its facilities and conducting research over those two years.

But by 1931, with movie production entering a slump due to the Depression, the company pared its payroll to 230. Still, Technicolor continued to work on improving its approach to color, since Kalmus was convinced that the public would eventually tire of the slightly surreal look and constrained palette of the two-color process. (In Technicolor's red-green world, as with Kinemacolor before it, blue skies didn't exist.)

Legong: Dance of the Virgins, one of the last silent films made in Hollywood, was also one of the last to use Technicolor's two-color system.

Eventually, the company perfected a three-color process, which produced a full range of colors and also gave the images on the screen crisper edges. The new approach used three strips of film running through the camera simultaneously, one each to capture red, green, and blue light. All three negatives were later printed onto a single piece of film stock.

Kalmus wanted to try out this new "three-strip" Technicolor process first with a cartoon. "But no cartoonist would have it," he wrote. "We were told cartoons were good enough in black and white, and that of all departments of production, cartoons could least afford the added expense."

The only place Kalmus found someone wiling to gamble on his three-color process was a fledgling animation studio run by the brothers Walt and Roy Disney, which four years earlier had introduced a new character, Mickey Mouse. But even at Disney, Roy tried to discourage Walt from spending the extra money to make a Technicolor cartoon. And United Artists, the distributor of the Disney cartoons, said it wouldn't advance them any extra money for a color film – though if the Disneys paid the costs themselves, UA would be happy to distribute it.

Walt was already halfway through with one of his "Silly Symphonies" cartoons, *Flowers and Trees*. He acknowledged that making a cartoon in color would cost about 25 percent more in production expenses, and three times as much in film processing costs. But he was enchanted by Technicolor's potential: "At last! We can show a rainbow on the screen," Walt exclaimed.

At Walt's instruction, the Disney animators literally washed off the black, white, and gray paint from the cels they'd already finished. (Cels, transparent sheets of celluloid, served as a blank piece of paper for animators.) That left only the outlines of the characters and backgrounds, which they filled in again, this time in color. Midway through the work on the Technicolor version of the movie, Disney invited Sid Grauman in for a look; Grauman, who owned the Chinese Theatre on Hollywood Boulevard, agreed on the spot to book the movie when it was ready.

Released in 1932, *Flowers and Trees* was a smash, and also won the first Academy Award handed out for Best Animated Short Subject. Disney was wise enough to negotiate an exclusive with Kalmus. For a year, his competitors were barred from making cartoons with the new Technicolor process.

> "I do not believe that black and white will disappear entirely. It will still be the ideal medium for certain subjects, not merely for newsreels and shorts, but for full-length pictures."
>
> – *Becky Sharp* director Rouben Mamoulian

But Disney's cartoon blockbuster didn't persuade the studios that the new Technicolor process deserved an audition with a live action movie. The company was stuck in the doldrums, losing a quarter-million dollars in 1932 and 1933.

Coincidentally, Kalmus was a horse racing aficionado, and at the racetrack at Saratoga Springs, he met a wealthy would-be movie producer, John Hay Whitney. (Whitney, a nationally-renowned polo player, was known as "Jock.") Whitney had backed several Broadway shows, and he was eager to break into motion pictures. With a cousin, Whitney acquired a 15 percent stake in Technicolor, and he financed the first full-length, live action feature to use the three-strip Technicolor process, *Becky Sharp*. The film, an adaptation of the 19th century British novel *Vanity Fair*, was released by RKO, the smallest of the major studios.

Variety found the Technicolor tones of *Becky Sharp* "highly improved," but didn't have many other kind words for the movie.

Fortune magazine wondered "whether color can make black and white pictures as obsolete as sound made silent pictures.... [C]olor is not so pronounced a revolution as sound." Most studios, the magazine posited, felt that the extra cost of filming in Technicolor was better spent on stars' salaries, since studios "know that names have a box-office draw and they are not at all sure about color."

Studios withheld their biggest stars from color films, including Shirley Temple, Fred Astaire and Ginger Rogers, and Gary Cooper. "Color was still a novelty and having them appear, or even be associated with such a production, could jeopardize their futures," wrote film historian Fred Basten. Top actresses worried how they'd look: Bette Davis declined to star in Warner Bros.' first production using the three-strip process, and Carole Lombard, recalling the "over ripe" hues of *Becky Sharp*, said, "...[C]olor goes a little screwy at times and I'm not just sure I want to make a Technicolor picture." If having a top star in a picture could virtually ensure its success, and the stars wanted to continue making black-and-white movies, why spend the extra money on Technicolor? (Even Walt Disney waited until 1935 to cast his best-known character, Mickey Mouse, in a Technicolor release.)

At Technicolor, Kalmus seemed to have an endless list of improvements he wanted to make. He'd heard the complaints about the intense lighting Technicolor demanded – the lights were hot enough that flowers on the set would wilt almost instantly, and one cameraman swore he once saw smoke rising from an actor's hair. So Kalmus and his technicians developed a faster speed of Technicolor film, which cut the lighting requirements by half. The first production to use the faster film was *Gone with the Wind*. (Jock Whitney had put up half of the money to option the Margaret Mitchell novel.)

The movie was one of the most expensive and chaotic endeavors Hollywood had ever seen: three directors and three cinematographers worked on it. (The first cinematographer, Lee Garmes, was replaced because his footage was judged too dark.) When producer David O. Selznick was preparing to shoot the scene in which Atlanta burns, he demanded that Technicolor send him all of the three-color cameras it had on hand; he was burning a vast swath of the studio backlot, and he didn't want to miss an angle. The budget was nearly $4 million – astronomical for the time.

But *Gone with the Wind* earned more money than any movie that had come before it, and it won the Academy Award for Best Picture of 1939, beating out another Technicolor film, *The Wizard of Oz*. (Director #2 on *Wind* was

Victor Fleming, who'd just finished working with Judy Garland and Toto.) *Gone With the Wind*'s success helped convince other studios to start churning out movies in color. The phrase "Color by Technicolor" soon became a crucial part of a new release's promotional campaign, boosting a movie's box office by as much as 30 percent. In advertising, the studios touted "Glorious Technicolor," "Sizzling Technicolor," and "Magnificent Technicolor," and they made sure audiences knew when a starlet was making her first appearance in a Technicolor picture.

If 1939 can be considered the year that Hollywood was finally sold on Technicolor's merits, then it had taken the company nearly 25 years from its founding in 1915 to perfect its technology and nudge Hollywood to the tipping point. For innovators like Herb Kalmus who aim to change the workings of an industry, persistence is a pre-requisite.

Throughout the 1930s and 1940s, Technicolor controlled 90 percent of all color film production, and the company was more profitable than most of the studios. (Technicolor opted not to sell its cameras or equipment, but rented them to the studios, accompanied by a phalanx of technicians and a color supervisor – often Kalmus' ex-wife Natalie.) In 1947, the Department of Justice, as part of an on-going antitrust campaign against Hollywood, started chasing Technicolor, accusing it of conspiring with Eastman Kodak to keep the cost of making color movies high.

> In 1940, Technicolor was given a special Academy Award for "bringing three-color feature production to the screen."

Kodak and Technicolor eventually signed consent decrees. Technicolor began licensing its patents to anyone who was interested, and Kodak introduced its own competing system for making color films, which used a single strip of negative running through the camera instead of three. Though the film was initially marketed to amateurs, it soon improved enough for studio productions to begin using it.

Kodak's film didn't require a special camera – it would run through any black-and-white film camera – and it didn't need to be processed at one of Technicolor's labs. (Film buffs would eventually lament the disappearance of Technicolor's distinctive palette.) The number of color films released began to creep up steadily in the late 1940s and early 1950s, driven in part by the cheaper cost of producing them, but also by the need to compete with a new external threat to the motion picture industry: television.

•   •   •

When studios first evaluated television, they quickly saw its merits: a movie screen in every home. It didn't take a genius to realize that plenty of Americans would find it more convenient to stay in their living rooms rather than schlep out to the neighborhood theater.

So studios tried to buy into TV. Paramount operated the first experimental TV station in Chicago and, in Los Angeles, the first commercial station. The studio also bought a piece of DuMont, which made TV sets and broadcasting gear. During World War II,. Warner, MGM, and Fox each filed applications with the Federal Communications Commission to own stations in big cities.

But the studios were in the middle of a face-off with the Department of Justice. Like Edison's Trust before them, the biggest studios wanted to exert the most possible control over the entire movie industry. They not only set admission prices at their own theaters (Warner Bros. and Fox now owned the largest collections of cinemas, with about seven hundred each), but they dictated a minimum admission price to all the independent theaters that booked their films. Independent theater owners were also forced to book movies sight unseen, and buy a complete package of movies for the entire year – practices called "blind booking" and "block booking." The practices helped ensure that the studios would be able to get screen time for all their releases, no matter if they were good or bad.

In 1938, after the studios had survived the Great Depression and emerged from it stronger than ever, the Department of Justice filed suit against the eight largest studios, accusing them of monopolistic behavior. Five of the studios dodged a trial by signing a consent decree in 1940, agreeing to limit block booking, start showing movies to exhibitors in advance of their release, and get federal approval before expanding their theater chains. Eventually, all of the studios sold off their theater chains.

Given all the anti-trust tussles between Washington and Hollywood, as the FCC was drawing up its rules for television station ownership, the Justice Department suggested that it'd prefer not to have movie studios exercising the same control over television that they'd wielded with cinemas. The studios were effectively prevented from owning a parcel of the new television landscape.

In the post-war period, Hollywood sank into another depression. From 1946 to 1952, movie attendance dropped from 82.4 million a week to 46 million. Meanwhile, Americans were plugging in their new televisions; by 1949, there were about 56 stations broadcasting to a million TV sets in the U.S. In New York, where three TV stations were on the air, Paramount conducted a study and found that TV owners went to the movies 20 to 30 percent less often than people who hadn't yet bought a set.

If they couldn't build their own television networks, Hollywood's biggest studios decided they weren't inclined to help others make television a successful medium.

After a closed-door gathering in Hollywood in 1951, a group of producers and theater-owners issued a statement: "Films made expressly for theatrical distribution should not be funneled into television, nor should big-name personalities be encouraged to appear too frequently on video, because the public will tire of seeing them and thus their pictures will suffer at the box office." Jack Warner is alleged to have banned televisions from the set of any Warner film; why give the competition free advertising? Stars such as Bette Davis needed the studio's permission to appear on a television show, and studios also prevented TV producers from renting their facilities.

> "If I had my way, we wouldn't sell to television, ever."
>
> – Fox executive Alex Harrison

The major studios had one perfectly valid business reason not to license certain films to television: they knew they could make more money by re-releasing their old films to theaters. "...Video just can't pay enough," said Dore Schary, MGM's head of production. "We probably couldn't even get more than $75,000 the way things are now. But if we re-release something like *Mutiny on the Bounty* to the theaters it would probably bring in upwards of $200,000." There were rights issues, too, since with contracts drafted before television, it was often unclear whether broadcasting a movie's soundtrack over the air was permitted or not.

While the biggest studios kept their movies out of the living room, others were willing to supply television stations with content from Hollywood. Initially, they were small "Poverty Row" studios such as Monogram and Republic, independent producers, and foreign studios.

Some of the most popular movies broadcast during television's early days were westerns featuring Hopalong Cassidy. As it happened, Hopalong (played by the actor William Boyd) controlled the rights to 54 of his movies, and he wasn't hesitant about turning those rights into cash. Hopalong's strategy provided one hint that television might not prove to be the death of cinemas: attendance at his movies actually rose the more he appeared on TV.

Part of the problem for Hollywood was that the arrival of television wasn't just about the arrival of a new technology in the home (similar to radio in the 1920s). Television was accompanied by major lifestyle changes. Americans were migrating out of urban areas and buying homes in the suburbs, away from the downtown movie palaces. With more space in their suburban homes, they were inclined to stay in more often. They were commuting to the office in their new cars.

Entrepreneurs who paid close attention to these new trends saw an opportunity. They started opening drive-in theaters to serve the new suburban, car-oriented populace. Though the first drive-in opened in 1933 in New Jersey, the concept really accelerated in the 1950s, when there were about 4000 around the country. At one point, in the summer of 1956, attendance at drive-ins actually surpassed that of indoor theaters. One early drive-in operator was Michael Redstone, father of Sumner Redstone; his company would eventually evolve into Viacom. Many of the drive-in entrepreneurs later diversified, opening indoor theaters in the new shopping malls that were cropping up like clover around the country.

Drive-in inventor Richard Hollingshead invested $30,000 to build the first drive-in in Camden, New Jersey in 1933. Though the original closed in 1935, there are an estimated 527 surviving drive-ins around the world.

The studios, hunting for a way to take advantage of television while retaining control over the distribution of their product, kept trying to figure out the right response to the new technology, and the changing behavior of the post-war consumer. They made two attempts to create early video-on-demand systems. The first was called Phonevision (dial a special number, and pay $1 to see a relatively-recent movie) and the second, supported only by Paramount, was called Telemeter. During a test in Palm Springs, Telemeter, though expensive to install, was a mild success, generating revenue of a $10 per month from each of its 2,500 households. But local drive-in owners fought it, arguing that Paramount was violating the still-fresh consent decree, by producing and distributing movies, and also controlling the means of exhibition (the Telemeter box atop the TV.)

Studios and exhibitors also made an attempt to co-opt television technology, bringing live programming like boxing matches and baseball games to movie theaters via microwave relay or coaxial cable, and projecting it on screen with a variety of complicated systems (one involved capturing broadcast images and printing them rapidly onto celluloid, which was then run through a projector). It was called "theater television," and by 1952, *U.S. News & World Report* predicted, it would be in every important theater. But theater television was a technology with a short life span: the equipment and transmission costs were expensive, the projection quality was sketchy, and television sets were getting cheaper. As it turned out, by 1952, theater television was in just a hundred U.S. cinemas, at most.

•   •   •

Throughout the 1950s, as it became clear how pervasive television was becoming, the studios and independent producers launched a fusillade of new technologies, accompanied by neon-lit showmanship, intended to convince the public that the cinema would always supply a more spectacular experience than that small black-and-white screen in the living room. Movies now played in NaturalVision, Cinerama, and Smell-O-Vision. Who could resist?

Some of these technologies had been invented earlier, but didn't gain momentum until the 1950s.

Three-dimensional films arrived in theaters even before talkies. These used the same process that was revived in the 1950s: anaglyphic 3-D, which projected two complementary colors on the screen (like red and blue, or red and green) to deliver slightly different images to each eye. Audiences wore glasses with red film over one eye and green over the other, which created the illusion of depth.

The first 3-D exhibition for a paying audience took place at the Astor Theatre in New York, in 1915; the movie was *Jim the Penman*, accompanied by short subjects on rural America and Niagara Falls.

> In 1939, at the Chrysler Motor Pavilion at the New York World's Fair, the first 3-D film in color was shown. It chronicled the assembly of a 1939 Chrysler Plymouth.

In the early 1920s, there was a staccato burst of interest in 3-D movies, then called "plasticons" or "plastigrams," which used a single strip of film that had been coated with emulsion on both sides. As with the two-color Technicolor process, a red image was printed on the front of the film, green on the back. Optimistically, the cardboard glasses distributed to audience members often bore instructions like, "Retain these glasses for viewing plasticon pictures."

But the movie industry didn't truly embrace 3-D until 1952, when *Bwana Devil*, a story of railroad-building in Africa starring Robert Stack, made its debut in NaturalVision. (NaturalVision was simply a new marketing handle for anaglyphic 3-D.) The inventor of NaturalVision, M.L. Gunzberg, tried without success to shop it around to the studios before Arch Oboler, the independent producer and director of *Bwana Devil*, agreed to give it a try. The Santa Monica mountains north of Los Angeles stood in for Africa.

Once the movie was completed, United Artists bought the rights to *Bwana Devil* and scheduled a wide release. The ads promised, "A lion in your lap!" But converting a theater to show *Bwana Devil* wasn't cheap. Two projectionists were often required to keep a pair of projectors running in perfect sync, one showing the green-filtered image, and the other the red. Exhibitors had to purchase glasses, for 5 to 10 cents a pair. A new silver screen would enhance the brightness of the image, too.

Despite bad reviews, theaters where *Bwana Devil* was shown reported strong ticket sales.

> The occasional 3-D movie showed up in theaters in the 1960s and 1970s, including Andy Warhol's *Frankenstein* and *Disco Dolls in Hot Skin*, the only X-rated 3-D movie.

House of Wax, a Vincent Price film that Warner Bros. released in 3-D in 1953, stunned Hollywood executives when it grossed $1 million in its first week. In 1953 and 1954, Universal put out *It Came from Outer Space* and *The Creature from the Black Lagoon* in 3-D. Disney, not surprisingly, released the first 3-D cartoon, *Melody*. While there'd been just one 3-D film released in 1952 (*Bwana Devil*), in 1953 there were 23.

But the resurgence of 3-D film production didn't last. By the middle of 1954, *Variety* ran a story that was headlined, "3-D Looks Dead in United States," and that year there were just thirteen 3-D releases. (In 1955, the number would dwindle to one.) For theater owners, the expense of converting theaters to show 3-D simply wasn't repaid with increased business over the long run; for studios, the complexity of distributing films in both 3-D and 2-D versions created headaches like those suffered by some audience members.

•   •   •

As with 3-D, studios and independent inventors had been experimenting with ways to expand the size of the image projected on a screen even before sound and color found a permanent place in theaters.

In 1924, Paramount tried installing a magnifying lens on a projector, to create a wider-than-usual image for spectacular sequences, such as a sea battle in *Old Ironsides* and an elephant stampede in *Chang*. But the lens also magnified the grain of the film, so Paramount next tried using a wider, 56-millimeter film stock. (Wider film allows a larger, higher-quality image to be captured and then projected.) William Fox chose 70-millimeter film, which could produce an image twenty feet high and 42 feet wide. Warner Bros. this time followed the pack, shooting movies on 65-millimeter film and calling it Vitascope. But the widescreen systems required new cameras, new film processing equipment, new projectors, and new screens – not to mention bigger sets to fill up all the new real estate that had been created on the screen.

Exhibitors were reluctant to make the additional investment, and with few theaters in which to play their widescreen releases, the studios couldn't earn back the additional money they'd invested. And when it became obvious that theater owners would have to spend money installing sound equipment, widescreen took a backseat. Adolph Zukor, head of Paramount Pictures, said in 1930 that it "would be folly to bring out the wide film and place additional burdens on the exhibitors.... [T]he producers of America have decided to delay the advent of the wide film until such time as it is necessary again to provide an attraction to the public."

Twenty years later, the popularity of television made it necessary. Throughout the first half-century of cinema, nearly all movies were shown in the so-called Academy ratio – a picture that was almost square, with a width-to-height ratio of 4:3. (A traditional television set recreates the old Academy ratio exactly, while all new movies today are made in a much wider format, with a width-to-height ratio of about 2:1.) The expansion of the silver screen was begun by a group of entrepreneurs.

This is Cinerama was produced outside of the studio system, backed by former MGM chief Louis B. Mayer, Broadway producer Michael Todd, and Henry Luce, the founder of *Time* magazine. (Mayer, the architect of MGM's success and once the highest-paid executive in America, had been fired by his board in 1951 when the studio – and the entire industry – hit a rough patch.) Shot with three cameras joined together in a special rig, it was a panoramic two-hour travelogue that transported the audience to the Grand Canyon, Niagara Falls, the canals of Venice, and the front seat of a roller coaster.

This is Cinerama became one of the blockbusters of the early 1950s. The movie played for more than two years in Manhattan, commanded a higher-than-normal ticket price, and grossed more than $20 million. President Eisenhower went to see it at a special screening in Washington, getting so wrapped up in the experience that he sang along to "America the Beautiful" and "The Battle Hymn of the Republic" on the soundtrack.

The Cinerama system offered breathtaking visuals – three projected images lined up horizontally – and rich stereo surround sound, but at great expense. Making a movie in Cinerama, with three cameras rolling simultaneously, gobbled up lots of film. Actors also had to be careful not to stand in the "seams" between the three cameras, since the image was a bit blurry there.

> "A wide screen just makes a bad film twice as bad."
>
> – Samuel Goldwyn

Converting a theater to show Cinerama involved installing a new, curved screen that reduced the number of seats in the theater, and spending between $50,000 and $100,000 to install three synchronized projectors and a new sound system. Theaters that showed *This is Cinerama* and the movies that followed it, such as *Cinerama Holiday* and *Seven Wonders of the World*, had to employ a team of between twelve and sixteen projectionists.

Eventually, by the early 1960s, the supply of Cinerama films dried up. Part of the reason was that the studios threw their support to less-expensive widescreen systems, most of them developed in-house.

Fox president Spyros Skouras had been a theater owner – he'd gotten his start by opening a nickelodeon in St. Louis with his brothers – and he knew that hiring extra projectionists was anathema to them. Fox revived a quarter-century old process to create CinemaScope, using an "anamorphic" lens on the camera, which squeezed twice the usual breadth of a horizontal image onto standard-size 35-millimeter film.

The projector also needed its own anamorphic lens to unsqueeze the image. On the screen, the first batch of CinemaScope releases were more than two-and-a-half times as wide as they were tall. And CinemaScope offered enhanced four-channel sound, encoded magnetically alongside the image; there were left, right, and center speakers behind the screen, and a set of "surround" speakers positioned in the rear of the auditorium.

Skouras had gauged the market perfectly. Six months before the first
CinemaScope movie was released, 1953's *The Robe*, he had orders for more
than 700 installations. *The Robe* starred Richard Burton as the Roman
centurion in charge of Christ's crucifixion, and it was shot in the Academy
ratio as well as CinemaScope, so that it could be shown in non-
CinemaScope equipped theaters. Monaural versions of the movie were
available, too, for theaters that didn't want to invest in a new stereo sound
system. When adjusted for inflation, *The Robe*'s ticket sales put it in the top
50 box office hits of all time, above Peter Jackson's "Lord of the Rings"
trilogy.

By late 1954, almost half of all theaters in the U.S. were equipped to show
movies in CinemaScope, and all of the major studios, except for
Paramount, had licensed the technology from Fox.

Paramount developed its own widescreen process, VistaVision, which ran
ordinary 35-millimeter film horizontally through the camera, instead of
vertically. (The VistaVision camera itself weighed 105 pounds.) Each frame
was elongated to twice the width of a standard 35-millimeter frame, which
enabled VistaVision to produce a higher-resolution image than
CinemaScope. In 1954, the first VistaVision film, *White Christmas*, starring
Danny Kaye and Bing Crosby, debuted at Radio City Music Hall. For its
national premiere, it set a record for opening day box office revenues. But
other studios didn't adopt the process, and the publicity surrounding the
installation of VistaVision in one Times Square theater didn't help: the
costs were said to exceed $100,000.

After releasing epics such as *The Ten Commandments* in VistaVision,
Paramount itself started to question whether the costs of the process were
justified at the box office. An analysis of Alfred Hitchcock's *Vertigo* found
that it cost an extra $78,000 to shoot the Jimmy Stewart/Kim Novak
thriller in VistaVision – too high a price for Paramount executives, since
Vertigo didn't perform very well in its first release. Paramount abandoned
VistaVision in 1963, switching to Technirama, a widescreen process
similar to VistaVision that had been created by Technicolor.

The 1950s saw a succession of other widescreen technologies. Technicolor
touted Technirama and later Super Technirama (Stanley Kubrick's
Spartacus was released in Super Technirama, a format that used 70-
millimeter film to deliver sharp imagery.) National Theatres came out with
Cinemiracle, which, like Cinerama, required three cameras and three
projectors. The Roxy in New York and Grauman's Chinese in Hollywood
both played the only film ever made in Cinemiracle, *Windjammer*. (The

movie was a travelogue that chronicled a tall ship's voyage across the Atlantic.)

Michael Todd, a partner in the original Cinerama venture, brought out Todd-AO in 1955, a widescreen format shot on 65-millimeter negative and projected on 70-millimeter film stock, both at a rate of 30 frames per second, their own unique speed. (The standard speed is 24 frames per second, and when more frames are shown on the screen within a second, the picture appears sharper.) Todd convinced composers Richard Rodgers and Oscar Hammerstein II to allow him to film their popular Broadway musical *Oklahoma!* in the format. The second Todd-AO production, *Around the World in Eighty Days*, won the Best Picture Oscar in 1956 and, like its predecessor, was an enormous hit.

But in 1958, the same year that the third Todd-AO production, *South Pacific*, was released, Michael Todd died in a plane crash. Todd-AO began to wither, since theater owners assumed that the string of hits he'd made weren't likely to continue.

The specialized equipment required for studios and exhibitors – plus the additional labor and film processing costs – led to obsolescence for most of the majestic widescreen formats. They were replaced by a more flexible and less expensive system devised by Panavision, an optics company that had originally built its business by supplying projector lenses for Fox's early CinemaScope releases. Panavision's projector lenses were easily adjusted to show films shot in any aspect ratio, widescreen or not. Eventually, by the late 1960s, even Fox acknowledged the superiority of Panavision's system. But in a tribute to CinemaScope, whenever a movie is shot in a widescreen, anamorphic format (using lenses on the camera and projector that shrink and then expand the image), cinematographers and projectionists alike still refer to it as a "'Scope" picture.

· · ·

Some of the other innovations of the 1950s and 1960s can be seen, through the rear-view mirror, as either examples of brilliant showmanship or mounting desperation.

B-movie director William Castle was the Zeus of crass promotional gimmicks: novel effects intended to pique the curiosity of ticket-buyers sprang forth fully-formed from his head. In 1959, his movie *House on Haunted Hill* featured a plastic skeleton hidden in a box next to the screen, which popped out and flew over the audience on a guy wire during a climactic scene. (Castle dubbed this special effect, which was sadly never deployed again, "Emergo.") That same year, another Castle film, also starring Vincent Price, introduced "Percepto." Certain seats in each theater were rigged with motors that created vibrations at key moments during *The Tingler*; Castle also conspired to plant people in the audience who'd scream and pretend to faint.

Castle's gimmicks reached their apex – or nadir – with 1961's *Mr. Sardonicus*. Audience members could vote on whether the villain should be spared or punished. But only one ending existed (he got his due), and the audience's ballots were never tallied.

For a brief period, two visionaries in the Castle mold tried to introduce an olfactory dimension to cinema, an experience television surely couldn't duplicate.

In 1959, Charles Weiss and Walter Reade, Jr., introduced AromaRama, a system that pumped artificial smells through an auditorium via the air conditioning ducts. The following year, Michael Todd, Jr. gave the world Smell-O-Vision, which emitted fragrances from beneath each seat. Both were triggered by a special "smelltrack," which was encoded on the film.

> As far back as 1906, exhibitors had been tinkering with scents; during the showing of a newsreel about the annual Rose Bowl football game, one theater in Pennsylvania dipped some cotton in rose essence and placed it in front of an electric fan.

AromaRama was deployed in December 1959, for the release of a documentary about Communist China called *Behind the Great Wall*. It had been grafted onto that film at the last minute, in an attempt to capitalize on the impending "smellomania." There were 52 different smells, including jasmine, incense, and the smell of salt water. "A beautiful old pine grove in Peking smells rather like a subway rest room on disinfectant day," sniffed *Time*.

Less than a month later, *The Scent of Mystery* premiered in Smell-O-Vision, with thirty smells, including garlic, paint, boot polish, bread, coffee, and perfume.

Smell-O-Vision had been invented by Hans Laube, a Swiss professor who used a centralized "smell brain" (actually, rotating drums filled with fragrant essences) to pump aromas through a system of plastic tubing, with outlets hidden under each seat. Michael Todd had seen Laube's process in 1954. In 1958, after the elder Todd died, his son, who'd been an assistant producer on *This is Cinerama*, took over his production company. Michael Todd, Jr. was just 28.

Newspaper ads equated the earth-shattering importance of *The Scent of Mystery* with *The Jazz Singer*. "First They Moved (1895)! Then They Talked (1927)! Now They Smell!" The movie had been shot on location in Spain. It told the story of a British tourist played by Denholm Elliott, who overhears talk of a plot to murder an American tourist. The smells help Elliott find his quarry, who turns out to be Elizabeth Taylor, in an unbilled cameo. (Michael Todd, Sr., was married to Taylor at the time of his death.) *Scent* was preceded by a short cartoon, "The Tale of Old Whiff" – the only animated film made in Smell-O-Vision. It featured a bloodhound voiced by Bert Lahr who had lost his sense of smell.

At Chicago's Cinestage theater, a mile of plastic tubing was installed for the premiere of *Scent* at a cost of about $15,000 – three times the price of AromaRama. *Variety* said that Smell-O-Vision "odors are more distinct and recognizable and do not appear to linger as long as those in Aromarama." But both systems had problems dispersing the smells, and so each new odor tended to mingle with those that preceded it.

> Henny Youngman's review of *Scent of Mystery* was short and to the point: "I didn't understand the picture," he said. "I had a cold."

Michael Todd, Jr. lost his entire investment making *Scent* and deploying Smell-O-Vision, and left the movie business. No other movies were made in Smell-O-Vision, and when *Scent* was re-released several years later as *Holiday in Spain*, it was completely fragrance-free.

• • •

Columbia and Disney were the first major studios to start delving into the business opportunities presented by free broadcast television. Around 1950, Columbia started making TV commercials, and in 1952, the studio began producing half-hour television movies for NBC's *The Ford Television Theater*. Partnering with ABC, Walt Disney created *Disneyland*, a weekly hour-long show that often promoted his new theme park and his upcoming movie releases. (In 1954, an entire 60-minute episode plugged *20,000 Leagues Under the Sea*, helping to make that film a hit.)

In a spasm of copycat-ism, other studios created their own promotional series, among them *The MGM Parade* and *Warner Bros. Presents*.

Fox was the first studio to announce, in 1953, that it believed that selling some of the older films in its vaults, rather than just producing promotional shows, was inevitable. Fox president Spyros Skouras figured that as theaters converted over to showing movies in the new, widescreen formats, like Fox's CinemaScope and Paramount's VistaVision, the older, square format movies wouldn't be as attractive for theatrical re-releases.

But it took two outside pressures to crack the status quo, and nudge the studios to open their vaults and start renting out their old movies to television. One was a new Justice Department lawsuit, filed in 1952 against a dozen companies that included Fox, Warner, Universal, Columbia, RKO, and Republic, accusing them of restraint of trade for preventing TV from licensing past and current movies. The second pressure was color television. In November 1953, NBC broadcast the first color programming nationally; while color sets wouldn't arrive in most households until the 1960s, the early broadcasts had the studios worrying. Most of their vintage pictures were in black-and-white. If color TV took over, what value would that vault material have?

> "Color television! Bah, I won't believe it until I see it in black and white."
>
> – Samuel Goldwyn

By the time a judge dismissed the Justice Department's suit in 1955, the floodgates had already started to open. The billionaire Howard Hughes had sold the studio he owned, RKO, to General Tire & Rubber, which started running RKO movies on an independent station it owned in New York, and also licensed RKO's library of 700 features to other stations.

By 1956, all of the majors had decided to make their pre-1948 movies available for broadcast, except for Paramount and Universal. (At one point, a group of cinema owners made a run at buying Paramount's movie library, to keep them off TV and use them solely for theatrical re-releases.) Paramount was hoping that its experiments with Telemeter might take off, and so it wasn't until 1958 that the studio sold – rather than rented – its collection of pre-1948 titles to MCA, Lew Wasserman's dominant talent agency. The library, along with MCA's television production business, eventually generated so much money for MCA that it enabled Wasserman to buy Universal Pictures.

Broadcasting movies on television, it turned out, did alter people's behavior. When rumors started circulating that more recent, post-1948 movies would soon be available on TV, a study found that about 22 percent of people who'd considered going to the movies in July 1957 – but didn't — had stayed home because they figured the movies would eventually show up on television. That equaled about 36 million lost ticket sales.

But while the studios had frequently complained that they could make more money by re-releasing a movie to theaters, prices for television rights started to rise, from an average of $169,000 per title in 1962 to $500,000 in 1966.

By 1967, the Motion Picture Association of America reported that the studios were cranking out 500 features a year — but only 190 of them would ever show up on the big screen. The majority were being made especially for television. Hollywood product occupied 44 hours of the 74 prime-time hours each week on the networks. Though independent producers and smaller studios had been the first to license their movies to TV, they'd been shouldered aside by the establishment.

In 1985, revenues from licensing movies to television surpassed theatrical box office revenues for the first time.

In 1971, ABC paid $5 million to show *Cleopatra* twice. And new records were regularly set; in 1997, a few weeks before the sequel *The Lost World: Jurassic Park* arrived in theaters, the Fox television network agreed to pay Universal $80 million for the rights to air the movie over a period of a dozen years. The price was about $7 million more than the movie had cost to make, meaning that *The Lost World* turned a profit before it opened in theaters.

.   .   .

It was the crooner Bing Crosby, Danny Kaye's co-star from *White Christmas*, who helped spark the next technological revolution in Hollywood.

In the 1940s, Crosby was the host of a weekly radio show, "Kraft Music Hall," broadcast live on NBC. He had to perform each show twice: once for the network's east coast stations, and again three hours later for the west coast. But Crosby preferred the more relaxed atmosphere of the recording studio, where mistakes could snipped out, and any ad libs that proved funny could be retained. (Another rumor had it that recording appealed to Crosby, in part, because he thought it'd give him more time to play golf.) He hired a recording engineer, Jack Mullin, who was well-versed with using a German-made tape machine, and in 1947 started recording his radio show. NBC didn't appreciate the notion of a pre-recorded show at a time when nearly everything on radio and television was live, so Crosby crossed over to the talent-starved ABC network, where his show was called "Philco Radio Time."

Mullin thought that tape recording would also be useful as Crosby moved into the newer medium of television. In 1951, he and several other engineers at Bing Crosby Enterprises demonstrated a modified audio recorder that could record sixteen minutes of black-and-white video onto magnetic tape: Crosby Video, the first prototype of the videocassette recorder. The picture was flickery and fuzzy. But Crosby was impressed enough by the demo to agree to keep financing the work, with the goal of developing a broadcast-quality recorder.

4: Befriending
the Boston Strangler

In September 1976, the two top executives of Universal Pictures, Lew Wasserman and Sidney Sheinberg, flew to Manhattan to meet with their counterparts at a Japanese electronics company, Sony, that was best known for making transistor radios and the Trinitron line of color TVs.

Wasserman was the bespectacled super-agent who'd represented Ronald Reagan, Alfred Hitchcock, Marilyn Monroe, and Frank Sinatra, and helped build MCA, Universal's parent company. Working with his client Jimmy Stewart, in the 1950s he'd helped to reinvent the way stars were paid, ensuring that Stewart received a hefty percentage of the profits from the movies he was in. (Forever after, stars would boast not just about their salaries, but how many percentage "points" of the profits they'd been promised.) Sheinberg, trained as an attorney, was Wasserman's protégé, and a few years earlier he'd been installed as CEO of MCA and Universal, when Wasserman moved up to the chairman's office.

In 1976, Universal was on a hot streak, producing hits for television and the cinema; its summer 1975 release, *Jaws*, had earned more than $250 million on a budget of about $7 million, and helped establish 28-year old Steven Spielberg as a bankable director.

A week before Wasserman and Sheinberg's trip to New York, Sony's ad agency had sent Sheinberg a proposed newspaper ad for the Sony Betamax, a new videotape recorder aimed at consumers that had been introduced the year before. "Now you don't have to miss Kojak because you're watching Columbo (or vice versa)," the ad copy read; "Kojak" and

"Columbo" were two popular TV series that Universal produced, which aired on two different networks at 9:00 PM every Sunday.

But rather than getting a quick stamp of approval – why wouldn't Universal want to encourage viewers to catch both of its programs? – the ad prompted Sheinberg to start thinking about the nature of the Betamax product itself. "This machine was made and marketed to copy copyrighted material," Sheinberg concluded. "It's a copyright violation."

At the time, Universal was also planning to launch a home video system of its own, DiscoVision, which would only allow customers to play pre-recorded movies. (The system, which used a beam of laser light to read information from a large plastic platter, later became known as LaserDisc.) Universal's corporate parent, MCA, had invested millions in the DiscoVision technology, and set up a subsidiary to make the discs; one remaining task was to find an electronics company willing to make the players – and Sony was a leading candidate.

So when Sheinberg and Wasserman showed up at Sony's midtown Manhattan offices, overlooking the Plaza Hotel and Central Park, there was plenty to discuss. The foursome talked about a possible partnership, and debated whether Betamax would prevent DiscoVision from getting off the ground, or whether discs, which are cheaper to produce, and allow the viewer to skip to any point in a movie without fast-forwarding, might be able to coexist with videotape systems like Betamax. "Videocassette is the door opener of videodisc," Sony chairman Akio Morita hypothesized, suggesting that one technology would logically lead to the next.

Midway through a catered dinner in the Sony boardroom, Sheinberg produced a memo that had been written by Universal's law firm, and explained that Universal felt that the Betamax promoted copyright violation. Unless Sony pulled the recorder from the market, or suggested another solution, Universal would have no choice but to file a lawsuit.

Morita was dumbfounded by the threat of litigation during what he thought was a meeting about possible partnerships. Japanese tradition held that "when we shake hands, we will not hit you with the other hand," he said. But after the dinner, he told his colleague, Sony Corporation of America president Harvey Schein, that he didn't think Universal was serious about suing.

But by early October, a private investigator working for Universal was visiting retail outlets that sold Betamaxes, asking for demonstrations of how the device could record shows off the air – ideally, Universal-produced shows. Disney agreed to join Universal's suit as a co-plaintiff, and Warner Bros. promised to pay some of the legal bills, without actually singing on to the suit. On November 11, Universal and Disney filed suit against Sony, several retail stores that sold Betamaxes, Sony's ad agency, and a token Betamax owner.

•   •   •

Bing Crosby had continued to support the development of a videotape recorder in the early 1950s, and by 1955, engineer Jack Mullin and his colleagues had built a prototype that could capture color.

The following year, Ampex, a Silicon Valley company, unveiled the first practical, high-quality videotape recorder at a television industry convention. (Crosby had earlier invested $50,000 in Ampex, to help them produce commercial versions of the audiotape recorders he relied on.) Instead of moving the magnetic tape at high rates of speed past the stationary heads that recorded and played back the images, Ampex's engineers decided to have the heads spin while the tape moved more slowly; they also switched from amplitude modulation to frequency modulation, which allowed them to fit more picture information onto the tape. Ampex sold $4 million worth of the machines, at $50,000 each, to television broadcasters during the convention. Almost immediately, television began to shift from a live medium to a pre-recorded one. (Also in 1956, Crosby sold off his electronics group to 3M, the Minnesota conglomerate.)

> One of the engineers on the Ampex team that developed the first commercially-successful videotape recorder was Ray Dolby, who'd go on to start Dolby Labs. Dolby later helped convert the movie industry from monaural to stereo soundtracks.

But a consumer version of Ampex's tape machine wasn't much cheaper than the professional model. In the 1963 Nieman-Marcus Christmas catalog, shoppers were offered a giant cabinet that included black-and-white Ampex recorder, video camera, record player, loudspeakers, and television, for $30,000. The price included installation by a qualified Ampex engineer.

Other systems were cheaper, but didn't necessarily appeal to a broader audience. Sony's bulky U-matic recorder, introduced in 1971, sold for $1000, and the tapes only held a half-hour of video. (Universal's Sid Sheinberg even had one in his office, for watching tapes of new Universal productions.) Avco's CartriVision system, launched in 1972, was the first to offer pre-recorded movies for rental (mostly from Columbia Pictures). CartriVision cost $1600, and came with an integrated TV set. The system had two different kinds of cassettes — black cassettes (for recording TV shows and home movies using the included camera) and red cassettes (for pre-recorded movies.) The red cassettes could only be rented — not purchased — and there was no way to rewind them. If the viewer got up to answer the phone and forgot to pause the movie, that was her problem. As a condition of working with CartriVision, studios had mandated that viewers would only be able to watch a movie once.

But soon after CartriVision went on sale, it was discovered that the tapes disintegrated quickly, and that disintegrating tapes could damage the system. A product recall deflated the company's ambitions.

Two Japanese companies — Sony with Betamax and Matsushita with VHS — finally made home video viable in the mid-1970s. They relied on some intimate knowledge of the Ampex machines, gleaned when that company tried to enter the Japanese market, and they took advantage of a technology that had come from AT&T's labs, the birthplace of talkies: the transistor, which with its compact size allowed home video machines to shrink to consumer-friendly proportions.

> November 8, 1972: Home Box Office starts broad-casting to 350 homes in Wilkes-Barre, Pennsylvania. The first film shown is *Sometimes a Great Notion*, a Paul Newman-Henry Fonda drama released the previous year.

Though Betamax, a successor to Sony's U-matic system, arrived on the market first, in 1975, Matsushita's equipment cost less, and the company willingly licensed its technology to other manufacturers, such as General Electric and RCA. Matsushita was also quicker to introduce longer-playing six-hour tapes, even if most judged Betamax's picture quality to be better. (Sony also forbade the production of Betamax tapes containing X-rated movies, so adult material was available only on VHS tapes.)

The studios, in full-on preservationist mode, found plenty to dislike about the new machines. They weren't sure that they wanted to distribute their movies on pre-recorded tapes, and they didn't like the idea of consumers buying blank tapes to capture their movies when they were broadcast on free TV or cable. Not to mention the possibility of renting or buying a pre-recorded movie on tape and using a second videocassette recorder to make a few copies for friends. But the overarching fear was that home video would diminish the revenues that studios wrung from each of their titles, as they licensed them to television and re-released them in theaters. Disney, for instance, was accustomed to bringing its animated classics out in theaters once every seven years, so they could be seen by a new generation of children.

"The videotape machine would be used to steal our property," said Disney's general counsel, Peter Nolan, "and we could never be fully compensated for the loss that would occur."

•   •   •

Andre Blay, an entrepreneur in the Detroit suburb of Farmington Hills, had built a fairly successful business as a dealer of audio-visual equipment, and he'd even made some money producing and duplicating videos in the U-matic format for corporate training departments and ad agencies.

Even before the Betamax appeared in the U.S., Blay reckoned that it, along with the VHS recorder, would create a new business opportunity. "I said to myself, 'It's time to move,'" Blay said.

In 1976, Blay sent a letter to every Hollywood studio but Universal, asking for the rights to market their movies on videocassettes, and got back just two replies – one of which, from MGM, simply said that the studio was evaluating the idea in general. (Universal was already engaged in its lawsuit against Sony, and so Blay decided to focus his energies elsewhere.) Fox was the only studio willing to experiment with Blay's business, offering him fifty movies that were already airing on television. If those movies could already be taped for free, Fox figured, what harm was there in charging Blay a royalty of $7.50 for every tape he sold?

"I was surprised to get one affirmative," Blay said. "If I didn't, I'd have just gone to the independents to get titles."

Fox was strapped for cash at the time, and executive Steven Roberts also sensed that a real shift was happening. "I took the position that I never wanted to see our company let a new technology come along and bury its head in the sand," he said later.

Blay picked Fox movies that had done well at the box office, including *Hello Dolly*, *M.A.S.H.*, and *Butch Cassidy and the Sundance Kid*. He took out a full-color ad in *TV Guide* to advertise his new Video Club of America, which launched just about the time that prices of videocassette recorders dropped below $1,000.

"The magazine hit the stands on a Thursday," Blay recalled. "Even before the weekend, we'd gotten a few coupons returned, and by Monday, we probably had a thousand checks for $10 each. By the end of the week, we had 14,000 $10 checks. We were breaking open champagne bottles." (The $10 membership fee was deductible from a member's first purchase.) "I picked up one phone call from a veterinarian who was calling on his mobile phone," Blay said. "He said, 'I've been waiting for this all my life. Here's my Visa number. I want all fifty tapes [from the ad].'"

The average price consumers paid for a tape was $49.95. By the end of 1978, Blay had sold 250,000 units, but aside from the movies from Fox, other titles were hard to come by. He did, however, manage to get the videotape rights to seven Elvis Presley movies, most of the Charlie Chaplin library, and *The Graduate*. Just one year after Blay started the company, Fox acquired it for $7.2 million in cash.

"Most corporations want to plan everything to death," Blay said. "But Fox literally gave me a blank check to build the business." (Decades later, Fox would still bring in more money from home video than many of its rivals.)

Paramount was the next studio to start test-marketing movies on tape, in 1979.

"It just seemed obvious to us, since we approached the movie business from television," said Barry Diller, then the chairman of Paramount Pictures. (Diller had previously developed programming for the ABC network.) "But the truth was, we didn't know how it would affect our other revenues, so we tried it out. Our instinct was that it wouldn't gut the theatrical release." When Paramount's *An Officer and a Gentleman* was released on video – even as the movie lingered in some theaters – "what happened was, instead of [the video] hurting theatrical, the box office went up," Diller recounted.

But in those early days of home video, rival, incompatible technologies muddied the waters of the new market: different tapes were required for Sony's Betamax, Matsushita's VHS tape deck, and a third, short-lived system, Quasar's VR-1000. (Blay's Video Club of America offered movies in both Betamax and VHS formats.) No one was sure which system would win out.

•   •   •

Universal's lawsuit against Sony got underway in 1979, in U.S. District Court in Los Angeles.

"The case was really about leverage," Sheinberg said. "If we won, we would have the leverage to get a royalty on the sale of the machines and blank tapes, and have a system where content owners were compensated. The issue never really was that the machine would've been prohibited."

Sony argued that consumers had the right to record programs for their own private use. Disney and Universal asserted that home recording would completely upend the economics of making movies, since the studios would no longer be able to command a high price for repeated television showings or theatrical re-releases if consumers were building up their own movie vaults using blank videocassettes. The studios had gone to court to defend their existing revenue streams.

Sid Sheinberg waited until 1981 – just before the appeals court reversed the lower court's decision on the legality of home taping – to decide that the time was right for Universal to start selling its movies on videocassettes. (It was also in 1981 that Universal laid off most of the employees at its DiscoVision laserdisc subsidiary, after losing an estimated $30 million.)

Laserdiscs were "a good technology," Sheinberg said later, "for the twelve people who used them."

During the trial, Sony's lawyers got Sheinberg to confess that he'd used his Sony U-matic to record a few minutes of a television program. But Sheinberg claimed he'd only done it to see if the system worked. When asked if he'd want consumers to be able to view two Universal TV shows that happened to air at the same time, by taping one and watching the other as it was broadcast, Sheinberg had a curt answer: no.

Universal and Disney lost the case. The judge ruled that "home use recording from free television is not copyright infringement, and even if it were, the corporate defendants are not liable and an injunction [against the sale of Betamax recorders] is not appropriate." But two years later, an appeals court reversed the decision, partly on the basis that the lower court had been too strict in requiring the studios to prove how their businesses had been stung by home recording. The case headed for the Supreme Court.

•   •   •

Jack Valenti was the movie industry's man in Washington as Universal and Disney campaigned to squelch the Betamax. Valenti, an attorney from

Houston, was known for his eloquence and sartorial elegance, and before he'd been lured to take on the presidency of the Motion Picture Association of America, he'd been a special assistant to President Lyndon Johnson. Not insignificantly, it was Lew Wasserman who recruited Valenti to the post at the MPAA, paying him a stratospheric $200,000 salary.

As Universal's suit against Sony wended through the courts, Valenti visited elected officials, often with Charlton Heston in tow, to try to convince them that VCR makers should pay a $50 fee for every VCR sold, which would make up for the income lost because of home taping. (The studios also wanted $1 for every blank cassette sold, and a bill introduced to the House and Senate would have forbid cassette rentals without a studio's permission, inevitably leading to higher rental fees.) If the courts wouldn't remove Betamax machines from the market, at least the studios might get some compensation.

Valenti and Universal tried to bring all patriotic Americans to their side by repeatedly noting that the leading companies that made VCRs and videotapes were all Japanese. Foreign companies, Sheinberg said, were getting "a free ride on the backs of the American creative community." Valenti pointed out that "Japanese machines do not create entertainment. The American film industry does."

The Washington lobbying campaign occasionally stumbled, as when Sheinberg visited Speaker of the House Tip O'Neill. "I saw he had two or three [video recorders] in his office," Sheinberg remembered. "His assistants were recording the network news for him, and I'm in this man's office to tell him what he's doing is illegal."

In 1981, manufacturers were selling 1.4 million videocassette recorders a year. Matsushita's VHS format was also overtaking Sony's Betamax format in the marketplace, and more companies were producing VHS devices.

At a congressional hearing in 1982, Valenti famously declared that the 3.5 million VCRs then in use posed the same kind of danger to the American film industry as "the Boston Strangler [posed] to the woman home alone." Left unchecked, free home recording would eventually choke the revenues of the studios; by Valenti's estimate, home taping was already costing his constituents $2 billion a year. Attorneys for Universal and Disney threatened that the result could be that the studios would no longer allow their movies to be shown on free television. But advocates for home recording painted the royalty on tapes and VCRs as a tax, lambasting Valenti as "the troll under the bridge," and no royalty was ever enacted.

Harvey Schein, the president of Sony's U.S. division, decided that the movie industry's hostile reaction to the Betamax actually helped Sony market its product. "When people saw how worked up the movie industry had gotten, they said, 'Wait a minute! These guys here must be offering us something worthwhile if those people out in Hollywood are so afraid.' And the other perception was, 'Well, Jesus, we'd better go out and buy one soon, because otherwise we're not going to get the chance,'" Schein said.

Seven years after Universal had first filed suit against Sony, the Supreme Court issued its decision in the Betamax case.

The Supreme Court ruled 5 to 4 that consumers ought to be allowed to videotape television programs, since the technology was being widely used for legitimate purposes, like not missing a favorite TV show, and since many copyright holders (among them Fred Rogers, host of "Mr. Rogers Neighborhood") didn't object to recording or copying of their shows. The testimony of Mr. Rogers, one observer speculated, may have tipped the scales at the Supreme Court. By 1984, when the decision was issued, nearly 40 million VCRs had been sold worldwide. The following year, Disney released *Pinocchio* on videocassette, and experimented with dropping the price from the standard $79.95 to $29.95; the movie, made 45 years earlier, became the best-selling tape of 1985.

Sheinberg thought the Supreme Court's decision was poorly-written, and speculated that one of the justices had changed his vote at that last minute. "I don't have any question whatsoever that we were legally right," he said more than two decades later. "None."

By 1987, the vast majority of Hollywood's product was available on videotape; that same year, 60 million cassettes were sold to retailers for eventual sale to consumers, and 62 million were sold as rental tapes. Video revenues were $3.3 billion.

As the Betamax case was ascending through the courts, entrepreneurs were opening up storefronts to rent and sell tapes in every suburban strip mall. Most were opened by businesspeople like Blay, who had no connection at all to the entertainment industry – much like the nickelodeon proprietors of the early 20th century. The chain that would eventually dominate the industry, Blockbuster Video, was founded in 1985, and by the following year, there were at least 25,000 video stores in the U.S. But as video stores were proliferating, studios were coming to the conclusion that they'd gotten short shrift. They sold a tape to the rental company for $50 wholesale, and the rental company could then rent it dozens of times at $5 a pop, and eventually sell the "pre-viewed" tape to a bargain-hunting consumer. Companies such as Warner Home Video, MGM/CBS Home Video, and Orion Home Video tried to institute pricing plans where rental companies would share revenues with them. (Studios also explored repealing the First Sale doctrine, part of copyright law that gave rental companies permission to buy tapes and then freely rent them out.) But the plans didn't catch.

So studios, led by Paramount, started dropping the prices of their cassettes, down to the $20 range, enticing consumers to buy movies instead of renting. Movies like *Top Gun*, released on tape at $26.95, sold millions of copies and earned about half as much ($40 million) as a video product as they'd earned at the box office ($82 million).

Universal's Sid Sheinberg acknowledged that his studio may have initially under-estimated the positive aspects of home video, but he never changed his opinion about the VCR's impact on the movie industry.

By 1990, studios' revenues from home video had surpassed those earned from theatrical release. In that year, studios earned $5.3 billion from ticket sales, and $6 billion from home video.

Sheinberg said, "With the benefit of hindsight, I think it has been even more harmful than we thought. The harm is not only in the copying of material, which deprives us of subsequent potential revenues...but in the continuing degeneration of the concept of copyright."

But Sumner Redstone, chairman of Viacom (which owned both Paramount Pictures and Blockbuster Video), later termed home video "the bonanza that saved Hollywood from bankruptcy."

5: From Shotguns to Software

At the climax of the 1982 movie *Poltergeist*, a suburban house that has been visited by malevolent ghosts implodes and is violently sucked into a vortex.

To get that image onto film, model-makers at Industrial Light & Magic built a scaled-down version of the house and its surrounding yard, and placed it atop a giant funnel. Each piece of the house was attached to a strand of monofilament that threaded down through the funnel and was attached to a forklift.

The *Poltergeist* visual effects team planned a version of the old childhood tooth-pulling scheme: the forklift would start moving slowly, pulling the monofilament until the house and all its pieces disappeared into the funnel. But when the forklift shifted into gear, pieces of the house got jammed in the neck of the funnel. They needed another model, and a strategy to counter the clog.

"Our solution was that we got three shotguns, and when the model jammed, we opened fire on it, blowing it to pieces so it'd fit through the funnel," said Jeff Mann, who was a model-maker at ILM at the time. (ILM was founded in 1975 by George Lucas to develop the visual effects for the first *Star Wars* movie, and soon evolved into the movie industry's most accomplished producer of never-before-seen effects.)

Scale models had been a mainstay of visual effects technology for decades (even if shotguns were a somewhat less common tool). Producing a convincing world of fantasy, ever since the advent of cinema, had involved ingenuity and painstaking labor. It entailed building pose-able monsters and then shooting them one frame at a time, as Willis O'Brien did for *King Kong* in 1933; running the camera at slower or faster speeds than normal; or painting minutely-detailed backgrounds on glass – known as matte paintings – and then combining them with action shot elsewhere using a technique called optical printing. (Optical printing had been around since the 1920s as a way of combining multiple elements on film; it involved projecting two pieces of film simultaneously, and capturing the single merged image with a camera. In *The Wizard of Oz*, when Dorothy and friends stride toward the Emerald City, its shining towers are a matte painting, blended with the live action using optical printing.) For animated movies, the characters and backgrounds were drawn by hand, colored by hand, and then each individual frame of action was captured on film using a special camera.

In the 1980s, a group of innovators set out to prove that computers could be applied to visual effects and animation, expanding the realm of what was possible, and making the work more efficient. At the time, producing digital effects and animation was far more labor-intensive than the existing, analog ways of doing things – which is often the case with nascent technologies. They required expensive computer hardware and custom-crafted software. And the results looked nowhere near as realistic as the work being done by the most talented model-makers, matte painters, and traditional animators. Established players in the movie industry wondered why anyone would bother sinking money into the new approaches, when they were so obviously inferior.

Steven Lisberger was an unproven independent filmmaker and animator from Boston. His most ambitious project, a hand-drawn animated movie called *Animalympics,* about animals competing in the Olympics, had tanked when the U.S. boycotted the 1980 games. Somehow, after that project bankrupted his small studio, Lisberger persuaded Disney to take a gamble on a movie idea he had that would combine live action and computer graphics. The plot of *Tron* involved a videogame developer pulled into the virtual world he has created, where he must do battle with an out-of-control, Orwellian piece of software called the Master Control Program.

"When we first starting working on [*Tron*], we didn't know how we would do it," said Bill Kroyer, the "computer image choreographer" on the picture. "It was just an idea about a guy and a computer. But when we showed up at Disney, something started happening; it was almost like putting a blue light on the back porch and having flies from all over the neighborhood come to it. Every guy in the United States of America that was into computer graphics showed up to work on it. It was like the Crusades."

At the time *Tron* began production, a few visual effects had already been conjured by computers. Computer-generated imagery had shown up in

Futureworld in 1976, *Star Wars* in 1977, the title sequence of *Superman* in 1978, *Looker* in 1981, and *Star Trek II: The Wrath of Khan* in 1982. These digital effects didn't try to pass for reality; instead, the goal was to create tech-y images that appeared on computer screens, like a wire-frame image of the Death Star in *Star Wars*, or Susan Dey's rotating head in *Looker*. (The movie is about an evil advertising corporation that is trying to replace its imperfect human models with perfect digital replicas.) During production, it was hard to envision what the effects would look like when they were completed, since no one had much experience, and it took the computers a long time to render (or draw) each frame of imagery.

Tron would rely on more computer-generated imagery than any of its predecessors: about fifteen minutes of the movie involved computer environments, characters, and props designed by four digital effects firms using the fastest computers they could get their hands on, like a turbo-charged minicomputer from Digital Equipment that was given the tongue-in-cheek nick-name the Super Foonly F-1. Elements that had been created in the computers, pixel by pixel, were printed onto celluloid, and optical printing was still used to combine those images with the live action sequences shot on set.

"When we did *Tron*, there was very much a feeling of standing at the frontier, that it was all possible," said Lisberger. "Even if it failed, it was gonna be revolutionary."

"We looked at it like a *Fantasia* kind of thing: this is what artists do when you give them freedom. They go for it," he said. Disney's animators didn't quite feel like *Tron* should've been mentioned in the same sentence as *Fantasia*. "There was no rapport with them," Lisberger recalls. "We couldn't get any help." The entire movie was made over the course of one year.

Tron cost $17 million to make – nearly twice as much as *Poltergeist* – and it was released a month later, in July 1982. *Tron* didn't do very well at the box office (*Poltergeist* earned $76 million domestically, compared to *Tron*'s $33 million), and oddly, it wasn't nominated for a Best Visual Effects award from the Academy in 1982. Lisberger heard through the grapevine that Academy voters viewed using computers to create the effects as "cheating," and not true artistry. (*Poltergeist* was nominated, but the award went to the year's biggest hit, *E.T.: The Extra-Terrestrial*, which relied, like *Poltergeist*, on puppets, models, and other traditional visual effects methods.)

"We thought that *Tron* was going to open the floodgates, but it tanked," said Jeff Kleiser, who developed a character named Bit (really just a geometric shape) for the movie. "There wasn't this conclusion that computer animation equaled box office," Kleiser said, "so for about ten years, computer animation waited around for something to happen." Lisberger directed a few more movies (coincidentally, he was briefly considered to direct *Poltergeist 2*) before turning his attention to screenwriting and woodworking.

And the gurus of computer effects weren't quite ready to take over the industry. "Every production was a grueling, horrible experience," remembered George Joblove, an Industrial Light & Magic employee. "The machines were so slow, you were limited in what you could do, and there was no software. You had to write it yourself."

Nearly five years of development work at ILM were required before the firm had the ability to produce an animated character called the Stained Glass Man for *Young Sherlock Holmes* in 1985. (In one hallucinatory

> 1984: A small firm called Digital Productions, founded by people who'd worked on *Tron*, contributes 27 minutes of computer-generated imagery to *The Last Starfighter*, which tells the story of a teenager who is recruited by a video game to join an alien air force. But the effects reportedly cost $14 million, and the movie grosses just $28 million in its theatrical release.

scene, a stained-glass image of a knight inside a church comes to life and tries to kill a priest.) ILM also used its growing software expertise to remove the wires and cables used in flying sequences, and, in the Ron Howard film *Willow* in 1988, to morph a character from goat to ostrich to peacock to turtle to tiger to human, as the title character casts a spell.

Many of the companies that helped settle the frontier of computer-generated imagery fell victim to its expense, and the lack of consistent demand from movie producers. The Cray supercomputer leased by Digital Productions cost approximately $12,000 per month in electricity, and $50,000 in maintenance. Digital Productions and Robert Abel Productions (which had done computer-generated work for Disney's *Tron* and *The Black Hole*) were bought by another company, Omnibus, to create the world's largest computer graphics company. Omnibus declared bankruptcy in 1987.

Digital effects were allowing filmmakers to create things that hadn't been possible with the traditional tools, or to erase problematic pieces of reality that intruded upon their fantasy worlds, but they weren't exactly making movies cheaper. The visual effects budget for *Terminator 2: Judgment Day*, with its morphing chrome T-1000 robot, was $17 million. The original *Terminator* movie, a sleeper hit in 1984 that launched director James Cameron's career, had cost just $6.4 million in total.

The industry didn't really pay attention to the possibilities of digital effects until *Jurassic Park* came out in 1993. "*Terminator 2* was so advanced that I don't think L.A. really got it," said Dennis Muren, the visual effects supervisor for both movies. But a hit movie directed by Steven Spielberg, featuring digitally-animated (and also animatronic) dinosaurs with an appetite for humans, got everyone's attention. And it marked a tipping point, where digital technologies could do something dazzling that model-makers couldn't duplicate: give life to ravenous velociraptors.

Jurassic Park earned nearly a billion dollars worldwide, and was the top-grossing movie of 1993. Several other blockbusters in the early and mid-1990s relied heavily on computer-crafted effects, from *Forrest Gump* (ILM was able to remove the legs of Lt. Dan, an amputee played by Gary Sinise) to *Independence Day* to *Titanic* (in which doomed digital passengers fell flailing from the sinking ship into the ocean).

Thanks in part to long-running research at ILM and other companies, different elements – whether visual effects images created in a computer or actors filmed on a set – could now be scanned into the computer at high-resolution, and pieced together (or "composited") there, without relying on optical printing.

"There was a big flurry of excitement, where the studios set up their own visual effects units, or bought companies," said Doug Trumbull, a visual effects supervisor on films such as *Blade Runner* and *2001: A Space Odyssey*. But the studios' entry, along with the growing number of independent shops cranking out digital effects, made it more expensive to recruit and retain employees – and caused intensely competitive bidding for projects.

"These companies were perpetually struggling for survival, with everybody bidding against each other, to the point where no one could make a profit," said Trumbull. "They all had to buy computers that were un-amortizable. They'd buy these Silicon Graphics workstations, and the computers were obsolete within 18 months."

The studios were finally grasping the significance of the innovations in visual effects, and they began bringing groups in-house to try to control costs and quality. But weaving visual effects shops into studio culture was another matter. In 1996, Fox bought a small company called VIFX for $8 million, and sold it in 1999 for $5 million. Disney acquired a visual effects company of its own in 1996, Dream Quest Images, but slunk out of the business in 2001. Warner Bros. also dabbled temporarily. Sony was the only studio to hold onto its visual effects group, Sony Pictures ImageWorks.

Any time a director or visual effects supervisor wanted to try something new, they often faced questions about whether they could guarantee that it wouldn't bloat the budget or blow the movie's production schedule.

"It's always hard to make the case when you want to do something for the first time," said producer Steve Starkey, "like in *Back to the Future Part II*, when we had three characters played by the same performer who were in the same scene, and we had to create a new motion-control system for the camera." (Motion control systems allow the camera to be programmed so that it repeats exactly the same moves in take after take.) "You have to present your argument to the studio while you're in development, and explain the requirements, and why this can't be cut, or be done some other way," Starkey said.

Even with *Forrest Gump*, Starkey said, "from a budgetary standpoint, we met resistance. But what you have to ask the studio is, 'OK, you tell me another way to remove the legs off of Lt. Dan.'"

"We kept getting resistance on visual effects, because it's expensive," said George Lucas. "The attitude was, 'We'll pay the actor $20 million, but we're not going to pay $5 million for the visual effects,' even when you have a crew of 250 people [working on them]."

"Generally speaking, the studios don't understand what you're doing," said James Cameron. "As long as you're on budget, and they don't have to leave their offices, everything is OK."

As the digital tools improved, traditional visual effects artists started to feel threatened, since they seemed destined to reduce the need for model-makers, matte painters, and shotgun-wielders.

"It seems like it's really hurting our business," industry veteran Chuck Gaspar told *Variety* in 1993. The first film Gaspar had worked on, in 1963, was Alfred Hitchcock's *The Birds*. "Right now, there's a lot of people out of work and it seems like they're trying to do as much work as they can visually through the computers," Gaspar said, adding that he wasn't much impressed with what digital effects could achieve, circa 1993.

Not all effects artists were willing – or able – to learn how to push pixels after years of making models and matte paintings. Lucas acknowledged that the skills required at ILM in 2006 were vastly different from those required two decades earlier, and that the employee base had changed dramatically over that period. (Muren was one of those who made the transition, but more characteristic of the new ILM was John Knoll, who'd help invent the digital image editing software PhotoShop, and later supervised visual effects for the *Pirates of the Caribbean* trilogy.)

Some producers worried that digital effects could sometimes be used by directors as "a crutch," as producer/director Frank Marshall put it. "You don't want to make people lazy, because they can just paint something out," he said. "If you're having a problem in setting up a shot, you should be able to work around it, not add to the budget by trying to paint it out later."

Visual effects budgets did sometimes seem to be soaring out-of-control, as when Warner Bros. spent a reported $100 million on the visual effects budget for *Superman Returns*. (Critics often charged that more care had been given to the effects than to the script.) But studios felt that their expensive gamble could pay off if a movie's novel effects, included in a trailer and in television ads, could help whet the audience's appetite and generate buzz once a movie opened.

In 2005, Richard Hollander, president of the film division at Rhythm + Hues, a Santa Monica effects firm, said that the age of synthetic filmmaking had begun: a director could choose to shoot a movie on location with real actors and props, or replace almost any element digitally. (Though Hollander, who had earlier co-founded VIFX, admitted that replicating human actors, close-up, was still a challenge.) And while digital effects may not have brought down the cost of making movies at first, he argued that the "green screen" approach was obviating the need to build expensive sets or shoot in far-off locations. ("Green screen" technology is a replacement for matte painting, where actors can be shot against green or blue backdrops. The colored backdrops can later be swapped for real-world environments shot elsewhere, or digital sets created in computers.)

"There are stories that five years ago could not have been told, or made as movies," Hollander said. "But it is becoming economically feasible to get them out now, and do a good job."

By the time of Hollander's comments, it was no longer necessary to write custom software or purchase high-powered supercomputers to produce impressive effects. Rob Legato, the visual effects supervisor for *Titanic*, was using software from Adobe running on personal computers to tell epic stories – such as the life of Howard Hughes – without requiring an epic budget.

Legato had produced 408 effects shots for *The Aviator* on an allowance of less than $8 million. By comparison, he said, it had cost $45 million to produce a similar number of shots for *Titanic*. He said he'd used Adobe's AfterEffects software to create a whole neighborhood in Beverly Hills using just three or four houses that'd been shot on film, and that he'd been "tweaking" scenes on his laptop up to a week before the film's premiere. Legato also used software to help director Martin Scorcese emulate the look of two-strip and three-strip Technicolor, the color processes that Howard Hughes used for his own movies.

> 2006: Computer-generated imagery had replaced models, miniatures, and matte paintings as the preferred way to put the impossible up on screen. Industrial Light & Magic was finding it a challenge to keep its model-makers busy, and in June, the company announced it was selling off that division of the company to a long-time model-maker, Mark Anderson.

"You can make a film today by yourself, with CGI [computer-generated imagery] software on your laptop," said Jim Rygiel, the visual effects supervisor who won three consecutive Best Visual Effects Oscars for the *Lord of the Rings* trilogy. (In the *Rings* movies, artificial intelligence software was used to guide the actions of digital extras in battle scenes, making them behave realistically without having to script their every move.) The first movie Rygiel had worked on was *The Last Starfighter*. "When I started out, it was really tough to do one spaceship flying around," he said. "Now, anyone can do that at home."

Visual effects artists tended to see technology as a fast-growing beanstalk that could take them to new places each time they climbed it. "Whenever I finish a show, I imagine the work I just did as already being obsolete, but I don't know what's next," said Dennis Muren.

•   •   •

Richard Chuang spotted Ed Catmull standing in a hotel lobby at the SIGGRAPH computer graphics convention in Boston, and only hesitated for a second before deciding to go up introduce himself. It was 1982 – the same summer that *Tron* and *Poltergeist* were playing in theaters. Two years earlier, Chuang had helped start a company called Pacific Data Images, and Ed Catmull, a West Virginian who'd been inspired as a child by Disney's animated classics, was the first employee of the computer division at Lucasfilm, which was starting to use computers to produce visual effects in movies like *Star Trek II: The Wrath of Khan.*

"Our sole purpose was to apply digital technology to entertaining people – not necessarily just in film," Chuang said. As an employee of Hewlett-Packard just a few years earlier, Chuang had become progressively more obsessed by computer graphics, and he had enrolled in a Berkeley course taught on videotape by Catmull, Alvy Ray Smith, and Loren Carpenter – all of whom wound up working at the Lucasfilm Computer Division.

The field of computer graphics was still incredibly primitive – for most of the 1960s and 1970s, just putting individual, monochromatic dots on a screen was tough enough, let alone coaxing movement out of them. The software didn't exist to create pictures and animate them, though people like Chuang and Catmull were furiously writing it; another constraint was the expense and speed of the fastest computers available at the time. But progress in computer animation began to accelerate in tandem with the advances being made in digital visual effects, relying on some of the same software, hardware, and people.

Pixar president Ed Catmull's left hand was the first computer-generated graphic to appear in a feature film, 1976's *Futureworld.* The animation had been developed initially by Catmull and Fred Parke at the University of Utah.

Chuang approached Catmull, one of the pioneers of the field, with a simple request: "Mr. Catmull, do you mind taking a look at these pictures we made?" Chuang had brought a few 8-by-10 Polaroid prints of images he'd created with a Digital Equipment PDP-11 minicomputer, using rendering software he'd written: a few still lifes, and a planet with a spaceship orbiting it. "Ed's encouragement during that brief meeting helped push us forward," Chuang said. "We were unknowns at the time, and getting positive responses from Ed was very uplifting for us."

While Catmull appreciated Chuang's achievements, no one in the traditional animation business at the time really grasped what they had to do with the art of animation. The computer jockeys were drawing mountains that looked like they were made of toothpicks, with rigid lines, hollow interiors, and no surfaces whatsoever. When they did create higher-quality pictures, such as an image of several pool balls on a green felt table that the Lucasfilm Computer Division produced in 1983, they were stills, frozen in time. But the people pushing computer animation ahead, like Chuang and Catmull, knew what they were ultimately trying to do, and they had the innovator's blind faith that with sufficient smarts and persistence they could get there.

Most others didn't share their faith. Catmull remembered talking to people at Disney's animation group about the potential of computer animation, including Frank Thomas, part of Walt's original cohort of animators. (Thomas had been responsible for many famous Disney scenes, such as the moment in *Bambi* when Bambi and Thumper slide playfully on the ice.)

"Frank Thomas was intrigued, but the animators didn't know what it meant," said Catmull. "Our color images were fairly crude, and they definitely weren't up to the standards there." Computer animation's boosters understood that the software was always improving, and their computers were getting faster every year, but most people, Catmull realized, "didn't measure the technology against the arc that it was on." They didn't understand how fast it was progressing, and so they dismissed it as a science fair project.

"Disney was a place that was kind of frozen in time," said John Lasseter, a gregarious young animator who started working at the studio in 1979. "When Walt died, the desire to experiment died, too." Lasseter was one of the few Disney animators intrigued by possibilities of computer-assisted animation, in part as a result of having seen an early screening *Tron*. "What blew my mind was the potential of having a truly three-dimensional environment that you could control like hand-drawn animation," he said.

Lasseter wanted to make some experimental short films to see how computers could be used in future Disney projects, but "I kept bumping up against people saying 'no,'" he recalled. "My reasoning was, we should try this. With *Tron*, for the first time in decades, Disney is really ahead of everybody else in an area. But the work for *Tron* had been done by outside companies, and all of that knowledge was going to be gone. But there was tremendous resistance in the animation leadership."

The executive who'd been in charge of *Tron*, Tom Wilhite, gave Lasseter the green light to create a snippet of animation based on the Maurice Sendak book *Where the Wild Things Are*. (Wilhite was part of Disney's live action group, not its animation studio.) It would blend scenery, lighting and shadows produced by a computer with characters drawn by hand.

"I had this vision where we'd show the 'Wild Things' test to Ron Miller [the president of Walt Disney Productions, and Walt's son-in-law], and there would be no way they could say no to 'Brave Little Toaster,'" the computer-animated short that Lasseter imagined would be his next project.

Instead, Miller asked about the costs of computer animation, and Lasseter told him that they were comparable to producing hand-drawn animation. "'The only reason to do computer animation is if it makes it cheaper or faster to make animation,'" Lasseter recalls Miller telling him. "Then he stood up and walked out," Lasseter said. Later that day, Lasseter was fired from the animation group – and immediately rehired by Wilhite, who wanted him to finish up the "Wild Things" test. In 1984, Lasseter moved to northern California and started working for the Lucasfilm Computer Division as an artist. There, he said, "Ed's dream became my dream, of doing an animated feature film someday."

•   •   •

Some of the early computer animation and computer-oriented tools got a more hospitable welcome in the world of television.

In the late 1970s, Hanna-Barbera adopted a computerized system developed at Cornell University to assist with painting colors onto animation cels, hoping to lower the cost of producing Saturday morning cartoons. And Pacific Data Images scraped together work producing spinning corporate logos for TV commercials and corporate videos. "Later, we did the Pillsbury Doughboy in computer-generated animation," Chuang said. "He'd traditionally been done with stop-motion animation, frame-by-frame," the same way King Kong was brought to life in 1933. PDI created a computer-animated character for The Jim Henson Hour on NBC, and was developing a project with the Muppets creator that could've become the first fully computer-animated feature film. But that was halted by Henson's sudden death from pneumonia in 1990.

Disney used the CAPS system for one shot in *The Little Mermaid* in 1989, and more extensively in *The Rescuers Down Under* the following year.

Lucasfilm's Computer Division established a tentative foothold in Hollywood by developing a system for Disney called CAPS (for "computer-aided production system.") CAPS allowed animators to scan their drawings into the computer, paint them digitally, and then assemble the images into an animated sequence. Disney bought the system in 1986, but swore the supplier to secrecy. Alvy Ray Smith, one of the computer division employees, said that Disney thought any sort of disclosure would take away the magic.

The CAPS technology wasn't a clear money-saver for Disney. "Disney concluded that [CAPS] wouldn't save any money, but Roy [Disney, the studio's head of animation and Walt's nephew] said, 'I don't care. I just want the reinvigoration that you get with bringing in new technology,'" said Ed Catmull. "The budget department said there was no benefit, and Roy said, 'Do it anyway.'" Roy was willing to take the same kinds of risks with CAPS that Walt had taken fifty years earlier with Technicolor.

Also in 1986, George Lucas decided to spin off the Lucasfilm Computer Division, selling it to Apple co-founder Steve Jobs for $5 million (Jobs also promised at least $5 million in further funding for the company); it became known as Pixar.

"There was a little competition going on with all of the SIGGRAPH guys," Lucas recalled, "and that was, who is going to be the first one to make the first digitally-animated movie. But that wasn't my agenda. I needed [computers] for special effects, and I personally didn't think that doing a digitally-animated film would give you any advantage over a hand-drawn film."

As an independent company whose strategy at first was to sell specialized hardware and software for manipulating digital images, Pixar struggled. Like Chuang's Pacific Data Images (PDI), the small animation group turned to producing TV commercials for products like Listerine mouthwash and Tropicana orange juice, and trying to advance its abilities by making short films for the annual SIGGRAPH convention. Over the first five years that Jobs owned the company, he poured about $55 million into it.

Lasseter kept pitching Disney on letting Pixar develop a full-length computer-animated feature, but "they said no," he recalled. "Their position was that all Disney animated features are made at Disney."

Lasseter credits Steve Jobs, Pixar's chairman and CEO, with helping change Disney's position. Though he's not sure the story is completely true, Lasseter heard about a pivotal meeting between Jobs and Jeffrey Katzenberg, who then headed Disney's studio.

"Steve goes, 'So, is Disney happy with Pixar?' and Jeffrey says, 'Oh yeah, it's really innovative,'" Lasseter recounted. "Then he says, 'Jeffrey, do you think Pixar is happy with Disney?' It was one of those Steve Jobs questions that just throws you. Jeffrey said he supposed that Pixar *was* happy. And Steve says, 'In fact, no we're not. We have this animation group that's doing pretty amazing stuff, and they should be doing a feature film.'"

By March 1991, Pixar had a contract with Disney to make three feature films that Disney would distribute and market. The first would be a buddy movie starring two toys.

"We had a thousand animators who were so invested in the status quo," Katzenberg said later. "The only way we could [get into 3-D animation] was to finance Pixar. Computer-generated animation could not have occurred inside the [Disney] enterprise. We could never have revolutionized our business the way Pixar did, because they were independent and entrepreneurial." (In animation, "2-D" usually refers to movies drawn mostly by hand, and "3-D" refers not to movies where the audience wears glasses and marvels at things popping off the screen, but movies where the characters and backgrounds have been built as three-dimensional objects in a computer, and brought to life that way.)

But after Katzenberg left Disney to start DreamWorks SKG, a new studio that would make live-action and animated movies, Disney did try to develop its own ability to make computer-generated, 3-D films, the first of which was *Dinosaur* in 2000. (That film wasn't entirely computer-generated, but it did have the distinction of being the first to combine 3-D animated characters with live-action backgrounds.) Disney also kept turning out two-dimensional movies, a few of which were hits (*Lilo and Stitch*), and others which slipped off theater screens quickly (*The Emperor's New Groove, Atlantis: The Lost Empire*).

"You had so much tradition and history there – people who'd grown up at Disney, who personally knew Walt," said Ed Leonard, the executive responsible for setting up Disney's computer infrastructure. "They'd tell stories about *Snow White*. Getting them to change was like turning a cargo ship."

At Pixar, Catmull and company weren't trying to make animation a faster or cheaper process, like Disney was; rather, they wanted to introduce a fresh look. "We believed that we could create these made-up worlds that had the look of the real world," he said. "The goal was to do something totally new."

Just after *Toy Story* was released in November 1995, Pixar went public, raising $150 million from investors on Wall Street. Reviewers gushed over the movie. "Although its computer-generated imagery is impressive, the major surprise of this bright foray into a new kind of animation is how much cleverness has been invested in story and dialogue," wrote Kenneth Turan of the Los Angeles *Times*.

Turan continued, "... *Toy Story* creates the kind of gee-whiz enchantment that must have surrounded *Snow White* on its initial release. True, computer imagery still has trouble creating people that don't look like space aliens, but this film compensates by sensibly shoving the humans to the background and focusing on those darn toys."

To produce the final version of *Toy Story*, it took 117 powerful Sun Microsystems workstations rendering each element of each frame for a total of 800,000 hours. But from Catmull's perspective, it took two decades.

"I'd wanted to make a feature film ever since I was in grad school," Catmull said. "I knew full well what the standards [for such a film] were, and I viewed it as a ten-year project. But it took twenty years."

Though Disney was the only major studio pursuing 3-D animation before *Toy Story*, with its Pixar partnership and its small in-house effort, once the movie was released, suddenly Richard Chuang's phone started ringing. "We spoke to a lot of studios," he said, "including Warner Bros., Paramount, and Fox." Now that Pixar had proven there was an audience for computer-generated animation, everyone wanted a production facility of their own. DreamWorks SKG, the studio formed by Steven Spielberg, Jeffrey Katzenberg, and David Geffen, bought 40 percent of PDI in 1996 to augment its hand-drawn animation division, and started working on a computer-generated movie that became *Antz*. Fox bought Blue Sky Studios in Westchester, New York in 1997, which led to the successful *Ice Age* movies. (Chris Wedge, the founder of Blue Sky, had earlier been involved with the visual effects team for *Tron*.)

Even after *Toy Story*, Disney didn't abruptly abandon 2-D animation, and neither did the DreamWorks studio, which was making 3-D animated movies in northern California, and hand-drawn movies in Los Angeles.

"I didn't think that 2-D was becoming obsolete," acknowledged Jeffrey Katzenberg. His position harkened back to the thinking that silent films would co-exist with talkies, and black-and-white films with Technicolor spectacles.

But by the time 2000 arrived, the 2-D movies both studios were releasing were playing to empty theaters. DreamWorks' last 2-D animated movie,

Sinbad: Legend of the Seven Seas, cost $60 million to make, $30 million to market, and earned just $73 million in its worldwide theatrical release. Disney's last, *Home on the Range*, cost $110 million to produce and sold $103 million worth of tickets worldwide. (Both movies likely turned a small profit after their home video releases.)

"Even older kids will understand that Pixar does it so much better, not because of their computers but because of an intelligent attention to script and character and craft," Boston *Globe* critic Ty Burr wrote in his review of *Home on the Range*. The headline read, "'Home' looks like last, not best, of Disney's hand-drawn films."

Asked what he thought had caused the apparent shift in tastes, Chuang brought up his two children. They "are used to immersive worlds, and playing games on the computer that are animated in 3-D," he said. "That's an environment they're comfortable in. They like to see that richness. The 2-D work just doesn't look interesting to them."

But Catmull didn't agree that it was the aesthetics of 3-D animation that had soured the audience on hand-drawn, two-dimensional animation. "People blamed the shift on the audience, and said that the audience has rejected 2-D for 3-D," Catmull said. "But that was all B.S." Catmull attributed Pixar and DreamWorks' success to fresh stories, empathetic characters, and clever screenplays. "For us, it was very sad when they closed down 2-D animation at Disney," Catmull said.

Whatever the reason, suddenly the animation field was full of would-be Pixars, not would-be Disneys: studios such as Blur Studios, Alligator Planet, Wild Brain, Vanguard Animation, and even an Israeli telecommunications company, IDT, began working on 3-D computer-animated features of their own.

In 2006, after a long stretch of haggling over a renewal of its distribution deal with Pixar, Disney decided to purchase the company, for $7.4 billion. Catmull became president of both Pixar's and Disney's animation studios, and Lasseter was named chief creative officer. Jobs joined Disney's board of directors.

Both Pixar and DreamWorks seemed obsessed with developing new software in between each release, to expand the scope of what they could achieve. Programmers toiled to create more realistic rain and lightning, hair and clothing, and more nuanced facial expressions. Sometimes, they wrote software to make characters less-realistic, too, as when DreamWorks sought to have its *Madagascar* animals emulate the rubbery movements of a

Tex Avery character from the golden age of Warner Bros.' hand-drawn cartoons. Animators were still waiting, though, for the combination of hardware and software that would allow them to give their characters direction and see them respond on the computer screen immediately, the way actors would on a real-world set. As it was, each frame of a movie took between an hour and twenty hours to render.

"I still feel like these are the very early days of this industry," said Rex Grignon, a long-time employee at DreamWorks Animation. "We don't have a full palette of paints yet. Once we do, I think that will allow a lot more creativity and expressivity by the artists."

As Pixar was getting ready to release its seventh feature film, *Cars*, Catmull was feeling the same sort of restlessness. "There's a recognition here that creativity takes place within an environment of change," he said. "Everyone's rational reaction to change is to get to a stable place," which was why most studios, he felt, wanted known actors, known writers, and known stories for their movies. Pixar's movies had all been based on original stories – not fairy tales or popular children's books.

> 2006: Shortly after taking over the top jobs at Walt Disney Feature Animation in the wake of Disney's acquisition of Pixar, Ed Catmull and John Lasseter announced that they'd encourage the studio to return to its roots by developing a limited number of traditional hand-drawn, 2-D animated movies. The first such project they put into development was *The Princess and the Frog*, scheduled for release in late 2009.

Catmull said one of the main challenges of his job was stoking the fires of originality and experimentation. "The message has to be that technological change is good," he said. "It's the air you breathe, the water you swim in."

6: Movie Editors' Slow Cross-Fade

L ike the founders of Technicolor, Bill Warner and Eric Peters were engineers with no connection at all to the movie business. In the 1980s, the two were working for Apollo Computer, a booming minicomputer company in the northern suburbs of Boston. Warner sometimes shot videotape of family get-togethers, and Peters had made a few short eight-millimeter films for a road rally club he belonged to. Both had run into the frustrations of trying to impose some kind of order on the scenes they'd captured, but it wasn't until Warner tried to put together a sales video for Apollo that the frustration turned to inspiration.

"There was no script, and no shot log," Peters recalled, referring to an ordered list of the material an editor has to work with. "It was just, 'Here are the tapes.'" The two days that Warner had booked in a videotape editing suite weren't sufficient to whip the sales video into shape. But when he finally finished the painstaking work, Warner approached Peters with an idea: what if they worked out a way to digitize videotapes, feed them into one of Apollo's minicomputers, and write software that'd make it easy to trim some scenes, delete others, and alter the sequence of the action.

It was hard to tell from their early demonstrations that digital editing would ever amount to much. "You could only store about 10 seconds of video in the computer's RAM [random access memory]," Peters remembered. One of their first experiments involved mashing together a few seconds of a Disney cartoon featuring Pluto with a fighter jet from *Top Gun* blowing something up. Getting the video to run on a computer in the first place was a big accomplishment – Peters and Warner had to invent their own way of compressing the images – but executives at Apollo didn't want the pair to pursue the project.

In August 1987, Warner quit to form a start-up company, which he named Avid Technology. A year later, after he'd raised $500,000 in funding from a local venture capital firm, Peters joined him.

•   •   •

In cinema's early days, after editors made a cut and then spliced the film back together, they had to hold the strip of celluloid up to the light, or load the film onto a projector to see the result.

Iwan Serrurier, a Dutch-born engineer, invented the first machine that editors could use to review film as they worked on it. The Moviola was essentially a personal projection system that showed footage on a small screen. In 1924, Serrurier sold the first Moviola to Douglas Fairbanks' production company for $125.

"When Moviolas first came in, in the mid-1920s, editors had always edited by looking at still frames, and they developed a knack for it," said editor Walter Murch. "Even then, people who edited on the clattering [Moviola] machines were seen as somehow wimpy. 'You're not a jungle fighter. You're going into the jungle with Pellegrino on your back.'"

"I had a wonderful teacher, Dorothy Arzner, who had been a woman director in the 1930s. She'd cut silent movies, including *The Covered Wagon*. She told me that in the old days, when she used to cut silent, she would cut in hand. You'd extend a length of film in your hand, and you knew that one arm was a certain amount of time those images would be on the screen. So if a kiss lasted two arm-lengths, that was a good kiss. But if it was three arm-lengths, that was a very sexy kiss."

– Francis Ford Coppola

Though there were updates to the Moviola technology – like replacing the original hand-cranked version with a motorized model – the Moviola remained the most commonly-used tool in editing suites for most of the 20th century.

The editor's job was to start organizing film footage as soon as it was shot, working with the director (and often a few assistant editors) to produce a series of "rough cuts" that got progressively less rough, until the movie was finished (or until a release date loomed.) Traditionally, editors watched hours of footage on their Moviolas, marked the places they intended to make a cut with a white china marker, lined up the film in a cutting block, and guillotined it with a hinged razor blade. Pieces of film that were waiting to be spliced into a sequence hung on hooks in a "trim bin," which resembled a laundry cart.

"An editor's tools were pretty low-tech," admitted Steven Cohen, a movie and television editor. "We used glue and tape to splice pieces of film together, paperclips to join things temporarily, and rubber bands to hold together a small spool of film." Since a Moviola's screen was small, when a director wanted to check on an editor's progress, the film was usually brought to a screening room and threaded through a projector.

New editing systems, such as the PicSync, Steenbeck, and KEM, came along occasionally, offering incremental improvements on the Moviola, but they tended to be more expensive and complicated.

Flatbed systems like the German-made KEM and Steenbeck, for example, could handle many reels of film at the same time – useful when a director had shot a vast amount of footage. (They were called flatbeds because they resembled a desk, with a broad, flat work surface.) Still, many editors chose to stick with the Moviola, which made editing a physical, tactile process. "I used to stand up with my two Moviolas," recalled editor Mark Goldblatt. "I'd throw a clip in the air, and my assistant would catch it. I'd ask her for this close-up or that one. The film was alive. I'd throw it around my neck, keep it in my mouth. It was kind of like a dance."

In the 1970s and 1980s, new technology was developed that made it possible to edit movies using computers in conjunction with videotapes, laserdiscs, or digital storage devices that held a low-resolution copy of the film. The computer could keep track of which version of a take was where, access it quickly, and integrate it into the sequence an editor was working on. Proponents of the new technology compared the difference between editing on film and editing with one of the new "non-linear" systems to the difference between typing and using a word processor. (The new approach was generally referred to as "non-linear" editing, since it allowed editors to grab sequences and insert them into the movie-in-progress in a more flexible, less regimented way.)

But even as the systems got better, most editors stuck with the dance steps they knew. And there was no pressure from the studios to do anything differently.

Murch remembered encountering an early non-linear editing system in 1971. At age 28, he had just worked as a sound editor on Francis Ford Coppola's *The Rain People*. The system he saw was the CMX-600, released in 1971 by CMX Corporation, a joint venture between CBS and Memorex. It could handle only black-and-white video, and it relied on a Digital Equipment Corp. minicomputer, and disk drives the size of washing machines.

"I saw it in Los Angeles, where they were using it to edit commercials at Dove Films, the commercial agency that [cinematographer] Haskell Wexler had helped to start. You could edit about five minutes of footage at a time," Murch said. With him were Coppola and George Lucas. "This is the future, I thought, and it'll be here in five years. Francis and I produced a paper looking at the feasibility of using that machine to edit *The Godfather*," Coppola's upcoming project.

They concluded that they could work around the limitations of the CMX-600. But the executives at Paramount weren't comfortable taking the risk.

The new systems, to be sure, had drawbacks, and they didn't operate the same way as the trusty Moviola or Steenbeck. Some of them had screens that showed footage in black-and-white instead of color, usually at lower resolution than film. Instead of simply cranking out a "work print" for the editors to snip and splice, they required converting the footage to videotape, a laser disc, or a digital file.

And once the editing was done, it wasn't always easy to get the final film to match the choices the editor had made, since the systems would output "shot lists" that instructed how a film lab should cut (or "conform") the original film print so that it matched the edited version; when Coppola put together his own cut of *Apocalypse Now* using a videotape system, it took editors nearly a year to get the film version to look the same way.

> **1986: Editor Andy Mondshein convinces director Sidney Lumet to use the Montage Picture Processor for the political drama *Power*, after walking Lumet through a demonstration editing session. While the movie is considered the first to use a modern, non-linear editing system, the Montage wasn't totally digital: it stored footage on a bank of 17 VCRs.**

But there were plenty of advantages, such as being able to find a given shot more quickly, or try a number of different cuts or transitions in a short period of time. And the technology was getting better each year. Companies such as CMX, Ediflex, Editing Machines Corp., E-Pix, Montage, and Lightworks tried to persuade editors that they'd be able to work more efficiently with their new non-linear systems. At Lucasfilm, a team of engineers was developing a system called EditDroid, which made its debut in 1984 and relied on laserdiscs to make footage easily accessible. But the new systems were expensive. A Moviola editing system rented for $70 a week at about the time that an EditDroid rented for $1700 a week.

And no one – not studio executives or directors or producers – was pushing editors to change. Editors felt that their film-based systems worked perfectly fine. "Once you get comfortable with certain tools," Goldblatt explained, "it's easier to use those tools than some new set of tools."

· · ·

In an old machine shop north of Boston, Warner and Peters were grinding away on improvements to their Avid editing system. A key breakthrough happened in 1989, when they showed their system at the SIGGRAPH computer graphics conference, which had returned to Boston. An Apple Computer executive who saw their demo suggested that they build it to run on Apple systems, instead of Apollo. "The next day, they FedEx'ed us two top-of-the-line color computers," Peters said, "and they sent us a programmer, too." While Apollo's systems were on the way out, Apple's less-expensive computers were being adopted widely by all sorts of creative professionals.

The company focused its marketing at first on the editors who worked on television commercials, especially young editors just starting out in the business; they were most likely to be tech-savvy, and also most likely to appreciate the way the Avid system could speed up the process, while also letting them present several variations on a TV ad. Slowly, the company moved into music videos, movie trailers, and then television shows.

At a trade show in Los Angeles, Warner happened to meet Steven Cohen. Cohen had been a commercial editor in New York, using Moviolas and KEMs to edit TV spots for Volkswagen, Clairol, and Alka-Seltzer. After moving to Los Angeles, Cohen edited several documentaries, then worked as an assistant editor on *Foul Play*, a Goldie Hawn-Chevy Chase vehicle. In the mid-1980s, Cohen dabbled with the Montage Picture Processor, a PC-based editing system that controlled an array of tape decks; he was interested in new technologies, and especially in any system that would allow him to preview a cut without actually having to make it on film. But cuts were sometimes imprecise with the Montage. While Cohen had reservations about the image quality of the Avid, he called Warner, and Warner sent him a free Avid system to use for an HBO movie, *Teamster Boss*, starring Jeff Daniels and Brian Dennehy. (Cohen later became a paid consultant to Avid.)

Cohen urged Avid to teach its system to be more fluent with film footage shot at 24 frames per second (film differs in that respect from video, which captures 30 frames every second). That would help him make sure that the work he did on the Avid would stay in sync with other departments, like sound. The company promised it would deliver a new system by the time for his next project, a film version of *Lost in Yonkers*, the Neil Simon play, which would star Richard Dreyfuss and Mercedes Ruehl.

Cohen and director Martha Coolidge had to meet with production executives at Columbia Pictures to make the case for editing the movie on the Avid.

"There was some resistance," Cohen recalled, "but they trusted Martha, and wanted to make her happy. Besides, this wasn't the biggest film to them. We made the case that it'd bring down the costs – though in hindsight, I'm not sure that was true."

Cohen did several tests and trial runs, to make sure Avid's new Film Composer product would be able to perform under pressure. The Avid cost $60,000 – much cheaper than the EditDroid. But it had its drawbacks, such as 600 megabyte hard drives that cost $5000 and were so fragile they could only be shipped once without potentially causing internal injuries.

While Cohen was finishing work on *Yonkers*, he became an evangelist for the Avid technology, inviting other editors into his cutting room for demos. (Directors such as Robert Rodriguez and Barry Levinson visited as well.) "Every one of [the editors] said, 'It's bullsh—t.' 'It's not going to work for features.' 'It's not fast enough.' 'I can barely type. I'm not going to learn your computer.'"

But a few other editors, more open-minded, were willing to give the Avid system a try. Shortly after Cohen finished *Yonkers*, Dean Goodhill approached Avid to explore the idea of using an Avid system to edit part of *The Fugitive*, starring Harrison Ford and Tommy Lee Jones. (There were several teams of editors working on the film because of a tight deadline; Goodhill was responsible for the pulse-quickening train crash sequence in the beginning of the movie, just before Ford's character, Richard Kimble, goes free.)

Goodhill had tried using a non-linear system before, from E-pix, to edit a movie called *All I Want for Christmas*, but he found the interface unnecessarily complicated. Goodhill explained, "It was difficult to operate the machine, and you had to be able to write [computer] code in DOS [an early Microsoft operating system]."

Goodhill switched to Avid for *The Fugitive,* a film with an unbelievably hectic production schedule. Shooting started in February 1993, and the movie was released that August. Of the six editors hired to work on the film (and 27 assistants), Goodhill was the only one using a digital system. "I was like the pariah," he said with a laugh. After working on *The Fugitive,* Goodhill never went back to cutting film.

> 1993: Avid Technology acquires EditDroid from Lucasfilm, agreeing to incorporate some of EditDroid's features into future releases, and to adapt the system to run on computers made by Silicon Graphics. Though George Lucas had spent millions developing the EditDroid for his own use, he never actually used it to cut a feature film. Only about two dozen of the systems were ever made.

At Disney, an early user of the Lightworks, EditDroid, and Montage systems, "editors would look at them and see the limitations first," said senior vice president Bob Lambert. "And if we had an A-list editor working on a project, they knew these systems were out there, but they were totally booked on films. They didn't have a break in their work [that would give them time to learn one of the systems.]"

"There were a number of old editors who vowed that they were never going to use electronic editing," Peters said. "They were like concert pianists who were told that instead of playing on a Steinway, they were going to have to perform on a Moog synthesizer."

Disney tried to nudge editors to use the new systems just for wrangling raw footage from dailies into order, or working with a visual effects sequence that had been produced by an outside contractor. Lambert said the idea was to make more senior editors feel like there was nothing big at stake; these were less-significant tasks than doing a final cut of the film. "An assistant editor might take video from the camera tap and cut it together. The older editors had the attitude of, 'Sure, kid, go ahead and do it.'" [A camera tap is a system that simultaneously captures on videotape the images that are also being recorded on film.] The result was that they saw the speed at which the digital systems could work. Eventually, when schedules and budget got tighter, editors started using the digital systems more often.

"A lot of editors were concerned that their skills would become obsolete," Goodhill said.

"I used to joke with Laurie, my assistant, 'You better not come in late, or I won't know how to turn the thing on,'" said Richie Marks, who'd been the supervising editor for *Apocalypse Now*. "It was true."

It was also hard for the editors to figure out which of the competing systems they should learn. Marks first worked with the EditDroid on James L. Brooks' *I'll Do Anything*, and later switched to Avid for movies such as *As Good As It Gets*.

Fine details of an image were sometimes indistinct on the computer screen, which didn't offer the same resolution as film shown on a Moviola. "Night scenes were nightmares to edit," said Marks. And "[system] crashes were constant, where you'd lose cuts and have to start again."

Even some editors who were willing to try working with a non-linear system like the Avid still had reservations. "Editors were afraid of too many cooks, of too many people looking over your shoulder," Cohen said. "With a Moviola, the screen was really small – really big enough for just one viewer. But with the Avid, a bunch of people could be in the cutting room watching while you worked." And indeed, directors did start spending more time in the editing room than they had before. "The work used to be so slow, and the screen so small, that they couldn't really contribute," Cohen said. "I think there was, and is, a legitimate worry that too much communal critiquing can sometimes hurt the end product."

"In the old days," Murch said, "the editor and the director had all kinds of spurious reasons why they couldn't make a cut that the producer or studio executive suggested." (Murch compared it to a plumber who explains, in a roundabout and incomprehensible way, why he couldn't replace a faucet.) "With the Avid, a producer can walk into the cutting room and say, 'Let's see it if you cut from the knife to the girl's face, and lose that shot of the taxi. It's easy to do, and it emboldens them," Murch said.

There was also concern that the ease of non-linear editing encouraged editors to make more cuts, just because they could, whether or not they served the story. And Murch said he would miss the endless scrolling forward and backwards, looking for a particular shot within an entire reel of film. How else would an editor develop a deep, back-of-the-hand familiarity with the raw material he was working with?

Another fear was that the new technology was being used as an excuse for trying to compress post-production schedules, in search of cost savings.

Editors, even technology-savvy ones like Cohen, also viewed the democratization of editing tools as a threat to their future livelihoods. Computers were getting cheaper by the month, and starting around 2000, Apple was even including its simple iMovie video-editing software for free with every computer it sold. "Every kid in college can edit now," Cohen said. "They're coming in and competing with me [for jobs], and they're twenty years old. They didn't used to do that, because they couldn't get time on a Moviola to learn. So they didn't have the experience with it."

•   •   •

Ever since he saw the CMX-600 in 1971, Murch had become an advocate for adding new technologies to the editor's toolbox.

In talking with director Anthony Minghella and producer Saul Zaentz about how he would edit *The English Patient*, which was being shot in Rome, Murch pushed to use the Avid, but said it was regarded as "too expensive." Besides, the company didn't have support technicians in Italy, and any problems Murch ran into might take days to fix.

But there was another issue underlying Minghella's resistance to using the Avid: meddling. "Anthony had witnessed friends of his cutting their movies with an Avid, and he felt it made the film more accessible" to studio executives who might want to tinker with it. With film, it was expensive and time-consuming to copy a work print, and have a second editor, guided by studio execs, working on a "ghost cut" of the film outside of the director's supervision. But with Avid, it seemed all too easy to copy a few hard drives and hand them off to another editor. (Miramax, the studio that financed *The English Patient*, was notorious for doing ghost cuts.)

So Murch wound up in Rome, editing *The English Patient* on a KEM flatbed system. Five weeks into the shoot, he got a call from his wife in California that his son had had a seizure, and been diagnosed with a brain tumor. Murch had to return to the U.S., and he guessed he'd be off the project for at least two months. "I thought about it on the plane ride back, and sent an e-mail to Anthony and Saul, suggesting that we switch over to Avid, which would let me take two months off but still catch up with the post-production schedule," Murch said. At the time, Murch hadn't yet edited a feature on the Avid – though he had used it for two music videos.

He had an Avid system set up in the barn next to his home in Bolinas, in rural Marin County. *The English Patient* became the first (and perhaps only) film to switch from film-based editing to digital in the middle of the production schedule.

"The thing about film technology is that it's like the four-stroke automobile engine – there isn't much opportunity anymore to make investments in it that are going to pay off with major improvements," Murch said. "But with digital technology, it's still at the bottom of the curve. If you invest in it, there's a lot of room for it to grow and get better."

* * *

In 1996, *The English Patient* became the first digitally-edited film to win an Academy Award for Best Editing, and the following year, another movie edited on an Avid system won. James Cameron had assembled, in a guest house on his property, "the biggest Avid system ever, to deal with three million feet of film that he'd shot for *Titanic*," Warner said. In 1999, Warner and his colleagues received an Oscar at the Academy's Scientific and Technical Awards ceremony.

By the late 1990s, Eric Peters reckoned that Avid had hit the halfway mark: about half of Hollywood feature films were being edited using his company's technology. A few years later, Murch was using a new Macintosh-based system, Final Cut Pro, which cost less than $1000, to edit *Cold Mountain*. That film was recognized with an Oscar nomination for Best Editing.

Once veteran editors had started using the new non-linear systems, Bob Lambert said they became "just like reformed smokers. They were the most evangelical about it. If they were converts, they sat around the [American Cinema Editors] clubhouse talking about it to their compatriots."

By 2006, editors said they knew just one person in Hollywood who still regularly used a Moviola and a KEM, and worked with actual celluloid: Michael Kahn, the editor who regularly worked with Steven Spielberg.

But Kahn wasn't a Luddite. He'd offered advice and pointers during the early development of the EditDroid, while he was at Skywalker Ranch editing *Indiana Jones and the Temple of Doom*; edited Jan de Bont's *Twister* on the Lightworks system; and was using the Avid for a Morgan Freeman movie, *10 Items or Less*.

"I was afraid of [the technology] initially because I didn't think I had the capacity to learn all this stuff," Kahn said. "But then I realized that I only have to learn just enough to edit, and I can let somebody else take care of all the details. For me, the important question is, 'How do I keep my craft pure, and keep my thinking right, when there are so many mechanics to be involved with?'"

Kahn explained that the only time he used the Moviola and KEM was when he worked with Spielberg, for whom he'd cut *Saving Private Ryan*, *Schindler's List*, *Munich*, and many others. "Steven likes to work with film," Kahn said, "and it doesn't bother me at all, because that's where we come from, anyway." (*Saving Private Ryan* won the Oscar for Best Editing in 1998, the year after *Titanic*'s sweep.)

Kahn said he didn't necessarily wish that he was editing more movies on film, but he did sound a bit nostalgic. "After Steven drops film," Kahn said, "we're not going to see any more film editing. It'll all be electronic."

7: Digital Cinema Pioneers

S tefan Avalos and Lance Weiler were friends who had met in the film department of Bucks County Community College. Avalos, 30, was working as a teacher's assistant, and Weiler, 28, was taking classes and hustling for work as a production assistant on film and TV shoots. Weiler was taller and more boyish looking, with jug-handle ears; Avalos had a goatee, round glasses, and a prematurely-receding hairline. Both were still trying to figure out a way to crack the movie business from their base in Pennsylvania, midway between Philadelphia and New York City.

As a child, Avalos had been enchanted by *The Adventures of Robin Hood, Star Wars*, and *Raiders of the Lost Ark*. "I knew I wanted to make movies from the time I was ten," he said. His first feature film, *The Game*, about a counterfeiting scheme that goes awry, cost $180,000 to make. It was shot on 16-millimeter film – Weiler worked on it for a few days as a camera assistant, loading film – and edited on a traditional flatbed film editing system. Like many independent productions, it never came close to recouping its costs.

Avalos and Weiler had heard that some cash-strapped filmmakers were starting to use digital video cameras to make movies on the cheap, but "we weren't excited about shooting on video," Avalos said. "We were kind of film snobs." That was, until Avalos, tinkering around with the way his computer could manipulate video footage, stumbled across a way to make the images look much more like film, shaking off some of their TV-like sharpness.

So Avalos and Weiler set out to make a movie about the Jersey devil, a mythical creature, and the fate of a television crew that ventures into the pine barrens of New Jersey to investigate its possible existence. To make *The Last Broadcast*, the pair used a personal computer, editing and visual effects software from Adobe, and a semi-professional digital video camera from Sony, the DCR-VX1000. (For some sequences, they also used an $80 toy video camera made by Tyco.) They shot the movie in the winter of 1996-1997, in Pennsylvania and New Jersey. By the time they'd finished the month-long shoot, working mostly with friends and actors willing to donate their time, they tallied up the costs of videotape and food for the cast and crew, and came up with a total budget of $900.

"We kind of did it on a lark: How little can you make something for?" said Weiler. They spent about nine months in post-production, editing the movie and applying Avalos' "film look" to their digital footage.

Before they'd finished, Avalos and Weiler were invited to Belgium to speak about digital movie-making at the Flanders International Film Festival, and it was there that they first saw a high-resolution digital projector, made by Barco, a Belgian company. "It looked amazing," Weiler said.

Even though it was simply a souped-up version of the liquid crystal display (LCD) projector that might sit in a corporate conference room, "most people wouldn't have known the difference between this projector and a film projector," Weiler said.

Back in the States, they began thinking that if they could get their hands on a projector like the one they'd seen in Belgium, they wouldn't have to shell out several thousand dollars to make a 35-millimeter celluloid print of their movie. They hoped to premiere *The Last Broadcast* in March 1998 at the County Theater in their hometown of Doylestown, Pennsylvania. So they started sending e-mails to different manufacturers of digital projectors, asking them to donate some equipment for the showing. "Nobody responded," Weiler said.

As the date for the premiere drew closer, "the movie still wasn't done rendering, and we didn't have a projector," Weiler said. (Rendering was the process of filtering the original video through software to apply the "film look.") Renting one, they learned, would cost about $3,000 a day. So Weiler decided to get crafty. He sent another batch of e-mails to the projector manufacturers, this time mixing up the names of the companies, so that each company received an e-mail addressed to one of their competitors. That sly strategy sparked a response from Digital Projection, Inc., a Georgia company that had been the first to license a new technology from Texas Instruments that used an array of tiny mirrors to reflect light onto the screen. Digital Projection signed on as a sponsor of the premiere of *The Last Broadcast*; Weiler and Avalos, scrappy indie filmmakers that they were, didn't spend a dime.

The projector that Weiler and Avalos helped lug into the County Theater's projection booth had come straight from the White House, where Tom Hanks had used it to show President Clinton an HBO documentary he'd made about the Apollo space program. It was a tight fit: on either side of the projector, there were about two inches to spare.

"For the duration of the one-week run, we had to be the technicians," Avalos said. "We had to learn to change the bulb." The projector was connected to a tape deck that would play the movie from a DigiBeta digital videotape. The final "film look" processing of the movie was finished about three hours before the first screening.

"It was an incredible feeling as the lights went down and the projector started up, and then at the end of the movie when people applauded," Weiler said. "The movie itself felt like it went by really quickly."

"People paid money to go to the movies, and for probably the first time, they were watching digital video be projected," Avalos added.

Over the week-long run, *The Last Broadcast* grossed $5,040, earning a 560 percent return on the duo's initial investment. A film critic for the *Philadelphia Inquirer* called it "a smart, assured work – no matter how exactly it was made," awarding it three-and-a-half stars out of four.

•　　　•　　　•

A handful of Hollywood soothsayers had been predicting the arrival of digital cinema (earlier, they called it "electronic cinema") for a half-century. In 1949, the independent producer Samuel Goldwyn, who'd helped to launch three Hollywood studios (Paramount, MGM, and United Artists), anticipated the development of video-on-demand systems that would allow movie fans to view the movies they wanted to see at home, as well as methods for delivering a movie electronically to thousands of theaters, saving the studios the cost of making film prints.

A few years later, in 1954, Albert Abramson, a CBS television engineer, published an article titled, "A Motion-Picture Studio of 1968." In it, he sketched out how digital cinematography and a film-free distribution system would work: movies would be shot with electronic cameras, and then "sent by radio-relay or coaxial cable to the theaters. Five or fifty theaters in an area may be receiving the same program. An area may cover the whole state, a county, or just a large city. But no theater is shipped the actual picture tape." Abramson also expected that by 1968, a new generation of electronic cameras would be totally self-contained and

In the 1990s, the telecommunications company then known as Pacific Bell created an initiative called "Cinema of the Future," to promote the use of its fiber-optic lines for movie distribution. PacBell successfully sent the movie *Bugsy* from the Sony Pictures lot to a trade show at the Anaheim Convention Center in 1992.

But a 1995 demonstration for cinema owners didn't go so well. Telecommunications snafus interrupted the presentation of clips from movies such as *A River Runs Through It*, and *Variety* dismissed the demo as "a shabby display of makeshift technology at a Las Vegas strip mall."

Though the company had seriously considered building a nationwide fiber optic network to deliver movies to every theater in the U.S., after SBC Communications acquired Pacific Bell in 1997, executives grew impatient of waiting for the future of cinema to arrive and shut down the initiative.

cordless – capable of capturing 3-D imagery and transmitting it wirelessly back to the production center.

In 1955, Abramson followed up with a book, *Electronic Motion Pictures*, which began with the declaration, "The cinema has entered the electronic age… Motion picture production is changing from a mechanical process to an electrical one…"

Anyone involved in the movie industry at the time could immediately grasp the benefits: producing film was an industrial process that involved noxious chemicals and expensive machinery. Once a movie was ready to go to the theater, it was shipped in a set of battered metal canisters that weighed about 60 pounds. The quality of film prints wasn't perfect from the start – they were graded, with A being the top mark, and many prints getting Bs or Cs – and every time they ran through the projector there was the chance to accumulate dust or scratches. Once a movie's run was over, it was returned to the distributor, where it would be either reconditioned and sent to a second- or third-run cinema, or destroyed.

In those early days of television, shifting to electronic distribution and projection felt inevitable. But like many enthusiastic visionaries before them, the only mistake Goldwyn and Abramson made was expecting change to come quickly.

Even on the verge of the 21st century, filmmakers, cinematographers, studios, theater owners, and the movie industry's equipment suppliers remained stubbornly attached to celluloid, and the companies that sought to make film a digital medium encountered countless cold shoulders. Upgrading an industry with such a vast web of interdependent players, each with its own financial motivations and a long list of justifications for preserving the status quo, is rarely an easy task.

•   •   •

Paul Breedlove was born in Texas, a small town called Overton, and he hadn't spent much time living outside of the Lone Star state. His accent, twangy and thick as barbecue sauce, made his origins clear. An engineer by training, Breedlove seemed unable to address a topic any way other than head-on, but he managed to mix his straightforwardness with warmth and humor.

At Texas Instruments, Breedlove gravitated towards the most exciting new technologies. First it was pocket calculators. Then Breedlove helped to invent an electronic learning aid called Speak & Spell, intended to teach children how to spell; more than two million of the talking toys were sold around the world, and the earthbound alien E.T. even used one, modified somewhat, to phone home. Breedlove also helped Texas Instruments get into the personal computer business, working on laptops and desktops in the early 1980s.

By 1996, as the result of a management shuffle, Breedlove wound up in a division that was trying to commercialize a technology that the company had been developing for about fifteen years. Texas Instruments had bestowed upon the technology (and the division) a three-letter acronym: DLP, for digital light processor. It was a chip whose surface was made up of a field of miniature mirrors that reflected colored light onto a screen.

Texas Instruments had licensed the technology to Digital Projection to make projectors that were used in conference rooms and for big trade show presentations, but neither Digital Projection nor TI could figure out how to crack the cinema market. (Not counting their little experiment with Avalos and Weiler.) Breedlove felt the DLP chip might fit well inside consumer television sets, as high-definition television arrived. But he also suspected that HDTV would be a market that'd be slow to develop.

"I began to look at the digital cinema market as a way to build awareness in the consumer marketplace for this DLP technology," Breedlove said. "By doing digital cinema, we'd be showing the world that this technology is good enough to be the technology of choice in the industry where pictures are valued most." If DLP was on display at the neighborhood theater on

Friday night, Breedlove figured, when DLP-powered television sets began appearing in the window of the local electronics store, consumers would have positive associations.

How many people did Breedlove know in the movie industry? "Not one soul," he admitted. "But I never let that stop me. I didn't know anybody in the PC business when I went into that. And one of the first people I met was Bill Gates."

Breedlove's engineering team had developed a next-generation DLP chip that he thought might be good enough to show to Hollywood. It produced a higher-resolution image than the chips that were in the projector Avalos and Weiler had used. (Each projector relied on three chips: one each to bounce red, green, and blue light onto the screen.) A few executives from Viacom, the parent company of Paramount Pictures, traveled to Texas to see an early version that could only produce still images.

Not much came of the visits, but Breedlove, skilled at working the system within TI, still managed to get approval from his higher-ups to spend more time and money on the new chip, and actually incorporate it into a prototype projector.

As soon as the prototype was done, Texas Instruments finagled an invitation to bring it to the Paramount Studios lot on Melrose Avenue for a demonstration. The projector wasn't going to win any beauty pageants. It was too big and clunky to fit into the projection booth of Screening Room #5, so Paramount's carpenters built a platform for it in the back of the theater, extracting a few seats to make room.

TI had been given clips from Paramount movies such as *The Godfather*, *Top Gun*, and *Indecent Proposal*. The Paramount executives who trooped in, including Wayne Llewellen, head of distribution, didn't exactly gush. One said, "Well, it ain't cinema, but I'd sure like one of these in my house."

William Friedkin, a director who was married to Sherry Lansing, the chairman of the studio, was more positive, exclaiming that he didn't believe he was seeing video. (Friedkin had made *The French Connection* and *The Exorcist*; Lansing herself wasn't at the demo.) But when Paramount invited a group of cinematographers in to see the demonstration, they rattled off a list of things they'd like to see improved. The most common criticism: the blacks on the screen just weren't black enough. The cinematographers also complained that if they sat close enough to the screen, they could see spaces between the pixels —a problem dubbed the "screen door" effect, because it was like looking at the image through a screen door. And the colors just weren't right.

"It was enough to work on for a long time," Breedlove said. They went back to Texas, realizing they'd need to ask management for more money to make the projector better.

•   •   •

Avalos and Weiler were savvy promoters, and they didn't just take their $5,040 in ticket sales and go home. They'd generated a few press clippings and local TV stories, and Web articles with their all-digital premiere at the County Theater. They realized that what they had was not just a movie, but a marketing hook.

Avalos realized that sending DigiBeta tapes around to theaters probably wasn't going to be the new means of movie distribution – it wasn't a whole lot easier, after all, than the existing approach of shipping reels of celluloid – and he'd heard a bit about the concept of sending movies to theaters via satellite. So he and Weiler started calling companies that had satellite transmission capabilities, pitching them on the idea of being the first to actually send a movie to a theater by way of earth orbit.

"Trying to get companies to support us was the hardest thing I've ever done," Weiler said. "I'd tell people that the studios were just going to be on the sidelines. They wanted to wait and see what'd happen. But we were willing to do this now..."

They convinced a division of Loral Space & Communications, called CyberStar, to provide free transmission for a new, national release of the movie that they were planning for October 1998. Ron Maehl, president of the division, was game to be part of motion picture history, and at the same time promote his company's ability to beam digital files of all kinds anywhere in the world.

They went to Plano, Texas to try to get some financial backing from Texas Instruments. "We said that all innovation has always come from the ground up in Hollywood, from the independents," Avalos recalled. "We told them they needed a two-pronged approach, to work with the big studios and the small-time, independent filmmakers." Texas Instruments agreed with Avalos. But TI executive Doug Darrow "told us that the independent they were really interested in was George Lucas," Avalos recalled.

Texas Instruments did wind up supporting the national release, as did CyberStar and Digital Projection. CyberStar installed a satellite dish atop each of the five theaters that were showing the movie, and Digital Projection installed projectors temporarily. The movie was packaged into a nine-gigabyte file and sent from CyberStar's network center in northern California up to the Telstar 5 satellite in orbit 22,300 miles above the earth, and then down to theaters in Orlando, Minneapolis, Philadelphia, Providence, Rhode Island, and Portland, Oregon. There, the file was stored on a server until showtime.

"We helped make sure the dishes were aligned with the satellites, and we ran cables down from the roof to the computers. We were as hands-on as it gets," said Avalos. "I was sweating bullets up in the projection booth." During the first showing, they held their breath. "We were promoting the fact that the digital version could never get scratched, and that the movie would look perfect, but the truth was, back then, the computers would hiccup more than you would've liked," Avalos said.

After a week of trouble-free screenings, *Variety* reported the box office totals (*Broadcast* had grossed about $18,000 so far), and Weiler fielded a trickle of calls from studio executives. "They'd read about it, and they were interested in knowing about the ticket sales, and whether the technology had worked OK." Weiler told them that it had, but the conversations didn't go further than that. Theater owners, Avalos added, "weren't interested at all [in digital cinema]. The equipment was just too expensive, from their point of view."

The filmmakers brought their digital dog-and-pony show to the Toronto International Film Festival, South by Southwest in Austin, Texas, and the Sundance Film Festival. Usually, they were regarded as heretics. "Sundance was not interested in digital or the word 'video,'" Avalos said. "A lot of the little indie guys said, 'I'll never shoot digital. Film is film.'"

They were invited to show *Broadcast* at the Cleveland International Film Festival, but the organizers requested a 35-millimeter print. "We didn't have one, and we couldn't afford to make one," Avalos said. "They said, 'We're a film festival, not a video festival.'" Avalos told them that the projector they had been using was not like the video projectors that the organizers might have seen in the past, and eventually, the organizers consented. But they also took the time to issue a notice that even though they were going to bend the rules to project a movie that had never existed on celluloid, this wasn't a permanent change to the festival's entry criteria.

In November 1998, the Independent Film Channel offered *The Last Broadcast* as a download on its Web site, making it among the first movies made available as a legal Internet download.

•   •   •

Around the same time, Texas Instruments returned to Paramount with a new version of the projector. They'd increased the amount of light it could put on the screen, and also improved the DLP chip's ability to produce a range of darker colors (again, they planned to show *The Godfather* as part of the demo, so being able to put represent shadowy scenes was key.)

The new chip had a nickname: "the black chip," because the engineers at TI had realized that the shiny aluminum surface underneath all of the tiny mirrors was unintentionally bouncing too much extra light onto the screen. If they used a black-colored alloy beneath the mirrors, they discovered that it would absorb much of the excess light that they didn't want cast on the screen. It was the high-tech version of putting dark velvet curtains in the windows.

They set up the projector this time in the biggest theater on the studio's lot, the 528-seat Paramount Theater, built in 1994, but designed to look like it had been there forever, with a sleek, curved entrance. In addition to *The Godfather*, they had collected clips from *The Truman Show*, *Braveheart*, and *Grease*. Breedlove was much more confident about the projector this time around. They were showing it on a much bigger screen – fifty feet wide – and also allowing the digital image to be shown side-by-side with film, in a split-screen format, for comparison.

"We invited everyone in Hollywood that any of us knew, or could find, or could get word to," Breedlove said. "This was our first big push into Hollywood."

Some of the directors and cinematographers who'd made the movies being shown came to see the demos. Peter Weir, director of *The Truman Show*, was impressed. (In one clip, actor Ed Harris' face filled the screen, and the close-up was so crisp that some dubbed it "the face that launched digital cinema.") But Bill Butler, the cinematographer who'd shot the hit musical *Grease*, felt like the colors weren't being reproduced accurately. One thing that bothered him: the projector wasn't precisely matching the brick-red color on a sweater John Travolta wore.

Even TI's advocates admitted that there was still work to be done. "*Braveheart* looked good, but film looked better. There were greens on those

Scottish hills that we just couldn't get exactly right," said Loren Nielsen, a consultant who was working with Texas Instruments. She admitted, too, that since the projector didn't yet have a wide enough dynamic range, there were plenty of movies that TI wouldn't have included in the demo. (Dynamic range, sometimes called contrast ratio, is similar to an opera singer's range. Bigger is better.) As an example, she mentioned some of the movies made by cinematographer Conrad Hall.

"There were lots of people who were still unconvinced," Nielsen said. "They said that it just didn't look as warm as film, or that they just didn't like the way it looks, or that they thought it was important that the TI projector didn't have a shutter like a traditional film projector, so the eye was seeing the images on the screen in a different way." And even with the improved chip, some people still complained about the "screen door" problem. If they sat close enough, they could see lines between the pixels.

"It wasn't soup yet," said Rob Hummel, who at the time was an executive at DreamWorks SKG, the studio founded by Steven Spielberg, Jeffrey Katzenberg, and David Geffen. Hummel had brought a few cinematographers with him. One of them, coincidentally, was Conrad Hall. To cinematographers, Hall was a revered figure: he'd shot movies such as *Cool Hand Luke, Marathon Man,* and *Butch Cassidy and the Sundance Kid,* and he liked to say that cinematography was "the language of storytelling."

Though Paramount had agreed to host some of the early demonstrations of the TI technology, the studio still didn't seem very eager to develop a strategy for releasing movies digitally. Studio executives believed that if anything was going to replace film, it had to not just replicate the quality of film, but surpass it.

"We didn't want the parade to pass us by," said Gino Campagnola, who was Paramount's executive vice president for domestic distribution. "We wanted to keep ourselves apprised of what the developments were, but we felt that this was going to be a gradual process."

But several Disney executives made the trip across town to see the demonstrations at Paramount, and they thought the images on the screen didn't look too bad.

•   •   •

Another person who attended the Texas Instruments demo at Paramount in the fall of 1998 was Dave Schnuelle, director of technology at THX. (THX, part of the Lucasfilm family of companies, was founded to improve the audio and visual quality level of the typical movie theater.) Schnuelle had been tracking the projector's development from afar. "Every year, we'd go to trade shows and look at the projectors, waiting for one to be good enough to release a movie with," Schnuelle said. He thought Texas Instruments was within spitting distance, and so he invited Breedlove to come up to Skywalker Ranch in Marin County, Lucasfilm's headquarters, and set up the prototype projector during the company's holiday party.

"Ostensibly, it was to show the projector to the THX guys during their party, but underneath that was the idea of maybe trying to get [Lucasfilm producer] Rick McCallum to see it, and if he saw it, maybe he could get [George] Lucas to come," Breedlove said. It was a gamble. Late 1998 was a busy time at the Ranch, since Lucasfilm was readying *Star Wars: Episode I – The Phantom Menace* for release in May 1999, its first new "Star Wars" movie in fifteen years.

The TI crew set up their projector in the Stag Theater, the largest screening room at the Ranch. The 300-seat Stag has a streamlined, Art Deco interior, and it was designed by Lucas himself to be the ideal place to watch a movie with an audience.

Breedlove, Doug Darrow, and their crew fired up the projector and ran the demo for the THX employees: many of the same clips that had been shown at Paramount, plus a 12-minute demo reel of Lucasfilm material, complete with a rousing John Williams soundtrack. But McCallum didn't show up, and neither did Lucas. Breedlove was crestfallen; the gamble hadn't worked.

Just as they were thinking about packing up the projector, McCallum and Lucas materialized in the theater, sat down, and asked if they might see the demo. Breedlove was told that, at the very most, Lucas would be able to stay for 15 minutes.

They rolled the Lucasfilm demo reel, but after that, the pair asked to see more, and so the Paramount clips were projected.

McCallum was on his feet even before the house lights came up. "The digital had no weave," he exclaimed, meaning that since there was no film running through the projector, the image didn't shift slightly from left to right on the screen as it would with a film projector. It was rock solid. McCallum and Lucas had long been frustrated by the sub-par quality of film projection in most cinemas, and they hoped that digital projection could offer a more consistent experience. "All of our dreams are coming true," McCallum said.

McCallum and Lucas started peppering Breedlove and Darrow with questions: How were the images created? Were they manufacturing the projectors in large quantities yet?

"The THX guys were all gathered around us, listening to Rick and George's reactions," Breedlove recalled. "It was like a huddle in the theater." The fifteen-minute demo stretched to over an hour.

Before they all filed out of the Stag, McCallum asked, "How can we help?"

Breedlove knew that he had to aim for the big prize. He'd heard that Lucasfilm had already been talking with another company, CineComm, about showing the movie using a competing projector technology that had been developed by the defense contractor Hughes, and JVC, the Japanese electronics company. "Well, you can let us do a demo of your new *Star Wars* movie when it comes out," Breedlove replied. He thought the TI projector would be able to hold its own against the Hughes-JVC projector – if McCallum and Lucas would give it a chance.

McCallum didn't need to think for more than a second: "OK. Call me, and we'll work out the details," he told Breedlove.

Breedlove and Darrow went back to Texas, having bagged the biggest independent in the movie business.

•   •   •

Every March, several thousand cinema owners descend on Las Vegas for an industry gathering called ShoWest. They schmooze with the distribution representatives from the studios, watch advance screenings of a handful of movies, listen to speeches analyzing the prior year's business conditions, and roam the aisles of a trade show floor.

The show floor offers a hint at the realities of being a cinema owner.

Most numerous, it seems, are the booths offering up new ways to make money selling concessions: Rico's Nachos, Nestle's new dark chocolate Raisinets, several different strains of popping corn and artificial topping, and all sorts of candy vending machines. Since exhibitors make the lion's share of their money at the concession stand, not the box office, the focus on food makes sense.

Also on display are ATM-like ticketing kiosks, miniature searchlights, and bright LED signs to advertise what's showing. There are high-backed black leather seats that would look perfect in a millionaire's basement screening room, and companies that will come out and re-upholster ragged old theater seats. Janitorial services hand out fliers, and one booth sells bottles of a fabulous solvent called Rid-A-Gum, guaranteed to divorce chewing gum from carpeting and cloth seats. There are makers of digital projectors and servers across the aisle from companies that make film projectors.

Lavish parties are also an essential part of the ShoWest agenda, intended to get theater owners excited about booking a studio's forthcoming films, and then promoting them heavily.

In 1999, the 25th anniversary of ShoWest, one of the most memorable parties was sponsored by Disney to promote its latest animated release, *Tarzan*. The studio showed the movie in its entirety (though some sequences were still in rough form), followed by a live performance by Phil Collins, who'd written the music. When the hour-long concert was over, guests were treated to a sumptuous buffet and a jungle-themed party. They meandered through vines and foliage, peering at an African spotted leopard and an Indian Bengal tiger (both caged), and Disney chairman Michael Eisner, who was roaming free.

"People couldn't make up their minds about whether they were more impressed with the movie or the party," said Phil Barlow, who ran Disney's distribution arm, Buena Vista Pictures. "What they knew was that they had to play the movie."

At that year's ShoWest, on the night of March 9th, Texas Instruments and Lucasfilm executives were still working out the details of their digital cinema collaboration. Breedlove was in a hotel suite at Bally's, talking to McCallum by phone. Faxes zipped back and forth from Las Vegas to California. "This had never been done before," Breedlove said, "and so everyone was trying to cross all the t's and dot all the i's."

The next day, Lucas planned to announce to the nation's theater owners that *The Phantom Menace* would be shown digitally in four theaters, two of them operated by CineComm using the Hughes-JVC projector, and two of them operated by Texas Instruments. "We were all sleep-deprived the next day, but we managed to get the contract worked out by one or two in the morning," Breedlove recalled.

Scheduled for the following day was the first public "shoot-out" between the Texas Instruments projector and the Hughes-JVC model. It was to take place in the Jubilee Theater at Bally's, a venue more regularly occupied by long-legged showgirls wearing feathered headdresses and not much else. Both of the new digital projectors would be shown alongside a projection of Kodak 35-millimeter film, the roots of which stretched back to George Eastman and Thomas Edison. The Texas Instruments contingent was feeling confident, having set up their projector early; they sat back and watched as technicians from Hughes-JVC made an endless succession of small adjustments to their projector as showtime approached.

About 45 minutes before the shoot-out was scheduled to take place, Breedlove was onstage, doing a sound check and figuring out where he and the other presenters would sit. He looked up and noticed a commotion in the projection booth. Someone was taking the entire head off of TI's projector – tantamount to removing the engine from a stock car just before a race.

Up in the booth, no one was exactly sure what had happened, but the projector had just stopped working. So two of the TI technicians went down into a basement storage area and got a spare projector head. (The projector was made up of two basic components, a standard lamphouse, which supplied the light, and the DLP projector head, which used prisms to separate the white light into red, green, and blue light; reflected it off three separate DLP micro-mirror chips; and then cast it onto the screen.) The technicians coolly bolted on the new head, replaced a few of the cables, and switched on the power. There was no time for any fine-tuning, and they couldn't even project a test onto the screen, since the audience had already started filling the theater.

Thankfully, the hastily-reassembled system worked fine. (It was later determined that someone had stepped on or kicked out a power cord, which caused an arc of electricity that blew out a circuit in the projector.)

Breedlove, looking back, considered the mishap "one of the most beneficial things to happen to us. A lot of the people we knew in Hollywood were up there in the booth, and either saw it happen or heard about it afterward." It became a commercial, essentially, illustrating that the TI projector didn't require the constant care – and lengthy warm-up time – that the Hughes-JVC projector needed. Just take it out of the crate, plug it in, and it worked.

During the shoot-out, Breedlove and CineComm executive Russ Wintner tried to emphasize the advantages of digital projection, pointing out that the last showing of a movie would look exactly the same as the first, while a film print would accumulate dust and scratches the more it was shown. Kodak executives emphasized what they described as the richer depth and tonality of film, and boasted that the company was continually improving the quality of its film stock.

"And by the way," Kodak executive Bob Mayson asked with a smirk, "where are you going to find the people with hands small enough to polish all of those tiny digital mirrors?" It was a great line, and Wintner couldn't help chuckling.

But Mayson also proclaimed that digital wouldn't take off until directors and producers decided to back it. And that, he said, hadn't yet happened.

Mayson's statement, correct when uttered, was rendered wrong a few hours later. Lucas appeared onstage at ShoWest to make three big announcements: he was moving the release date for *The Phantom Menace* up by two days; he planned to show the new movie digitally on four screens; and he was expecting to shoot the next installment in his *Star Wars* series with a digital camera. Brimming with optimism about the new technology, Lucas said, "I can't think of a better time to be in the motion picture business," and then he premiered a new trailer for the much-anticipated movie.

"That sound you heard during the *Star Wars* trailer was 20 guys from Kodak jumping off the roof of the hotel," quipped one exhibitor.

•   •   •

The lucky streak didn't last forever for Lance Weiler and Stephen Avalos, the ambitious indie filmmakers. In April of 1999, they were starting a tour to promote the idea of electronic cinema, along with all the equipment companies that had been supportive. It began in midtown Manhattan, at the Director's Guild of America Theatre, and eventually took them to Cannes, France.

A tiny Topeka, Kansas company called QuVis had recently volunteered to provide a prototype server to Weiler and Avalos. The server was the computer that stored the digital movie and funneled it to the projector (it replaced the tape deck they'd used at the County Theater premiere).

At the Director's Guild showing of *Broadcast*, "we were now playing to a large room of absolute professionals – people who know the business in and out," Avalos said. About twenty minutes into the movie, "the damned thing just locked up on us." The picture froze, then skipped ahead to a point later in the movie, then back. QuVis executive George Scheckel was in the theater, and he sprang up and raced toward the projection booth. A few audience members got up to leave.

There was a tense pause as the server was restarted, and then snickering as *Broadcast* was fast-forwarded on the screen to the point where it had stopped playing. (There was no way to skip to a particular point in the movie, as one would do with a DVD at home.) "It was inelegant," Scheckel acknowledged. Weiler said it was his "worst nightmare."

Then, later that year, another movie made cheaply, in part with a digital video camera and in part with a 16-millimeter film camera, was released. Like *Broadcast*, it was about a group of people venturing into the wilderness to see if they could find a mythical, evil creature. The filmmakers asserted that they'd never seen *The Last Broadcast*, and that they had begun writing their movie years before *Broadcast* came out.

The Blair Witch Project opened in the summer of 1999, earned $1.5 million on its opening weekend, and went on to sell $140 million worth of tickets, without relying on satellites or digital projectors.

•   •   •

Dave Schnuelle was the catalyst who'd helped broker the introduction between Texas Instruments and Lucasfilm, and later it fell to him to actually make sure that the movie would be ready to play in the four digital theaters. Thousands of movies had been released on reels of celluloid; this would be the first time that audiences would have a chance to buy tickets for a digital showing of a major motion picture, and no one knew exactly how the process would work. The goal was for the digital shows of *The Phantom Menace* to start on June 18th, a month after the film version of the movie had opened. They needed the extra month – at the very least – to get ready.

"We weren't worried so much about the projectors," Schnuelle said, "but the rest of the hardware we'd need didn't really exist. But when [Lucas and McCallum] asked me in February whether we could do it, I said, 'I think we could probably pull it together." Schnuelle and his many of his colleagues wound up working 20-hour days for the next four months. "There was a blur there," he said, "between February and June, when the movie opened."

In Burbank, two separate facilities were set up to get *The Phantom Menace* ready for its digital debut. One, at Modern VideoFilm, had a projector from Texas Instruments and one from Hughes-JVC, which were used to adjust the color of the movie, a process called "color correction." The movie had to be color-corrected three times, since it would look slightly different when it was projected on film, shown using the Texas Instruments projector, or played on the Hughes-JVC projector. At another facility in Burbank, International Video Conversions, they looked at the digital versions of the movie on a big screen, and occasionally compared them to the film print. The movie's editor, Paul Martin Smith, would stop in occasionally to offer his opinion on the results.

Schnuelle and his colleagues were growing frustrated with the Hughes-JVC projector. "It was a nice technology, but the color wasn't very stable – it floated around," he said. The color composition of a scene would look different from one day to the next. "The one thing you never wanted to do with the Hughes was turn it off. It could be days before it would stabilize again," Schnuelle said.

•　　•　　•

Interest in digital cinema was percolating at Disney, too, after executives there saw some of the Texas Instruments demos in Hollywood. And working with Disney, the industry's largest and most successful distributor of movies at the time, was one of TI's goals.

The studio had already been evaluating the Hughes-JVC projector at a research lab on Long Island. There, Disney "Imagineers" were trying to modify the projector so that it produced a brighter image on the screen. They were led by Bran Ferren, a red-bearded technology guru who wore a safari jacket to work every day.

"It used a tremendous amount of power," recalled Breedlove. "They'd put in a larger lamp, and they had a cooling system mounted on top of the thing that looked like a smokestack on an old wood-fired train. It was a sight to behold." (It was noisy, too, and when Disney demonstrated the projector for executives at a theater it owned on Hollywood Boulevard, the El Capitan, a special soundproof box had to be built to enclose it. It harkened back to the iceboxes that were used to muffle the cameras on the sets of talkies in the 1920s and 1930s.)

Texas Instruments brought its projector out to Long Island, and convinced Disney that its technology was the better horse to bet on.

"As soon as Lucas made his announcement about *The Phantom Menace* at ShoWest, the Disney guys came to us" to start to talk about their first digital release, Breedlove said. "They wanted to be one of the leaders, too."

"In a larger sense, we felt it was great that George Lucas had stepped up to the plate," said Bob Lambert, Disney's senior vice president for technology. "But there was also a minor amount of disappointment that we had been headed down the same road, and had been preparing a whole slate of movies for release, when he made his announcement." But Disney wanted to have more than just four digital screens, and persuading theaters to participate in the experiment ate up a lot of time.

Disney achieved a different first, however, when it became the first studio to name an executive to be solely responsible for digital cinema, just after Lucas spoke at ShoWest 1999.

As Disney's top distribution executive, Phil Barlow had presided over an unprecedented period of growth and profitability. He was tall and lanky, with a cutting, dry wit, and a penchant for squeezing a smoke into any free moment. Barlow had started his career in the movies in 1961, as an usher at a theater in Salt Lake City.

In 1999, Barlow was ready to retire. "I was getting bored," said Barlow. "I'd had a few heart attacks, and I owned a disco and a restaurant in Brittany," Barlow said. "France seemed more appealing." But Dick Cook, chairman of the Disney studio, asked Barlow if he'd help jump-start Disney's digital cinema effort. "It wouldn't be boring," Cook promised.

Barlow took the job, though he realized that other studios would probably see it as showboating on Disney's part to name the first executive responsible for what was then called "e-cinema." (As the term "digital cinema" overtook "electronic cinema" in the early 21st century, d-cinema also began to replace e-cinema as an abbreviation.)

"We were the first to say, 'This is the future,' and I think Paramount especially was pissed," Barlow said. "They'd been working with TI and doing all of the first demos, and here we were, announcing that we really wanted to make an effort on digital. They felt we were stealing their thunder." (Disney and Paramount had a long-running rivalry, and the two studios always seemed to wind up on opposite sides of industry debates.)

Meanwhile, Miramax, Disney's art-film subsidiary, was traveling on its own trajectory.

A consultant to Miramax had seen one of the Hughes-JVC projectors at a trade show, and agreed to do some tests with the company. At the National Association of Broadcasters convention in April 1999, Miramax's *Shakespeare in Love* was projected using the Hughes-JVC machine – while the movie was still playing in theaters. Later, Miramax co-chairman Harvey Weinstein decided to adjust the release date of *An Ideal Husband*, an adaptation of an Oscar Wilde play, so that it would open – and play digitally on two screens, using the Hughes-JVC projector – on the same Friday that the digital run of *The Phantom Menace* was to begin. (When the movie, starring Julianne Moore and Rupert Everett, had been screened at the Cannes Film Festival in April, its U.S. release date had been advertised as June 26th.)

Mark Gill, then president of Miramax, insisted that it wasn't a bid for publicity to open *Ideal Husband* on the same day as *Phantom Menace*, in the same two regions, New York and Los Angeles. "It just happened," he said. "The idea was just to try [a digital release]. Our feeling was that digital could be a huge opportunity to reduce print costs and transport costs, and maybe also get art films to play in places where art films don't usually play." (Miramax also gave permission for the movie to be shown digitally earlier in the week at a trade show in Orlando, edging *Phantom Menace*.)

But Breedlove didn't see it as a coincidence. "The nature of Miramax is just like that," he said. "They're an in-your-face kind of company."

•   •   •

As June 18th approached, Schnuelle's job shifted to supervising the installation of the servers and projectors at the two theaters in the Los Angeles area that'd show *The Phantom Menace*, an AMC theater in Burbank (which had the Texas Instruments projector) and one owned by the Pacific Theatres chain in Chatsworth, in the San Fernando Valley (which had the Hughes-JVC).

Usually, at the Pacific, Schnuelle would bump into Russ Wintner from CineComm, who was also working frantically to make sure the company's system would be ready. One problem was the temperamental Hughes-JVC projector. "The temperature in the projection booth couldn't change three degrees, or the color would go off," Wintner said. "We had to bring in a big industrial air conditioner to blow on the projector."

Wintner's family had been in the movie business for three generations. His grandfather had opened a drive-in theater in Cleveland, the Memphis, and then, with Wintner's father, built that into a collection of theaters in Florida, Ohio, and the Bahamas. Eventually, the company was sold to Regal Cinemas in 1994, which was on its way to becoming the country's largest theater chain. But Wintner held onto the drive-in, even as he ventured into digital cinema.

With *The Phantom Menace*, Wintner said, "we really felt that we were making history. We felt that when people would talk about *The Jazz Singer* and Al Jolson, they'd talk about *Star Wars* and CineComm," Appended to the credits of the digital version of the movie were the names of the Texas Instruments, THX, and CineComm employees who'd been involved with the digital release.

On the east coast, the movie was slated to play in two Loews theaters in New Jersey, and CineComm was determined to "get light on the screen first" at its theater in Paramus. "We hit the screen first, at one minute after noon on Friday," Wintner said. (The first showtime had also been moved up so that *The Phantom Menace* would be sure to start before the first screening of *An Ideal Husband*, according to Schnuelle. "We beat them by about half an hour," he said.) The theater was full. "We gave a little talk to the audience before every single show about digital projection, and we had t-shirts for the audience," Wintner said, adding that the CineComm equipment worked flawlessly, not missing a single show.

Just in case, though, throughout the month-long run of *The Phantom Menace*, at each of the four theaters a technician from THX was on hand to deal with any problems. If that was the belt, the suspenders were that there was also a film projector at the ready next to the digital projector. Its lamp wasn't on, but it was running a copy of the film, started one minute after the digital projector, in case the digital version suddenly died and the projectionist had to switch over to film. Patrons in the back of the theater could hear, faintly, the fluttering sound of the film projector even as the digital version filled the screen.

Both Lucasfilm and 20th Century Fox, the movie's distributor, were worried about the consequences if someone managed to steal one of the servers that held a digital version of *The Phantom Menace*. (The data files themselves weren't protected by encryption, or a system of software locks.) One day during the run, Francis Ford Coppola was touring the projection booth at the AMC in Burbank, and he asked how this security dilemma had been handled. "I said, the security was right here, and pointed to a guy with a gun who was watching the server," remembered

> Stealing the digital version of *The Phantom Menace* was likely more difficult than stealing the film version. In Wisconsin, a trio of young men stole a print of the movie from a projection booth in Menomonie in the middle of the night. They were quickly caught, and sentenced to five days in jail. They were also ordered to pay the theater for the cost of its lost business – and a replacement print.

Garrett Smith, a Paramount executive who was Coppola's tour guide. Guards had been stationed in the projection booths around-the-clock.

• • •

At Laemmle's Sunset 5, a theater in West Hollywood, Miramax's *Ideal Husband* played digitally on one screen, using the Hughes-JVC projector, and on celluloid in another auditorium. "On the first day, digital looked as good as 35-millimeter," Gill said. "But after about five days, there was no comparison between the film print and the digital version." The digital version hadn't changed, but the film print had started to accumulate dust and scratches after its many trips through the projector. Miramax conducted exit polls in New York and Los Angeles, and found that 91 percent of respondents felt that the digital projection was "as good or better than film." (Gill admitted, though, that in scenes with fast-moving objects or characters, "trails" sometimes appeared on the screen.)

Disney had decided to make *Tarzan* its first digital release, and in preparing a digital file, ran into many of the same technical issues as Schnuelle's THX team had encountered. There was also some internal foot-dragging.

"People can come up with a litany of reasons why it's not worth the trouble, as happens with any disruptive technology," said Bob Lambert at Disney. "People said that it was just a single-digit number of theaters, and a disproportional amount of energy was being put into doing it, with people preparing digital masters, and going out to check on the theaters."

Disney chose to play the movie from DigiBeta tapes, as *The Last Broadcast* had done, "purely because of the comfort factor," said Chris Carey, an employee of Disney's technical services group. They were anxious enough about the projector, and didn't want to also worry about a server crashing. The tape player – a kind often used for TV broadcasting – wouldn't crash.

Time was incredibly tight. "You were inserting yourself into a film post-production [process] that was really set up around using every last minute to do creative improvements on the film," Carey said. "They just barely had enough time to get the color timing done and go into mass replications of release prints, and here we were trying to do this digital mastering process."

Behind the scenes, studio chairman Dick Cook was assuring Disney's post-production executives that he understood that digital cinema seemed like a black hole consuming time and resources, but that the work was important to him.

•   •   •

People came to New Jersey from as far away as Maryland to see the digital version of *The Phantom Menace*. "I saw it the old-fashioned way, and this just blows it away," said one ticket-buyer, John Rybacki. Teenager Zev Eth pronounced it "30 times better this way." Executives from Disney and Sony dropped by, as did owners of other theaters.

A writer for the New York *Times* decided to compare the experience of seeing *The Phantom Menace* on the two different systems, using film projection as a benchmark. In Seacaucus, New Jersey, Rob Sabin saw the Texas Instruments projector. "The image was bright, with sharply defined edges around objects and excellent detail," he wrote. "Contrast, while not so deep as the best film can offer, was very good. ...The pixel structure, which can show up as a faint grid on this type of projector, was never obvious, even from the first few rows." Sabin concluded that the average audience member wouldn't have been able to tell that the image on the screen was digital.

In Paramus, Sabin wrote that the Hughes-JVC projector "produced a silkier, softer picture more in keeping with the film version and with film in general." But, he said, "at other times, the picture was more reminiscent of video, specifically of a projector or television set with the contrast control turned up."

While Sabin seemed to prefer the Texas Instruments projector, he concluded that both had passed the test: the typical moviegoer "would neither recognize nor fault them for being electronic. So the *Phantom Menace* run proved, at least to me, that the technology for electronic projection has indeed arrived."

Sabin's story estimated that it might take between two and ten years for the projectors to start showing up in local theaters, shepherded along by the studios.

"...Like it or not, the time has come to bid farewell to Edison's form of cinematic magic and swap it for another," Sabin wrote.

Sabin's review spawned a point-by-point response a few days later from Joerg Agin, Kodak's president of Entertainment Imaging, the division responsible for supplying film to the Hollywood studios (and the division that employed Bob Mayson.)

"Film has a unique look that other technologies try, without success, to emulate," Agin wrote. He objected that Sabin had made the arrival of digital cinema sound inevitable. "The truth is, with the exception of Disney, there is no 'mobilization' among studios, only cautious experiments."

He defended film: properly-handled celluloid prints can look good for a long time; cameras fed with film captured more "pixels of information" than digital cameras; and the dynamic range of a film projector was far better than a digital projector. (Dynamic range is the distance from the whitest white to the blackest black.) But Agin also mentioned that Kodak was developing a "higher quality digital cinema system that will...be twice as good as the best digital projection of today."

America's best-known movie critic, Roger Ebert, was in Agin's camp; he wasn't sure why the cinema needed a new projection technology. He wrote:

> Digital projection at best is seen as only "almost as good" or "about as good" as film. It is expensive, tricky, and if adopted will be perceived as no better than the high-def home TV in the consumer pipeline. Theaters have traditionally offered *better* pictures than TV, not the same.

Ebert would write repeatedly about his distaste for digital. (He'd also repeatedly plug a new system for film projection called MaxiVision, which aimed to improve the quality of images on the screen by projecting twice as many frames per second, but still relied on traditional celluloid. One of the developers of MaxiVision was the movie editor Dean Goodhill.) When one of Ebert's readers wrote in to say that he felt that the Texas Instruments projection of *The Phantom Menace* in Burbank was better than film, Ebert countered that the reader had seen "a custom-built installation with squads of TI acolytes hovering in the booth." Ebert added that digital projection systems were "likely to create nightmares for moviegoers" when they crashed. "How would you like it if the movie went down as often as the computers at your bank?" he asked.

•   •   •

A few days after the run of *The Phantom Menace* had ended at the AMC 14 in Burbank, Disney took over the theater for a press demonstration, which was to be followed by a digital run of *Tarzan*.

"We were relieved that we made it," said Disney's Chris Carey, who had raced to get the digital version ready. He was too busy to attend the press event on July 22nd, ensuring that the other theaters were in working order.

Clips from *Tarzan* were screened for a small group of reporters, and Disney executive Bob Lambert explained that "what was unique about this digital cinema screening is that these images didn't come from film, but came directly from the digital data generated by the filmmakers, without a film intermediate element. In any other transfer, you would see the artifacts of the source film material – a few scratches, a few color glitches." (Unlike Pixar's wholly computer-generated movies, though, *Tarzan*'s characters were drawn by hand, and the drawings were then scanned into a computer, and filled in with color there.) Within a few years, Lambert posited, live action films might start using digital cameras, but for the moment, *Tarzan* was the first film to be animated using digital tools, and then shown digitally.

> The voice of Tarzan in Disney's animated version was supplied by Tony Goldwyn, grandson of studio mogul Samuel Goldwyn.

Disney and Texas Instruments were confident enough with digital projection to show it side-by-side with film. They first used an "answer print," fresh from the lab, followed by a release print that had been in use for about four weeks. (An answer print is produced directly from the negative that ran through the camera; a release print, made for distribution to theaters, is a copy several generations distant from the answer print.)

The movie started playing digitally the next day in three theaters – two in southern California, and one at Walt Disney World in Florida. (Already, Tarzan had brought in $130 million in ticket sales.) Ads in the Los Angeles *Times* invited readers to "See the First-Ever All-Digital Major Feature Release!"

The Hollywood trades were impressed with the images, and so were ticket-buyers.

"...*Tarzan* showed sharper image definition and more stable colors (particularly deeper blues) in a split-screen comparison to film," wrote Matthew Doman of *The Hollywood Reporter*.

"I thought it was sharper, very vivid," said Nelson Wong, an audience member who saw *Tarzan* at a multiplex in Orange County, California. "I'd like to see all movies in digital projection."

Tarzan's digital run lasted three weeks. As Ebert had hinted, an engineer baby-sat the projection system for each of the 308 shows. Security was simple: the digital tape containing the movie was kept in a locked safe overnight. (One showtime was delayed when the engineer was late in arriving at the theater and getting the tape out of the safe.) As with *The Phantom Menace*, a celluloid version of the movie ran through a projector as a back-up.

There were a few scattered complaints about visible pixelization – blockiness in the picture – but mainly, the audience seemed to prefer the digitally-projected *Tarzan* to film. (Disney's Chris Carey said he was never content with the way that scrolling credits looked on the earliest TI projectors; the edges of the letters were never smooth.) In Orlando and at the AMC 14 in Burbank, *Tarzan* was shown digitally on one screen and on film in another, and the digital version attracted three times as many patrons.

> More than 50,000 people bought tickets to digital showings of *Tarzan* and *The Phantom Menace* in 1999. But that was just a sliver of the overall movie-going audience: nearly 1.5 billion tickets were sold that year in the U.S.

Disney staffers involved in the *Tarzan* release acknowledged that there were still kinks in the process of preparing a movie for digital projection that needed to be ironed out. Storing the movies on a digital tape wasn't an ideal solution, since tape, like film, would eventually wear out. The equipment needed to be easier to run, so that theater staff, rather than engineers, could operate it. But Disney's conclusion was that "the public accepts the technology," according to an internal company slide show, and that the company ought to "do more d-cinema releases to gain experience and help the technology mature faster."

To try to convince theaters that Disney was serious about continuing to supply digital versions of its movies, Barlow and Lambert decided to announce in November that a series of forthcoming pictures would be available digitally: Pixar's *Toy Story 2*, *Bicentennial Man*, starring Robin Williams, the animated *Dinosaur*, and Brian de Palma's *Mission to Mars*.

Texas Instruments was certain that the bobsled had begun sliding down the track. The company confidently predicted that hundreds of digital projectors would be in place within two to three years, and thousands within five years. "Change is seldom painless; however, the sooner the change starts, the sooner the benefits occur," the company declared in a Q&A document produced for the media. "The feedback we have received indicates that there is a very strong desire to begin the process and get to the benefits as soon as possible."

•   •   •

The press was trumpeting the start of the digital cinema change-over.

As 2000 arrived, *Daily Variety* took a look back at the previous year, and announced, "Hollywood (Finally) Goes Digital." The story began, "Some thought it would never happen, but a traditionally stodgy Hollywood went digital in 1999."

Technology advocates like Paul Breedlove, Phil Barlow, Russ Wintner, and George Lucas wanted it to be true.

But 1999 proved to be a false spring, and the earliest buds of digital cinema would soon be encased in a coat of ice.

Following the month-long digital run of *The Phantom Menace*, Wintner said, "the phone started ringing. People realized that digital cinema was going to happen." Despite the nibbles, CineComm was hampered by having linked its business to the finicky Hughes-JVC projector, and a shortage of funding. Wintner had some discussions with Technicolor about buying the company – or at least a piece of it – but the talks went nowhere.

What Wintner realized, slowly, was that even if people had to acknowledge that digital cinema was coming, "not everyone felt like they wanted to be first. And there were some people who seemed like they wanted to make sure it didn't happen during their lifetime." By 2000, CineComm was out of business. *The Phantom Menace*, it turned out, was the only movie that CineComm ever showed to a paying audience.

U.S. theater owners were starting to wheeze after a marathon of over-building. Since 1995, the industry had been adding more than 2,000 new screens every year, many of them with the newly-trendy stadium-style seating. At the Ontario Mills Shopping Center in southern California, a new 30-screen multiplex sprang up to compete with a 22-screen multiplex directly across the street.

In 1999 and 2000, eleven nationwide theater chains had declared bankruptcy – representing more than half of the country's 36,000 screens. AMC, which had built the world's largest multiplex in a Chicago suburb, featuring 30 screens, wide seats, and an espresso bar, planned to close or sell about 500 of its older screens – almost 20 percent of its total. Loew's

Cineplex, the country's second-biggest chain, shut 675 of its 3,000 screens. General Cinema shelled out nearly $40 million to get out of unprofitable theater leases.

"The timing is terrible," Carmike Cinemas CEO Michael Patrick said as the industry prepared to go to Las Vegas for ShoWest 2000, in March. "We are just ending the biggest building phase in the history of the business. It will be years before we are ready for digital." Six months later, Patrick's company filed for Chapter 11 bankruptcy protection.

The prospect of purchasing digital cinema equipment, which was estimated to cost anywhere from $100,000 to $250,000 per screen, wasn't very appealing in that environment, even if the cost was shared by the studios. At the National Association of Theatre Owners' fall conclave in Atlantic City, held in October 1999, Wayne Anderson, who ran a chain of cinemas headquartered in Maryland, distilled the new NATO party line: it was the studios that derived the biggest benefit from digital cinema, since it would reduce the cost of producing and shipping prints. So, Anderson concluded, the studios should pay.

But no studio, save Disney, had put an executive in charge of exploring digital cinema, and trying to understand how it would change the business. And more importantly, no studio chairman other than Dick Cook at Disney had publicly expressed his or her support for the concept of distributing and projecting movies digitally.

Hollywood is run by people with nuanced lists of priorities – which projects are hot and which are not, whose call to return immediately and who can wait – and digital cinema wasn't anywhere near the top of the priority list of the people running the other major studios.

•   •   •

Albert Abramson, the CBS engineer, was retired and living in Las Vegas. But he was keeping up-to-date on the evolution of digital cinema. In 2000, he sent an e-mail to Bob Lambert at Disney:

> The studios...have been weaned on film and it will take an act of Congress to break up this love affair. They are in love with the so-called "film look," which is merely tradition. (But don't tell them that.) They don't care how much a reel of film costs – as wasteful as it is, it is part of the process. So all this talk by people like Lucas [about] going digital is just that: talk. It will take some consortium (with Disney for example) to seed the

process, and it is going to cost millions.

Abramson, who had envisioned how digital cinema would work half a century earlier, concluded:

> I have long ago learned not to project the future, as it has a bad habit of doing whatever it wants to do...

8: 'Agreeing on the Weather'

Despite the rawness of the digital cinema technology and the theater owners' lack of enthusiasm, several companies and a few studios inexplicably kept investing in it. But as with all technological transitions, there are some players who want to see things happen fast, and others who'd prefer a more predictable, gradual shift.

Disney was in the former camp. "I was one of the few people who had digital cinema as his only job," said Phil Barlow, "and I was pushing like mad."

In November 1999, *Toy Story 2* was the first major studio feature to have its digital and film release occur on the same day, playing at six theaters, including Disney's El Capitan on Hollywood Boulevard. (The El Capitan, built in 1926 for live theater, also hosted the world premiere of *Citizen Kane* in 1941.)

The prototype projectors each contained three of the Texas Instruments digital micro-mirror devices inside, which were about two inches square. Each of the three DMDs was responsible for a different color of light: red, green, or blue. The DMDs operated by angling an array of tiny mirrors in much the same way that a stadium full of football fans might flip a cardboard sign to create a picture of the team mascot. If the mirror was angled in one direction, it would reflect light from the projector's bulb through the lens and onto the screen, and that color would fill one pixel on the screen. But if the mirror was angled just 10 degrees in the other direction, that pixel would be dark. Colors from each of the DMD chips could mix in the space of a single pixel. The mirrors themselves were small enough that about forty of them could be hidden underneath a grain of salt.

The mirrors on each DMD were laid out in a grid, with 1280 mirrors running horizontally, and 1024 running vertically. (As a short-hand, it was said that this projector's resolution was "1.3K," because it had roughly 1300 mirrors running horizontally. The grid of mirrors also created about 1.3 million pixels on the theater's screen.) Texas Instruments estimated that the projector would cost $130,000 to manufacture – though the prototypes had cost much more.

The system looked and sounded nothing like a typical film projector; instead of the purr of a motor and the loud, card-shuffling sounds of film spooling through gears and then past a blinking shutter, there was only the whirr of fans that kept the equipment from overheating. The digital system didn't require a shutter to open and close as film passed the lens. The micromirrors simply tilted, and a picture was always on the screen. An information sheet explained that because the DMD was "a virtually continuous display device," there was "no objectionable flicker." (Opponents of digital cinema would later argue that flicker – a totally black screen alternating with a screen filled with imagery, 24 times a second – was an essential part of the way audiences experienced motion pictures.)

Instead of relying on a digital tape player, as *Tarzan* had, the projector was fed by a server made by QuVis, which was about the size of a pizza box. Inside the server, the digital movie file was stored on four hard drives.

With *Toy Story 2*, Disney kept trying to communicate the economic rationale for digital cinema. As part of a "talking points" document that Disney prepared for some of the digital screenings of *Toy Story 2*, the studio explained that the movie industry spent about $850 million annually making and shipping 75-pound film reels to 33,000 screens around the United States, and that Disney alone spent $75 million a year.

"We wanted the best presentations for our audience," said Barlow. (Pixar president Ed Catmull later asserted that there wasn't a single Grade A, or top-quality, film print produced by Technicolor for the theatrical release of *Toy Story 2*.) But Disney also believed that digital cinema would eventually trim costs in its distribution business – and Disney wanted to convince other studios that they could benefit, too.

Barlow started making calls to distribution executives at other studios to discuss how they might move beyond the experimentation stage, and establish a network of digital cinema systems around the world. The collaboration became known as NewCo Digital Cinema.

"There were anti-trust concerns, and also concerns about what the exhibition community would think if all of the studios were getting together," Barlow said. "We didn't want to make everybody nervous." Anti-trust counsel was retained, and at some of the earliest meetings, the lawyers outnumbered the participants.

Some of the other studios suspected that Disney was such a strong supporter of digital projection because it made animated movies look good, but they feared that it wouldn't present live-action movies as favorably. (Shades of Hollywood's earlier response to Walt's success with Technicolor cartoons.) Lambert found himself frequently pointing out that Disney made many times more live-action movies than animated pictures, even when one counted the company's distribution deal with Pixar.

Within NewCo, Barlow thought of himself like a bulldozer: he'd simply level any obstacles in his way. "I knew that I was stepping on a lot of toes, but to me, the rationales for doing this were so obvious and so clear," he said. The studios would save money on prints and guarantee a more consistent visual experience, but Barlow also imagined cinemas evolving into "a multi-purpose entertainment center," presenting concerts and educational seminars and videogame competitions on their screens. Theater owners needed to "upgrade the experience, to keep pace with the increasing quality of the home system," he said. "In my opinion, [digital] was going to be the salvation of exhibition."

Disney laid out an ambitious goal at the NewCo meetings: getting 7500 digital cinema systems into theaters within five years. Each of the studios would pony up a certain amount to pay for the equipment – about $100 million over time, with the ability to shut down the project if it didn't seem to be working. NewCo would charge exhibitors a per-ticket fee for use of the equipment. After about seven years, the investment would start breaking even, and studios would be able to reduce their per-film distribution costs to a few hundred dollars – whatever it cost to transmit a movie via satellite, or ship a hard drive or set of DVD-ROM discs to the theater. "It was an idea that we put forward to stimulate conversation," Barlow said, and that it did.

Not everyone liked the large up-front investment required by Barlow's straw man plan for a digital cinema roll-out. "Warners said they couldn't accept it, and that they would come up with something better. But they never did," he said.

Later, NewCo shared the business plan it had developed with others, including Boeing, Technicolor, Kodak, and several investment banks, hoping that it might serve as the seed for a digital cinema beanstalk somewhere else. "There was no reason for us not to share it," said Barlow. "It wasn't a proprietary thing. The idea was just to get it done."

By the summer of 2000, there were 38 digital cinemas operating around the world, two-thirds of them in the U.S., but some in places like Seoul, Barcelona, and the AMC multiplex at Tokyo Disneyland. Barlow said his studio was releasing about 40 percent of its movies in a digital format, and the goal was to get to 100 percent by 2002.

Texas Instruments had already begun to realize that breaking in to Hollywood wasn't going to be easy, so the company hired the William Morris Agency to help craft a lobbying campaign.

"We had a list of the top hundred directors in Hollywood, and one of our goals with William Morris was to get all of them into a screening to see our projector," Breedlove said. Usually, the screenings were held in one of the Director's Guild theaters in Los Angeles. "We got a significant number of them there," he said, including Oliver Stone, who wrote a letter to Cody Alexander of William Morris after he saw a demo in October 2000.

"You cannot believe how excited I was after your presentation," Stone wrote. "I have been talking it up to many people. ...It was some of the purest film I have ever seen. Congratulations and may the winds speed your voyage."

Whether dealing with cinematographers, directors, or studio executives, Texas Instruments tried to listen, rather than pitch its products. "We were taking a 'what do they want to do?' approach," said Paul Breedlove. "We weren't trying to drive them, but trying to follow them." Texas Instruments kept improving the contrast ratio, to allow the projector to put blacker blacks on the screen. And while 1.3K was sufficient resolution for the first batch of digital releases, TI was hearing demands for more pixels, so the company started to develop a higher-resolution 2K chip.

Part of Breedlove's job also involved taking the projector around the country to theater chains, giving demos in their own theaters. "We met with most of the chains who had 100 screens or more, and almost 100 percent of the top 20 chains."

Later, it also became his responsibility to find companies that were interested in building projectors that would take advantage of the DLP chip. (TI wasn't in the projector business.) He was surprised that some of the biggest manufacturers of film projectors, like Germany's Kinoton and

Ballantyne of Omaha, either didn't have the interest or the resources to branch into digital projectors. But one venerable maker of film projectors was interested.

•   •   •

In 1929, when S.L. Christie started a venture in Los Angeles to make movie projectors, the film industry was still making the transition from silent to talking pictures.

As Christie's products found a place in projection booths, the company began introducing a series of improvements that made projectors more reliable and easy to operate. Christie replaced the temperamental and short-lived carbon arc lamp with the much more efficient xenon arc lamp in the 1960s; introduced "platter" systems that made the changing of film reels unnecessary; and invented gear-less and self-lubricating projectors. Before those innovations arrived, most projection booths were occupied by two projectionists. Today, projectors are so automated and dependable that one projectionist can supervise all of the theaters in a multiplex.

Jack Kline was Christie's chief operating officer in the late 1990s, as the company approached its 70th anniversary. "We were profitable, working six days a week, ten hours a day, making 35-millimeter projectors," he said. "We were at maximum capacity, and everything was really great."

The company had always dismissed the idea that video projectors, with their fuzzy colors and muddy images, would ever be able to compete with the crisp pictures that Christie's products cast onto the screen. "We said that video will never come about," Kline said. "If video came out first, and then film, people would say, 'Oh, film is so much better.'"

Still, like any good CEO, Kline felt it was important to keep an eye on the video technology as it developed, just in case it did improve to the point where it might threaten sales of 35-millimeter film projectors. In November 1999, one of his technicians attended a demonstration of several digital projectors organized by the National Association of Theater Owners in Denver. "It was supposed to be closed, for theater-owners only," Kline said. "But our guy got in."

"My engineer came back and said, 'It's much sooner than we thought. The TI stuff looks killer.'" At the time, Christie was poorly positioned to take steps toward digital projection. But the more research Kline did, the more he felt that the transition would be a sudden one, given the advantages of digital.

Christie had been acquired in 1992 by Ushio, a Japanese corporation that makes sophisticated light bulbs. Kline made a presentation to the board of directors, telling them that "in two years, we'll be out of business if we don't get into digital projection." The board agreed with Kline's assessment, and approved a plan to acquire Electrohome Systems, a Canadian company that produced digital projectors, for $60 million.

Then, in March 2000, Christie became the first company to license TI's DLP technology. Using the Ontario factory it had acquired with Electrohome, Christie started gearing up to make digital projectors. Kline was also such a believer in the digital future that the company also changed its name, from Christie, Inc. to Christie Digital.

•   •   •

An odd assortment of other companies were working out their own strategies for the digital cinema era.

No one was surprised to see Technicolor decide to get involved with digital cinema, since a giant portion of the company's business – developing film shot on movie sets, correcting the color, manufacturing prints, and sending them to theaters – was imperiled by the new technology.

But what *was* surprising was the company Technicolor chose to ally with in starting Technicolor Digital Cinema: Qualcomm, a San Diego company that made cell phones, wireless communications equipment, and software. In the early 1990s, Qualcomm had developed a method for compressing digital video files so that they could be stored and transmitted more easily, without sacrificing too much quality.

> When Thompson Multimedia bought Technicolor at the end of 2000, processing and distributing celluloid accounted for the largest part of Technicolor's $1.6 billion in revenues.

While many of the first digital cinema systems that Disney used for its releases were paid for by Disney and the exhibitors (70-30 was a typical split), Technicolor Digital Cinema paid the entire cost of more than a dozen early installations on its own. The company's strategy was to outspend any rivals and establish a digital cinema beachhead, even before there was a clear way to earn that money back. "They felt they'd circumvent everybody," said a former Technicolor executive.

"We clearly saw it as important to make sure that we were building our capabilities for digital distribution," acknowledged Joe Berchtold, president of Technicolor Electronic Distribution Services, the division that encompasses digital cinema.

Technicolor regularly alluded to its 80-year history of working with studios and theater owners. But the company stumbled when it announced its plan for earning a return on its investment in digital cinema. At ShoWest, in the spring of 2001, Technicolor executive Dave Elliot proposed that the company would convert 1000 U.S. theaters to digital projection within a year, and exhibitors would contribute 12.5 cents for every ticket they sold to cover the costs of the equipment. (This was similar to the per-patron usage fee that NewCo had been mulling.) Studios that released a digital version of their movies would pay 25 percent less to deliver it to a theater than they paid for a film print.

But the reaction from exhibitors wasn't what Technicolor had hoped for.

"Anyone who thinks exhibs can pay for these systems in their current state is not doing the math," said John Fithian, president of NATO, alluding to the exhibition industry's growing financial problems. *Variety* said that exhibitors' skepticism was "so palpable you could stick a fork in it." Both exhibitors and the studios worried that a company such as Technicolor might develop into a powerful gatekeeper, handling the majority of all digital film distribution and enjoying the freedom to set its own terms and prices.

Though Technicolor Digital Cinema had launched in mid-2000, it wasn't until December 2001 that the group distributed its first digital movie, Warner Bros.' *Ocean's Eleven*, which showed digitally in 19 theaters.

•　　　•　　　•

Hughes Space and Communications had a tenuous link to the movie industry: it was a descendent of Hughes Aircraft, the company that Howard Hughes formed in 1932. Hughes by then had already written, directed, and produced several movies, including *Hell's Angels* and *The Front Page*.

So it wasn't entirely out of character for Hughes' company to dip into digital cinema nearly seventy years later. After the Cold War ended, the company was trying to commercialize some of the projector technology it had created for the military to use in briefing rooms. That led to a partnership with JVC to market the Hughes-JVC projector, one of the two machines used to show *The Phantom Menace* in 1999. But Hughes also thought it might earn money by using its fleet of satellites to distribute movies to theaters, and in the early 1990s, the company created the Hughes Electronic Cinema Program.

> **Hell's Angels, made with $4 million of Howard Hughes' own money, began production in 1927 as a silent film about World War I flyboys. When Hughes decided to convert it to a talkie midway through production, he had to replace Norwegian actress Greta Nissen with Jean Harlow and reshoot most of the picture. (Nissen's accent was deemed too thick.) It was a hit when it finally debuted in 1930.**

But even executives at that program, later renamed Hughes Digital Cinema, weren't thrilled to be relying on the moody Hughes-JVC projector. In late 1995, Walt Ordway, the executive in charge of the group, recommended shutting it down. "The projection technology just wasn't there yet, and the studios knew it," he said.

The group dispersed until 2000, when another executive, Frank Stirling, was asked to take a second look at the opportunity. Stirling once again evaluated the Hughes-JVC projector, comparing it to the new Texas Instruments DLP projector, and decided to use the technology from TI. As he was getting ready to prove that Hughes could use its satellites to send movies to a theater, the company was bought by Boeing.

Somehow, what was now known as Boeing Digital Cinema wound up wedged inside Boeing's Integrated Defense Systems division, alongside such non-entertaining products as intercontinental ballistic missiles, B-52 bombers, the International Space Station, and smart bombs.

In late 2000, the company beamed a digital version of *Bounce*, a drama starring Gwyneth Paltrow and Ben Affleck, to AMC's Empire Theater in Manhattan for a press demonstration. Mark Gill, the same Miramax executive who'd overseen the digital screening of *An Ideal Husband* the summer before, decided he wanted to close the event with an attention-getting gesture. So just before the press conference ended, the speakers – including Affleck and Disney's Bob Lambert – walked in a single file line across the stage in front of the national media. Gill had given each of them a film canister, and instructed them to slam-dunk it into a big orange barrel labeled "Trash."

"I was still protesting the idea as the event started," Lambert said. The gesture was "more than a bit awkward, given that Kodak is one of Disney's largest, best, and longest-running corporate alliance partners, and we had long been genuinely stating that we did not expect to stop delivering some volume of film product for decades." Lambert — whose slam-dunking photo wound up in the trades — felt that the symbolic act made it seem as though the proponents of digital were trying to rid the world of film, and he worried about causing a backlash.

After the *Bounce* demo, Boeing handed out little Lucite models of a satellite to commemorate the first satellite delivery of a movie. Lambert put his on the credenza in his office. (Boeing conveniently ignored or forgot about the satellite delivery of *The Last Broadcast* two years earlier, made possible by its rival, Loral Space & Communications.)

•   •   •

A number of start-up companies also popped up like wildflowers, hoping to bring digital projection to theaters quickly, and take advantage of the slowness of the studios and other exhibitors.

Manhattan-based Madstone Films aimed to build a community of first-time filmmakers and finance movies with budgets of $500,000 to $1.5 million, shot with digital cameras. The company would then distribute the movies digitally to a network of existing theaters that would be given digital projectors. The goal was to have 15 to 20 theaters online by 2001. The company released one movie, "Rhinoceros Eyes," which won an award at the Toronto International Film Festival in 2003, before laying off 180 employees and ceasing operations in 2004.

Screening Room Entertainment, which since 1993 had operated a cinema café in Amherst, New York with a video projector, announced plans in 2000 to start franchising The Digital Cinema Café, which combined "the three hottest trends in movie exhibition today (VIP/Eatery Cinemas, Independent & Art Movies, Digital Technology) with a low-cost, modular designed business development plan." By March 2005, the company was still in the planning stages, aiming to open 100 "Digital Boutique Arthouse Cinemas" over the next year. But when that year had elapsed, the company was still operating just a single theater, in Amherst, New York.

A Los Angeles company called AndAction made a splash at ShoWest in 2000, angling to bring digital projection to theaters by giving away projectors. The company also planned to install four giant plasma screens in the lobby to allow patrons to play video games, collect demographic information, and allow them to give a thumbs-up or thumbs-down to coming attractions, providing feedback to the studios. It'd charge a screening fee for content that went to the digital projectors, whether a film or special event. The company announced plans to outfit three theaters in 2000, and then vanished.

•   •   •

Though the *Bounce* screening went off without a hitch, Boeing was discovering that the studios could be tough negotiators.

Stirling recalled one lunch with Jim Orr, who was in charge of domestic distribution for Paramount.

"We don't want to pay the virtual print fee," Orr told Stirling, referring to the fee that exhibitors would pay to get their movies played by the digital systems, covering part of the cost of installing and maintaining them. (This concept, of having the studios finance the equipment over time, had eclipsed the idea put forward by Technicolor and NewCo, of asking theater owners to hand over a portion of each ticket sold.)

"Well, how much would you be willing to pay?" Stirling asked. The average cost of getting a new movie out to a theater and then recovering it at the end of the run was as high as $3000, according to what the studios had told Boeing.

"$250," Orr responded. Stirling was flabbergasted. (Paramount never did distribute any of its movies through Boeing's system.)

Though the technology itself was improving, the issue of who would pay for what seemed like it might derail digital cinema.

At a panel discussion held in 2001 at the Pacific Theater in Hollywood, Thomas McGrath, chief operating officer of Paramount, said of digital cinema, "Is now the right time for deployment? No. The quality is not there. The methods are too expensive, and a plan to pay for implementation does not exist. And it's certainly the wrong moment in time to tell exhibitors, 'You gotta pay for it.'" (The Pacific, home for a time to the University of Southern California's Entertainment Technology Center, was built by the Warner brothers in 1927 for the premiere of the *Jazz Singer*, but wasn't finished in time.)

Exhibitors still weren't sold, either.

"It's just too expensive right now," Chandler Wood, executive vice president at Pacific Theaters, told the Los Angeles *Times*. "We were one of the four theaters first tested for digital when the 'Star Wars' prequel came out. A lot of people [in audiences] really could tell the difference." But when it came time to consider installing digital projectors in more theaters, Wood passed. "This may be the way of the future, but it's not the future right now – at least not at that price."

In Arizona, Harkins Theatres had put in the state's first digital projector in 1999, just in time to show Disney's *Bicentennial Man*. Dan Harkins, the company's chief executive, said, "The real film buffs would seek out the digital presentation, but its enhancement to the box office is almost negligible, unfortunately. Most moviegoers don't perceive it as enough of an advantage."

But Harkins also acknowledged that promoting digital cinema as a superlative experience to film, so that consumers would understand the differences, was something that theater owners were reluctant to do. "It would be like a person who has been selling you LP records all your life suddenly telling you about compact discs. 'But I thought you said the sound was perfect on the LPs!' It's a hard sell, when all along we've been saying we offer the best presentation," he said.

And some of the movie industry's long-time suppliers were swatting at digital whenever they had the chance. Denis Kelly, Kodak's film operations manager in Europe, declared that the quality of digital cinema was still not good enough, and that technology costs needed to fall at least 50 percent before digital would be welcomed by exhibitors.

"Kodak knew how Hollywood decision-making worked," said one ex-Kodak employee. "They knew which levers to pull to raise doubts. Their feeling was, it's going to happen, but how can we make it happen more slowly?"

•   •   •

John Fithian, president of the National Association of Theater Owners, cultivated one of the most articulate, thorough arguments against a swift change-over to digital cinema, and he delivered it often, in press interviews and at trade show speeches, on behalf of NATO's seven hundred members.

Fithian was a product of the Washington Beltway. His father had been a Democratic congressman from Indiana, and Fithian, after earning a law degree from the University of Virginia, ended up working at a D.C. law firm, where one of his clients was NATO. He assumed the post of NATO's president on January 1, 2000, just after the first crop of digital cinema releases had started appearing in theaters.

Fithian had one over-arching goal when it came to NATO's strategy on new technology: make sure that theater owners didn't have to foot the bill for the digital conversion. But in the half-century since the studios had been forced to sell off their own theater chains by the Supreme Court in 1948, there wasn't a precedent for the studios giving free equipment to exhibitors, who typically paid for their own projectors, bulbs, screens, and sound systems.

Fithian, however, argued that studios would derive the biggest benefits from digital distribution, by saving the cost of producing film prints, shipping them out, and recovering them once their run was over – even though there were numerous benefits for Fithian's members, too. Ticket-buyers who supported their local cinemas would likely notice the difference in quality if they went to see a movie after its opening weekend, since film presentations would decline in quality the more a print was run through the projector, while digital projection would remain consistent. Digital technology, in theory at least, would also give more flexibility to theater owners, allowing them to shift movies to more or fewer theaters based on demand, and even showing content other than movies on their screens: sporting events, gospel revivals, or rock concerts.

Disney executive Phil Barlow, who'd worked in theatrical exhibition for much of his career, was sure that digital projectors would deliver real economic advantages to cinema owners, and when he participated in panel discussions, he'd sometimes suggest, to provoke a reaction, that Disney would be willing to pay for all of the digital cinema equipment it installed if the theater owner would hand over to Disney any additional revenues that it generated. "Their response to that was, 'Aha! So you're after our revenue!'" Barlow said.

It was a classic Catch-22: theater owners didn't want to buy the equipment, but they also worried about any strings that might be attached if they accepted it for free.

"There was a game afoot," explained Michael Karagosian, who was hired by Fithian in 2000 to be NATO's digital cinema consultant. "Fithian laid it out really early. He wanted to get the studios to pay, and he wanted to get all of his members included in any roll-out of digital cinema equipment, whether they were a big chain or a single-screen mom-and-pop theater in the sticks," he said. Karagosian observed that the business of theatrical exhibition was "built on equipment that can be amortized over 20 or 30 years" – not more expensive, high-tech equipment that might need to be replaced or upgraded in ten years. Exhibitors also were comfortable with film, Karagosian added: "They didn't have the skills to deal with electronic equipment."

Karagosian supplied information to Fithian and NATO's members, but it was up to Fithian to continue making the case in public for why theater owners shouldn't pay, and raise the prospect of "dark screens," unable to play the 8 PM show because of technical glitches.

In an interview with *Forbes*, Fithian speculated that if theater-owners were asked to finance the digital upgrade, they might pass the costs along to movie-goers, who'd "scream bloody murder if they had to pay $45 a ticket."

Fithian also expressed his constituents' fear that the studios would be able to exert more control over exhibitors in a digital world, controlling (or at least monitoring) which of their movies played at what time in what theater. "Theatre owners do not want to be reduced to little more than brick-and-mortar businesses who build new complexes that the studios then operate remotely," he wrote in the NATO magazine, *In Focus*.

At one point, said Disney's Phil Barlow, "NATO's board took a position that no one should work with us on digital cinema. I didn't threaten to sue, but I did have to point out to them that what they were talking about was a boycott, and that would be illegal. But they put a lot of pressure on the exhibitors that did work with us."

In a confidential memo sent to exhibitors, Fithian did warn exhibitors about allowing digital cinema companies such as Technicolor or Boeing to put digital equipment into their theaters, even if the terms appeared favorable. He worried that the technology suppliers could develop into gatekeepers that would stand between exhibitors and the studios, exerting control and taking profits. "Gatekeepers offer unique terms for the first installments to incentivize exhibitors to install equipment," Fithian wrote. "However, exhibitors must know what the terms for a true rollout are before even the seeding can begin. We can't 'seed' intelligently if we don't know what type of crop we are trying to grow."

.   .   .

To those outside the movie industry, Roger Ebert, the movie critic, author, and television personality, was emerging as one of digital cinema's most vocal opponents. In December 1999, Ebert wrote a column in the Chicago *Sun-Times* in which he spun out a long list of reasons why backers of digital cinema were too bullish by far: the Texas Instruments system was expensive, and for the first wave of screenings, hard drives containing the movies had to be trucked to each theater; projectionists might be able to adjust the contrast and tint of the picture, "a frightening prospect"; projectionists managing digital equipment might need to be paid more; "armed guards" might be required to protect digital movie files in projection booths from pirates.

Ebert also observed, accurately, that the 1999-era projectors didn't put as many pixels on the screen as a high-definition TV set. But he also tossed out, without much scientific backing, the theory that digital projections wouldn't create as powerful a psychological state as film for audiences. "Some theoreticians believe that film creates reverie, video creates hypnosis," he wrote. "Wouldn't it be ironic if digital audiences found they were missing an ineffable part of the movie-going experience?" Hollywood should investigate the different brain states created by film and video, he suggested.

Ebert's concerns were echoed by others, as when *Variety* film critic Todd McCarthy fretted that audiences who bought tickets for a digitally projected movie would have the epiphany that "they're actually just watching TV with more people." That, McCarthy wrote ominously, "could be the end of movies as we know them."

Other critics prophesied that digital projection and satellite links would spell the end of cinema as art form. Godfrey Cheshire wrote in the New York *Press* that "if you take away film, what you have left may look much the same for a while, but soon enough you'll realize that it doesn't function the same." Screens would be filled with broadcasts of live events, movies that would aesthetically resemble high-quality TV, and big-budget, special effects-laden spectaculars. (Cheshire didn't think there'd be room for low-budget, artistically-motivated productions.) The studios backing digital "regard it as a money-saving, technically superior means of delivering their wares; they seem barely aware of how extensively it will reshape those wares and the culture and business surrounding them," Cheshire wrote.

•   •   •

In 2001, there was another management shuffle at Texas Instruments. Doug Darrow was promoted, and Paul Breedlove, then 61, was offered an early retirement package. At ShoWest in March, Breedlove finalized the contracts with the three companies, Christie, Barco, and Digital Projection, that had agreed to license TI's DLP technology and start manufacturing projectors. He left the company in April, just after ShoWest.

"I think I did my part. I advanced the ball a few yards down the field. We weren't on the goal line, but it felt like we were past the 50-yard line. Before we started, there wasn't even a game," he said.

But the pace of the game was still proceeding slowly. NewCo hadn't been able to come up with a business plan for digital cinema deployment that all of the studios would endorse. Barlow was getting ready to retire from Disney and relinquish his leadership of NewCo, but the group wasn't disbanding. It was being shaped into a more formal entity, which would have full-time employees to develop a business plan and technical standards for digital cinema, working with representatives from each of the studios. Barlow didn't want to remain involved with the new entity, sensing that his ardent advocacy for digital cinema at NewCo had "probably bruised enough feelings. I have the ability to make an enemy for each friend."

Companies touting digital cinema were still in the exhausting stage of having to turn over every possible stone to find willing exhibitors, said Frank Stirling of Boeing. But at ShoWest in March 2002, producer Rick McCallum defrosted some of exhibitors' reluctance when he gave exhibitors their first look at the next installment in the "Star Wars" series. The preview enticed several exhibitors to line up outside of Boeing's suite at the Paris Hotel the next day.

"The first guy in line was Kevin Ritz from Big Spring, Texas," recalled Stirling. Ritz operated two theaters in Big Spring, with a total of six screens. "I was in the middle of a lot of major markets, like Lubbock and Abilene and Midland," Ritz said, "and I honestly expected that digital would draw from those markets."

Ritz was the smallest cinema owner to sign up with Boeing, but Loews also committed to install six systems, as did Sony's Metreon multiplex in San Francisco, and the old Cinerama theater in Seattle.

Ritz had to spend $30,000 remodeling his 300-seat downtown theater, installing a new screen and pulling out the 35-millimeter projector because the booth was too small to accommodate both it and the digital projector. He paid Boeing a $22,500 "service initiation fee," and the contract he signed required him to pay Boeing 50 cents for each ticket sold in the digital theaters (with a minimum payment of $2500 a month).

• • •

Studios and theater chains had a big concern about digital cinema that hadn't really been addressed: making sure that all of the equipment being installed would speak the same language. If Warner Bros. sent out a movie in digital form, for instance, it needed to be playable on any system, no matter who made it or installed it.

Ever since *The Phantom Menace* had to be mastered twice to show on two different projectors, there had been worries about having to produce different versions of a movie for different digital systems. The Technicolor digital cinema systems required digital movies to be compressed in Qualcomm's own format, while the Boeing systems used a format called MPEG, and the QuVis servers used with some of the Disney/Texas Instruments installations had a third format, called Qubit wavelet compression. (Compression is a way of abbreviating data files, usually at the expense of quality, to get them to fit into less storage space. It's akin to making peach preserves – you throw out the pit and the skin, and get lots more peaches into a single Mason jar.) The studios weren't eager for digital cinema to make their distribution systems *more* complicated.

In order to start singing from the same technical hymnal, and to continue exploring possible business plans for making digital cinema financially feasible, the studios decided to turn the NewCo initiative into a more structured organization, with employees and funding.

In April 2002, the organization was made public for the first time – though it didn't yet have a name. The press release was headlined, "Major Studios Form Venture to Promote Development, Deployment of Digital Cinema Technology." (Members still referred to it as NewCo Digital Cinema.) The entity's timetable was set as two years. The objectives were to come up with a common specification for how digital cinema equipment would work by June of the following year, organize a beta test in the field by the fall, and report back to the studios in early 2004. (A similar standards effort had taken place in the early days of talkies.) Creating a plan for financing digital cinema equipment was also part of the mission.

Before long, the organization was dubbed Digital Cinema Initiatives, LLC. Each of the seven studios put $1 million into the DCI kitty, and named two representatives to the group. It took until June 2002 for DCI to hire a chief executive, Chuck Goldwater, who'd been an executive with several theater chains. The rest of the staff, including chief technology officer Walt Ordway, a veteran of Hughes Digital Cinema, started work that summer and fall.

"The goal was to create a single, open, non-proprietary architecture – patent-free, too," said Julian Levin, the Fox distribution executive who became chairman of DCI. "It wasn't a question of if digital cinema was coming, but when. We figured we could either bury our heads in the sand, or be a part of the solution."

Among the seven studios, Paramount was seen as the studio that most resembled an ostrich. And Universal still had done just one digital release, *Jurassic Park III*.

Gino Campagnola had started with Paramount in 1951, working in the mailroom and later collecting money from theaters. He became the studio's general sales manager, before being named executive vice president of electronic cinema in 2000. He was enormously well-liked within DCI, even if he wasn't the most avidly pro-digital member. "I was always of the opinion that if the picture had scratches and pops, it was a good movie," he said with a laugh. "That meant it had been in the marketplace for a long time."

DCI wasn't the first attempt to establish a standard for digital cinema. In 1995, the Technology Council of the Motion Picture-Television Industry started a feasibility study of what was then called electronic cinema, but didn't deliver a final product that satisfied the studios.

Representing Universal, Jerry Pierce said, "We wanted [digital cinema] to happen, but not if it was done in the wrong way. For us, it was about saving money first, and of course making the picture better, too."

Pierce was worried that Universal would have to create multiple digital versions of its movies to play on different digital cinema servers. So unlike Disney or Fox, which were freely giving movies to multiple companies to use in their digital cinema roll-outs, Universal decided to use what Pierce called "product leverage," being stingy about the movies it allowed to be distributed digitally.

Many in the fledgling digital cinema business saw the formation of DCI as an attempt by the studios to "slow things down and gain control," as QuVis executive George Scheckel put it.

"We didn't think the idea of a standards body was irrelevant," said Mike Blanchard of Lucasfilm, which wasn't involved with DCI, despite its experience with digital cinema. "But we just thought it was rigged to delay the production of an actual standard."

At Boeing, Frank Stirling concurred. "The studios really delayed things because of NIH," he said, referring to "not-invented-here" syndrome. They were reluctant to use technology that they hadn't had a hand in developing. "The studios don't like outsiders playing in their sandbox," Stirling said.

•   •   •

The creation of DCI put progress on pause, sending a signal to the market that the studios would let everyone know when they'd developed a satisfactory business plan and set of technical specifications.

Technicolor, which had promised in 2001 to launch a conversion of 1000 theaters in the U.S., laid off its business development and exhibitor relations employees at the end of 2002, though it continued supporting the 60 theaters it had converted.

"There was just a lull that happened when DCI was formed," said Joe Berchtold of Technicolor.

Qualcomm officially abandoned its digital cinema business the following year.

"Often, the pioneers in a technology get the arrows in their back," added Carol Hahn, who worked on digital cinema at Qualcomm. "We were ahead of the market, and when the studios put together [DCI], they effectively stalled it."

There were talks, according to Stirling, about merging Boeing's digital cinema business with the digital cinema groups at Technicolor, DeLuxe Labs, and Kodak. But Boeing eventually decided to get out of the digital cinema business. Boeing Digital Cinema had set up about thirty digital projectors in the U.S. and London, spending "at least tens of millions of dollars," according to *Variety*. The division, which had distributed 19 digital movies over two years, had dwindled down to just ten employees.

Though Boeing was essentially admitting that it didn't have the corporate patience to wait for DCI to develop its standard (and then for digital cinema to become a sustainable business), the company chose to declare victory anyway: in a statement, the company said it had "entered the digital cinema market to demonstrate the deployment of satellite-based technology for secure distribution of large data files…" and that Boeing had "successfully pioneered and demonstrated many technological advances…"

Christie chief executive Jack Kline, in the middle of a strategic shift from selling film projectors to selling digital projectors, said, "We continued investing, but we were shocked by all the roadkill: Boeing, Technicolor, Qualcomm." Now that Christie was building and marketing digital projectors, it needed the market to start developing – and it wasn't.

The number of digital cinema releases from the studios started to dry up once DCI was created, leaving exhibitors like Kevin Ritz in the lurch.

When he did have a digital movie to show, such as *Spy Kids 2*, he'd charge $1 more per ticket. "I'd do ten times as much business on the digital screen as on film," he said. "I had people coming in from Austin."

But as the studios released fewer movies in digital format, Ritz found that he was holding onto movies long after they'd stopped drawing crowds. (He'd removed the film projector from the under-sized projection booth, and so couldn't show any traditional 35-millimeter releases.) "I just assumed that everything would be available in digital," Ritz said. "But product was real scarce. I was getting frustrated."

•   •   •

The standard joke in Hollywood about any endeavor that involves representatives of the six major studios is that when gathered in a room, they have difficulty agreeing on the weather. That dynamic – and several others – made the work of Digital Cinema Initiatives, LLC challenging.

First were the late start and the tight timeline. By the time the DCI team came together and started making progress in the fall of 2002, six months of the planned two-year life of DCI had elapsed. The employees didn't even have an office at first, huddling in a conference room on the Fox lot. Later, they moved into a generic suite of offices on Hollywood Boulevard, across from the Kodak Theater, the home of the Academy Awards ceremony.

Who reported to whom wasn't clear. Chuck Goldwater seemed to think that Walt Ordway reported to him, and he reported to DCI's board of studio representatives, but Ordway was informed by the board that he reported directly to them. That created two separate fiefdoms within DCI: Goldwater's business domain, and Ordway's technical turf.

On the business side, Goldwater's goal was to develop a viable business plan that would help get digital cinema projectors disseminated in U.S. theaters. DCI also intended to conduct a small beta test of digital cinema equipment in about 30 theaters.

But one of the first problems Goldwater encountered was that the studios were reluctant to reveal to DCI how much they were currently paying to buy and ship traditional film prints. While many of them had deals with Technicolor and DeLuxe, the two leading film duplication labs, that ensured that they would be given the same price for prints as their competitors paid, they still viewed the information as extremely sensitive.

"The idea that studios were going to save a billion dollars a year with digital distribution was based on a cost of about $1500 a print, and that was a number that kind of came out of thin air," said a former DCI staffer. "We wound up assuming that the average cost of a print was a little over $1000, but it was a weird situation. People said, '$1000 is a little high.'" One studio delegate to DCI even suggested that the cost of a print and shipping, assuming a large enough release and a sweetheart deal with one of the labs, could be as low as $500.

Without an accurate number, it was hard to come up with a business plan. While DCI's predecessor, NewCo Digital Cinema, had floated the idea of adding a surcharge to tickets, Goldwater instead started concentrating on the idea of a "virtual print fee," where studios would finance the purchase of digital cinema equipment by paying a fee each time they sent a new movie to a theater. But without knowing current distribution and print costs, it was hard to come up with a plan that would appeal to the studios.

Goldwater and his business team also knew that if they wanted to make the prospect of financing the equipment attractive, they needed the equipment to be as inexpensive as possible. "We felt like $60,000 or $70,000 would've been an ideal number," said the former DCI staffer, "and even then, it's still a marginal proposition." The business side wanted the technological equivalent of a Honda, not a Ferrari. But it was hard for the business side of DCI to communicate that to the technology side.

"On the tech side, the *modus operandi* was, build any system, no matter what the cost," the ex-DCI staffer said. "They wanted a system that was so good you'd never need to replace it, and so secure no one could ever possibly hack into it. No one ever said, 'Make sure the all-in system cost is X,' even though we all knew that if X was over a certain number, digital cinema didn't make a lot of sense financially for the studios." If the virtual print fee to finance Ferrari-grade equipment exceeded the amount they were already paying for prints, what kind of economic incentive was there to go digital?

For the technology group, the biggest debates were about image quality, the format in which movies would be stored, and security.

Some studios believed that 2K, or two thousand pixels stretching horizontally across the screen, was sufficient. (Most of the earliest digital cinema releases were shown on either 1.3K or 2K projectors.) But others, such as Warner Bros. and Sony, felt that projectors that could paint four thousand pixels across each row of the screen, or 4K, were worth waiting for.

"The most important thing to me is not to be able to see the pixels on the screen," said Chris Cookson, chief technology officer at Warner Bros. Cookson and his colleague Rob Hummel had seen a prototype of a Sony 4K projector in Japan. But they had signed a non-disclosure agreement with Sony Electronics, and so they couldn't share information about it with the other studio representatives at DCI.

The digital release tally, as of September 2003:

Disney/Buena Vista: 19
Warner Bros.: 15
Fox: 8
Miramax: 4
DreamWorks: 3
Sony Pictures: 3
MGM: 1
New Line Cinema: 1
Universal Pictures: 1
Paramount: 0

Until others got a chance to see the Sony 4K projector, "people would laugh at us, and say that we were just trying to delay the roll-out of digital cinema," said Hummel.

Warner Brothers was in the midst of revamping its entire digital post-production process to handle movies at the 4K level of resolution. From a corporate perspective, it simply didn't make sense for the studio to complete movies as 4K files, then toss out half of that information when it distributed them digitally. So the studio campaigned hard for 4K, arranging demonstrations in its screening rooms once the top-secret wraps were taken off the Sony projector. Cookson and Hummel eventually persuaded a super-majority of the studios at DCI to support 4K.

"It looked like [the dispute over resolution] was going to break up the DCI venture," said Disney's Bob Lambert, who felt that even the 1.3K Texas Instruments projectors were good enough. "To us, there was no deliverable 4K projection technology, so you're basically just saying, 'We're not going to adopt digital cinema until some point in the future.' We were also uncomfortable with the lack of a competitive dynamic," he said, since only Sony was proposing to make a 4K projector.

At one point, in March 2003, 2K resolution was removed from the working draft of the DCI spec in favor of 4K. As a result, most technology manufacturers simply stopped cooperating with DCI. "Everyone in the industry hated the idea [of allowing only 4K projection of movies]," Ordway later conceded.

Ordway, along with Lambert and Cookson, negotiated a truce among the DCI members. (Disney and Universal were the staunchest 2K supporters, and Warner Bros. was every bit as adamant about 4K.) The compromise was a "layered approach," which allowed 2K projectors to simply peel off the layer of information that they needed if they were supplied with a 4K movie file. A 4K projector would scarf down all of the information the file contained.

By October, 2K had been put back into the spec, and "then we started moving again," Ordway said.

•   •   •

At a gathering of about 75,000 "Star Wars" fans held in Indianapolis before the release of *Clones*, Rick McCallum showed an excerpt from the movie on a Texas Instruments projector. He also encouraged the fans to contact theater managers and studio executives who might have influence over how soon digital projectors would appear in booths.

The fans took up McCallum's challenge, launching an e-mail campaign on sites such as TheForce.net.

"...Most people won't get to experience *Episode II* in full digital glory...[Digital cinema] is the greatest tech innovation for movies since sound, and the theaters are pushing [it] with all the exuberance of an air conditioning salesman in Siberia," wrote Chris Knight in an editorial on the site. Knight suggested that visitors to the site talk to the managers of their local theaters, asking when they were planning to install digital projection. TheForce.net also posted e-mail addresses for contacting the

National Association of Theater Owners and the Motion Picture Association of America.

• • •

Attack of the Clones, released in May 2002, would be the first time a digital movie was to be released on the same day at theaters around the world, and that meant lots of different languages. "There were 16 different digital versions, with either dubbing or subtitles," said Rick Dean, the THX employee responsible for the work. Much of the work was compressed into an intense two-week period at the end of April, when all of the required files – audio, video, and the text of subtitles – showed up at THX's Burbank office.

Adding to the complexity of releasing *Clones* in all those different languages was the fact that the different digital cinemas in which it would play used different servers, and so THX had to compress the digital versions in one of three different file formats.

Once a version of *Clones* in a given language was compressed into a particular file format, it needed to be encrypted and then be put through a quality check. Then, THX either encoded the movie onto a set of 16 DVD-ROM discs (along with the trailers that would run before *Clones*), or saved it onto an 80-gigabyte hard drive.

Lucas had hoped that by the time the second installment of the new "Star Wars" trilogy was released on May 16, 2002, there'd be hundreds of digital screens in the U.S. available to show the movie. But the number had stalled at about 100, 56 of which showed *Attack of the Clones.*

The release of *Clones* supplied one important new data point, however, for the case that digital cinema could be a draw for audiences. Box office revenues dropped off more steeply at conventional film theaters than they did at the screens equipped to show the digital version of the movie. In some markets, by the fourth weekend of release, one theater showing the digital version of *Clones* was raking in as much as three theaters showing the film version.

Even critic Roger Ebert seemed to be softening his position, writing in the *Chicago Sun-Times* that he preferred a digital presentation of *Attack of the Clones* he saw at the McClurg Court Cinemas in Chicago to a film presentation in the same theater. "The difference was dramatic," Ebert wrote. "More detail, more depth, more clarity."

"Readers familiar with my preference for film over video projection systems will wonder if I have switched parties. Not at all," he continued. "It's to be expected that [*Clones*] would look better on digital, because it was entirely filmed on digital. Therefore, the digitally projected version is generation one, and the film version is one generation further from the source. Lucas is right as far as a computer-aided special-effects movie like [*Clones*] goes, but may be wrong for the vast majority of movies that depict the real world on celluloid." Ebert remained convinced that movies "shot on film look better projected on film," while movies shot digitally, and studded with digital effects and characters, looked better on a digital projector.

Karagosian, the digital cinema consultant for NATO, was unmoved. "I thought the *Star Wars* digital showing looked very bad," he said.

•　　•　　•

As the result of the fan e-mail campaign, the in-box of John Fithian, the president of NATO, started to fill with pro-digital cinema missives. By July, Fithian had received 200 e-mails, and he dedicated his column in the NATO magazine, *In Focus*, to the correspondence.

"George Lucas and Rick McCallum have produced a wonderful picture, and we're grateful," Fithian wrote, acknowledging that their latest movie would be one of the year's biggest hits. "Having said this, I have to point out that these enormously talented filmmakers are completely wrong about the readiness of digital cinema and the importance of projecting their movie with that technology." The headline of his column was "Exhibitors Will Implement D-Cinema – When It's Ready."

•　　•　　•

Cinematographers and directors were well-represented in the audience at the Pacific Theatre in February 2003, when Texas Instruments demonstrated a new projector that almost doubled the resolution of its original crop of DLP projectors. This time, the company had squeezed nearly one million more microscopic mirrors onto the surface of its chip, and increased the contrast ratio to 2000:1. This became known as the 2K projector.

Among the footage that consultant Loren Nielsen had selected to show was a long stretch of *Road to Perdition* – a rainy, foggy scene featuring Tom Hanks and Paul Newman. The movie, photographed by Conrad Hall, had been released the year before, and Nielsen felt that the Texas Instruments projector was finally ready to do justice to Hall's moody blacks and grays. Sadly, Hall, who had worked closely with Nielsen and others to master his material so that it'd look right on the digital projectors, had died in January. (Later in 2003, he'd win a posthumous Best Cinematography Oscar for *Road to Perdition*.)

"After it ran, the audience was totally silent, and I was really nervous," Nielsen said. "Then they started to applaud."

•   •   •

Almost every time a representative of DCI appeared in public, the finish line moved again. At the Cinema Expo conference in Amsterdam in June 2003, Chuck Goldwater said the technical specs would be finalized by January of the following year. That fall, the date had slipped to March 2004.

In the spring of 2004, DCI got its first official term extension, a six-month stretch of the schedule that'd last until September 2004.

"At Sony Pictures, we felt strongly that it was better to do this right than to do it fast," said Joblove, the former Industrial Light & Magic employee, who now worked on digital cinema at Sony. "If we were creating a standard that would last anywhere near as long as 35-millimeter film had lasted as a standard, there was no reason to push to have it finished a year or two earlier."

When September 2004 arrived, there were bigger changes. Goldwater's contract wasn't renewed, but DCI's board, in a press release, thanked him for "facilitating the development of potential scenarios for the financing and deployment of digital cinema."

Goldwater had drawn up some plans to create a separate venture that would fund the installation of digital cinema equipment, but those plans faded away. It became clear, Lambert said, that some studios were very aggressive, and wanted to see the equipment rolled out quickly, and others who were more comfortable with a measured approach. And "some of the studios," Lambert added, "didn't really have any fire in the belly about getting it done at all."

•   •   •

Paramount had the reputation within DCI (and within NewCo before that) for approaching digital cinema with both feet on the brake pedal, and a hand on the emergency brake for good measure.

"If we were a brake, it was for two reasons," said Gino Campagnola of Paramount, who was one of that studio's delegates to DCI. "One was that we felt like exhibitors needed to be involved in the process, and two, we didn't want to pay for the equipment. We weren't going to spend $150,000 to equip a screen if that equipment was going to be obsolete in three years."

The studio's co-head at the time, Jonathan Dolgen, "was a bean counter," Campagnola said. "You couldn't go to him and say, 'I need $5 million for digital cinema, but I won't realize anything from it for a couple of years.' His attitude was, 'Let's see what the other studios are going to do.'"

When Campagnola retired from Paramount in 2004 after 54 years at the studio, he was replaced on the DCI board by Jim Orr, a distribution vice president. He and Julian Levin from Fox were the only distribution executives who showed up regularly; everyone else was a technologist, which meant that DCI's work tilted away from the business realities of implementing digital cinema, and toward drawing up a technical roadmap.

Characterizing the attitude of distribution executives, Ordway said, "They like their paradigm. 'Don't muck around with my box,' was the message we got."

MGM was perhaps the studio least involved with DCI. "We were the smallest studio, with the fewest resources," said Chris McGurk, former vice chairman of MGM. "We couldn't take the lead and push things. Our approach was to monitor digital cinema and make sure we were ready to move when everyone else did."

·   ·   ·

While studios in the U.S. were still haggling over the details of the digital cinema standard, Great Britain was preparing to leap ahead.

In Europe, as in the U.S., a similar cluster of filmmakers, producers, technology merchants, and exhibitors had been debating the pros and cons of digital cinema for several years. There had been seminars and conferences, and in 2001, the European Digital Cinema Forum was created. The difference in Europe, though, was that governmental bodies decided to put their weight behind digital cinema.

In February 2005, the UK Film Council, a quasi-governmental agency intended to promote filmmaking in the country, awarded a contract worth $20 million to a company called Arts Alliance Digital Cinema. The project would create a network of as many as 250 digital screens in 150 cinemas around the UK.

The Film Council's objective was to make it easier and cheaper for home-grown filmmakers to distribute their work, and give audiences outside of major cities a chance to see non-mainstream movies – what was referred to in Britain as "specialised film."

"What's important about the contract is that it serves a complete market – the art house market in the UK," said Thomas Hoeg, the chairman of Arts Alliance, shortly after the company had beat out fourteen rivals, including Dolby and Kodak, to get the contract. (A year later, Kodak executive Bob Mayson, a native of Yorkshire, criticized the roll-out for falling behind schedule and called it "a disgraceful waste of taxpayer money.") At the time, the company had just sixteen employees.

"There shouldn't be a reason to create a 35-millimeter print of an independent film that's coming out in the UK. That was the goal of the project, and that's what makes it unique," Hoeg said, The digital cinema network in the UK was one of the first to envision a movie being released to an entire nation without a single film print – rather than film prints and digital files co-existing for the foreseeable future. When it was announced, the UK Film Council Project was the biggest single roll-out of digital cinema technology in the world.

Theaters that were chosen to be part of the network would get the necessary projector and servers for free; all they had to pay was the maintenance costs (about $5000 annually), and the costs of any renovations or upgrade to their projection booth that were required. But they first had to apply to the UK Film Council, promising that they wouldn't just use the new equipment to screen Hollywood blockbusters. "They had to tell the Council that they'd go from 10 percent to 30 percent specialised film," said Howard Kiedasch, president of Arts Alliance Digital Cinema, "or 20 percent to 50 percent. And the Film Council wanted a good geographic spread."

Not surprisingly, there was more demand for the free digital equipment than supply. (The Film Council's budget came from revenues generated by the National Lottery.) In the end, the Film Council chose 238 screens. That was about 7 percent of the 3300 screens in the country.

The company developed what they called a "wallbox" that helped make the installation process less complex. It centralized the power feeds, network connections, and the automation controller (which did things like lower the lights and open the curtains) in one place. "The innovation there was that it helped standardize the installations," Kiedasch said. Arts Alliance sent two employees to each site. Kiedasch said the installations took two days initially, but that after the first ten were done, the employees shaved it down to a day-and-a-half.

By February 2006, they had 31 screens that were operational – a bit behind the target they'd set of fifty by the previous fall. "We never want someone to come out of a theater and say, 'That was a nice digital showing,'" Metral said. "We want them to say, 'That was beautiful,' and not know why."

There were two other measures of success, from the UK Film Council's perspective. One was that the technology proved reliable. The other measure of success would be whether the network helped British filmmakers compete against their counterparts in California.

Other countries were eagerly embracing digital cinema, too.

In Ireland, Avica Technology announced its intention to install digital projectors in 500 theaters – nearly every one in the country – by March 2006.

In Brazil, the independent cinema chain Rain had set up 77 digital screens in 22 art house cinemas in seven different cities.

In Asia, Singapore could lay claim to 21 digital cinema installations in 2005, including the first all-digital multiplex in the world. China surpassed the United States in 2004 as the country with the most digital cinema locations: 166. Twenty digital released were screened that year in China, including the digital-only release of *Looney Tunes: Back in Action*. Japan was just behind the China and the U.S. in total installations, with 44 digital auditoriums by the end of 2004.

While projection booths in India relied on a wide range of projectors, the research firm Screen Digest estimated that by the end of 2005 there were about 345 e-cinema screens in the country, and that there would be more than 5000 by 2010. (E-cinema was a term sometimes used to refer to theaters with projectors that were less than 1.3K resolution.)

One reason for India's speed was that the country's film industry – known as Bollywood – had never stopped to set a standard for projection quality or security.

"In Bollywood, the typical budget for a movie is between $1 million and $3 million," explained Marty Levine, executive vice president at DG2L Technologies, which was selling digital cinema systems to Indian theaters. "They can't afford to make enough prints to address all the theaters, and so movies get circulated around from town to town. Not only does the print get worn out, but you lose part of your audience to piracy. You've created demand with your advertising campaign, but most of the people in the country can't pay to see it in a theater." Digital cinema's ability to make a film omnipresent outweighed any concerns about security, and Bollywood studios regarded the image quality, even at about half the resolution as Hollywood demanded, as good enough.

Levine said that none of the major Bollywood studios had turned his company down when it had asked it for movies. It cost DG2L about $35,000 to convert one cinema to digital projection and satellite delivery of movies – less than half the cost what it cost to convert a U.S. theater to 2K digital projection.

•   •   •

In the States, a new kind of digital projector was starting to sneak into projection booths, though it wasn't being used to show trailers or the main feature.

The small projector usually sat on a high shelf in the projection booth, with its own special porthole cut into the wall. While the studios' representatives to DCI were deliberating over 2K and 4K resolution, two companies, Screenvision and National CineMedia, were installing thousands of 1K digital projectors at a cost of about $30,000 each, compared to a 2K projector that might cost $80,000 or more. Screenvision and National CineMedia delivered content to their projectors via satellite or a high-speed terrestrial data link, just as DCI was discussing.

But instead of showing movies, they showed advertising, and split the money with theater owners, who were thrilled to have the extra revenue. Regal Cinemas CEO Michael Campbell referred to pre-show advertising as "the biggest financial upside" of the digital cinema revolution. Theaters also had to pay nothing for the equipment. All they did was supply the captive audience.

"We're in a very emotional, engaged environment," said Jason Brown, a senior vice president at Screenvision. "People are outside of the home. They're not on the couch. The audience attentiveness level is huge, and there are no other distractions." Brown described the movie-going audience as young and upscale, and "a little more on the cutting edge than average." Advertisers paid Screenvision between $1.2 million and $2.7 million a month to air a 30-second ad over its national network of screens. (Screenvision was an independent company, formerly part of Technicolor, and National CineMedia was a joint venture of three exhibition companies: Regal Cinemas, AMC Entertainment, and Cinemark USA.)

Many of the ads weren't intended to air on television, or at least had their premieres in movie theaters; Directors Martin Scorcese and Baz Luhrmann created spots for American Express and Chanel No. 5, with stars such as Robert De Niro and Nicole Kidman.

Both Screenvision and National CineMedia touted surveys that said that consumers didn't mind the pre-show advertising, or in fact found it entertaining. National CineMedia cited its own research, which found that 75 percent of consumers had a neutral-to-positive opinion of pre-show ads. "Only 10 percent of the people said they'd rather see nothing," said Cliff Marks, National CineMedia's president of sales and marketing.

Advertising had been part of the movie-going experience at least since 1916, when Paramount began sending out trailers, intended to be shown after the main feature, to arouse interest in the studio's upcoming releases. But opponents of the new digital pre-show advertising were vocal. They felt that the new advertising was more intrusive than what theaters had traditionally shown: a series of advertising slides (sans audio) before the movie started, trailers, and a brief reminder to patronize the snack bar, where fizzy soft drinks awaited.

One group of advertising opponents created the Captive Motion Picture Audience of America to protest cinema advertising, and offered on their Web site a printable sign that movie-goers could use to hold their seats during twenty or thirty minutes of pre-show advertising that played at some cinemas. "Reserved: This patron is avoiding cinema advertising and will return when the feature begins," the sign read.

Roger Ebert wrote in his *Chicago Sun-Times* column, "…[W]hen I pay for a ticket, I am subsidizing the screening, and resent being made into a captive victim." Several consumers filed class-action lawsuits, complaining that the advertised showtime was misleading if the movie's start was delayed by advertising. Some theaters opted not to join the digital pre-show advertising networks, for fear of offending their patrons.

But in the four-year span between 2001 and 2005, the cinema advertising business grew from $200 million to more than $500 million, fueled in part by the digital networking and projection technology that made distributing ads more efficient. By late 2005, Screenvision was installing its equipment in 250 to 300 projection booths every month, and between the two companies, there were about 15,000 screens equipped to show digital pre-show advertising. National CineMedia said it had already spent $150 million building its network.

Those numbers dwarfed the total investment in digital cinema-grade equipment. While the studios were evaluating their technology options, digital pre-show advertising had become a half-billion dollar business, and found a niche in projection booths. It generated healthy revenues for Screenvision and National CineMedia, and for the theater owners who joined their networks – without having to spend a penny to buy equipment or upgrade their facilities. (There were also no worries for theater owners about equipment becoming obsolete – even if irate ticket-buyers did pose a new hazard.) Screenvision and National CineMedia took care everything.

• • •

Leading up to the release of *Revenge of the Sith* in May 2005, there were concerns that there might actually be fewer digital screens available to show the movie than there'd been three years earlier. But the final "Star Wars" release played digitally on nearly 100 screens (versus 56 for *Attack of the Clones.*) Part of the increase, however, was due to the fact that there were fewer digital releases from other studios competing for the available screens.

The worries about a dwindling number of digital projectors weren't unfounded. Since the supply of digital releases had slowed during the time of DCI's deliberations, many theaters had unplugged their digital projectors and pushed them into a corner of the projection booth, or removed them entirely.

Kevin Ritz, the Texas theater owner who'd been among the first to sign up with Boeing Digital Cinema, simply ran out of movies to play in 2005. "I had a dark house, and this was the biggest auditorium I had," he said. Since the booth was too small to fit two projectors, he'd removed the film projector. But now, he had no choice but to remodel the booth, and put the film projector back in.

He also had a problem, in that his digital projector, made by Barco, produced a 1.3K image, and it seemed that the studios were reaching a consensus that 2K would be the minimum resolution they'd allow. Ritz argued that the front row of seats at his theater were far enough away from the 38-foot wide screen that a 1.3K projector was perfectly adequate. "There's no way the people who made the decision that 1.3K is not compliant have seen the presentation in my theater," he said.

But Ritz wasn't expecting to get any more digital movies until he upgraded to 2K. "I now have an obsolete system," he said. "At the time we put it in, I had faith in Boeing. That was a big 'oops,' I guess."

• • •

"Security was the last thing left on the plate," Walt Ordway said, and a major reason for the final year-long extension of DCI's term announced in September 2004. Each of the studios worried about the consequences if a pirate got his hands on a perfect digital copy of one of their movies; it'd be like a counterfeiter obtaining the plate that the U.S. Mint uses to crank out $100 bills. And even if just one digital movie file was stolen, cracked, and duplicated in the early days of digital cinema, it could doom the whole digital cinema initiative by making studios reluctant to release more movies. Ordway hired three consultants to help evaluate all of the potential security holes.

"As grueling as it was to work out the decisions about resolution, and how many audio channels we'd have, and the color space, all that seemed simple and quick in comparison to doing the security piece," said George Joblove of Sony Pictures. "The studios needed to be confident that they could distribute their movies through this whole new pipeline and not be taking a risk." Every possible security breach – like someone unscrewing the cover from a server containing a digital movie – would be logged and reported, in case it was part of an act of piracy.

A majority of the DCI members had to concur with every point in the technical spec. As individual lines were approved, the color of the type went from red to black.

"The decision-making process was very complicated, since everyone involved was used to getting their own way," said the former DCI staffer.

DCI's final vote took place on July 20th. "It dealt with the wording of one last sentence on security," Ordway said. Of the 160 pages, about half were dedicated to security.

The planned beta test of digital cinema equipment never happened.

"The schedule was stupidly aggressive," Ordway explained. "To do a beta test, we would've had to make all of the decisions about the technical spec in [the first] four or five months."

.   .   .

The press conference announcing that DCI had finally crossed the finish line was held at the Beverly Hills headquarters of the Academy of Motion Picture Arts and Sciences, inside a 1000-seat screening room called the Samuel Goldwyn Theater; the stage was flanked by two statues of Oscar.

Walt Ordway kicked things off. "We are here today to celebrate the culmination of three years of hard work, an impressive collaboration with the various facets of the motion picture industry, and an exploration of the technical possibilities of the visual experience," he said. "One of our guiding principles was to create a digital cinema specification that introduces a benchmark of quality which would improve the movie-going experience for future audiences..."

Ordway clicked through a slide presentation that recounted DCI's history since its formation in 2002 (deftly avoiding, though, the missed deadlines), and some of the technical aspects of the specification (2K or 4K projection, 128-bit encryption, 16 channels of audio, etc.) Among the DCI "guiding principles" he listed on his fourth slide were equal or better reliability than film presentation, declining equipment cost over time, and the protection of intellectual property.

"We are convinced that moviegoers can tell the difference in higher quality digital picture and sound," said Disney's Bob Lambert, "and that with continued improvements in home technology, the need to convert theaters becomes that much more apparent." He ended his remarks with a bit of prodding: "The adopters who move toward the future first will be the ones who benefit first," he said, which suggested that he knew there was still plenty of reluctance left in the his fellow studio executives.

NATO president John Fithian called for a "significant test" of DCI's technical proposals in the real world.

But there was no discussion of the business arrangements that would have to underlie the roll-out of digital cinema, and the studio executives present, while supporting the new digital cinema spec in concept, didn't make any concrete commitments to releasing a certain number of movies digitally.

The lead sentence of the story that ran across the Dow Jones News Service that afternoon was, "Now for the hard part." The piece focused on the challenges of paying for the roll-out of digital cinema equipment, estimated to cost about $100,000 per screen. The Associated Press story focused on the same question as Dow Jones: who would pay, since theater owners weren't willing, and studios seemed reticent, too. The subhead of the day's *Variety* story was "Techies pass d-cinema torch to money men."

"DCI's work should've taken six months, not three years," said Chris McGurk, vice chairman of MGM. Director Robert Zemeckis made reference to the drawn-out process in the quote he supplied for DCI's final press release: "Hallelujah – It's about time!"

By *Variety*'s calculations, DCI's work had cost $8.4 million – $1.2 million each for the seven studios that participated.

9: Filming Without Film

I n the mid-1990s, as work on the first "Star Wars" prequel was getting underway, George Lucas and Rick McCallum, his producing partner, had been brainstorming about how they might design an all-digital moviemaking process. Lucas had long sought the freedom of being able to work digitally, from the storyboards to the shoot to the editing to the projection on the screen. He often referred to it as a more "painterly" way of working, with the ability to adjust colors or erase mistakes, exerting more control over the finished product. Some technologies were already fairly far along, like digital projectors and editing systems. But the most obvious missing tool was the camera.

"We were getting ready to shoot a million feet of film, and then I was going to have to spend $4 million or $5 million scanning it into a computer before I could even start to edit it or create digital effects with it," said McCallum. "Then, at the end, it looked like we'd have to spend millions again to get what we'd done printed back onto film. It was ridiculous."

McCallum got in touch with a Sony Electronics executive named Larry Thorpe to ask whether any Sony cameras in development might be up to the task of shooting an entire feature film. Thorpe thought it was too soon for one of Sony's high-definition digital cameras, then in development, to stand in for a film camera; at their core, they'd been designed, like all video cameras, to capture images at 30 frames-per-second, and the standard rate for film was 24 frames-per-second. They lacked a physical shutter, which film cameras had relied on since Edison and the Brothers Lumière. And they relied on light-sensitive microchips to translate the images before the lens into a seemingly-infinite stream of ones and zeros, instead of using a strand of chemically-treated celluloid to capture the light. The gulf was a big one – the difference between a TV look and a cinematic look.

Sony, with its corporate focus on the consumer and television broadcast markets, wasn't convinced that the motion picture industry represented a big enough market to warrant a custom-made camera. But McCallum kept needling, and in late 1997, Thorpe arranged a dinner in Los Angeles that included McCallum and several others from Lucasfilm and Industrial Light & Magic, and a group of Sony engineers and executives from Japan.

"You've got to do the selling here," Thorpe told McCallum before the dinner. "I've talked myself blue in the face, and their skepticism is really deep."

"None of them spoke English," McCallum recalled. "I said, 'Look, we want to take your high-definition camera and see if we can make movies with it and get them projected digitally.'" McCallum told them that if they'd build a 24 frame-per-second version of the camera, with a cinematic 2.35:1 aspect ratio, Lucas would use it to shoot *Attack of the Clones*. But although the wine was flowing over dinner, McCallum was skeptical that any amount of passionate lobbying would work. "I knew this wasn't going to happen. It was just so off-the-wall," McCallum said.

But after the Lucasfilm and ILM employees had explained some of what they'd need, the engineers started to make notes and sketches. "They were arguing with each other, and the translator wasn't translating – he was told not to," McCallum said.

After a long time, Sony executive Takeo Iguchi stood up and said, "We will do it." The dinner ended with a celebratory toast.

·   ·   ·

There had already been a few early attempts to see how electronic cameras might work on the set of a motion picture.

One of the pioneers was Lee Garmes, who had begun his career in 1918 as a camera operator for silent films, cranking the camera by hand. As a cinematographer, Garmes had shot the original Howard Hawks *Scarface* in 1932, and a large portion of *Gone With the Wind*. He'd also won an Academy Award for *Shanghai Express*, directed by Josef von Sternberg and starring Marlene Dietrich.

In 1972, at a gathering at the American Society of Cinematographers clubhouse in Hollywood, Garmes, a past president of the group, announced that he'd just finished shooting a feature on videotape, and "hoped never to see another piece of film." The movie was *Why*, a drama

Filming Without Film   **[151]**

about teen suicide, commissioned by Technicolor as an experiment in transferring material shot on videotape to 35-millimeter film for theatrical release. But Garmes may have made shooting with video sound too easy for his peers' liking, as when he told *American Cinematographer* magazine, "Looking at the monitors, the job was so easy. I could have phoned it in." Most cinematographers preferred for their work to seem complicated, mysterious, magical. (*Why* was the last movie Garmes shot.)

Other early experimenters had rockier experiences.

Around the same time Garmes was filming *Why* without film, cinematographer Donald Morgan brought several video cameras to New Mexico, along with two Ampex videotape recorders, to shoot the western *Santee*, starring Glen Ford. "Almost as an afterthought, Morgan decided to bring along his trusty

> **1972: Cinematographer Lee Garmes predicted that feature films would soon be sent to theaters via satellite, rendering release prints unnecessary.**

Arriflex IIC [film camera] and a few rolls of 35-millimeter color film for those situations where the cumbersome video cameras couldn't make it into inaccessible terrain," wrote cinematographer and film historian Russ Alsobrook.

Morgan gamely mounted the cameras and recorders in a four-wheel-drive vehicle to follow his cowboys through the waters of the Rio Grande, but the video cameras couldn't handle the high contrast of the sunny New Mexico landscape. And shadowy details were hard to see in night scenes illuminated by lanterns and campfires. "…[T]he smoking barrels of the old Winchesters looked like flame-throwers when recorded on video," Alsobrook wrote. Video just couldn't emulate the crispness of film.

Morgan wound up relying on the Arriflex to shoot most of *Santee* – using less than a minute of the video footage in the final film. "It was a grand experiment that fizzled," he said.

Cinematographer Giuseppe Rotunno, a long-time collaborator of Federico Fellini's, used a more advanced Sony high-definition video camera to shoot *Julia and Julia*, a racy psychological drama starring Kathleen Turner and Sting. The videotape was transferred to 35-millimeter film, and it was the opening film at the Venice Film Festival in 1987. Though film critic Roger Ebert complained in his Chicago *Sun-Times* column that there were "a few moments when quick movements seem to trail their shadows behind them," he labeled *Julia and Julia* "much better than any previous TV-to-film transfer I've seen."

But Rotunno himself wasn't a convert. "I am not an electronic person," said Rotunno, who had been the cinematographer for Fellini's *Amarcord* and *Satyricon.* "I prefer the film and not the tape."

Most cinematographers shared that preference, even as the cameras continued to improve in the 1990s.

•   •   •

Lucas and McCallum thought the technology in video cameras had come far enough. The cameras now captured images onto three light-sensitive chips – one chip each for red, blue, and green – converted them to digital ones and zeroes, and recorded them onto tape. Lucas and McCallum believed a digital camera would allow them work more efficiently, and cut their production costs. But staying on Sony to actually get it built, even after the engineers agreed it could be done, took effort.

"We'd started to get some movement," McCallum said, but then the project stalled – possibly because of Sony's concern about the camera's development costs.

Lucas and McCallum called in a favor, asking John Calley and Gareth Wigan, who were then president and co-vice chair of Sony Pictures, to talk to Nobuyuki Idei, Sony's chairman and CEO.

"I know one French proverb, and Mr. Idei speaks French," Wigan said. "So I said, in French, 'Take a step back in order to jump higher.' What I meant was, if and when we get into the digital age of moviemaking, Sony should be a leader."

Idei saw to it that the 24P camera project was moved to the front burner. (24 referred to the frame rate of the new camera; P to its ability to scan frames progressively – left to right, top to bottom – instead of in the interlaced manner common to video cameras, which switched between scanning every even horizontal line, and then every odd horizontal line.) *Attack of the Clones* was scheduled to start principal photography in Australia in the summer of 2000.

By March 10, 2000, Lucasfilm and Sony had produced ten minutes worth of test footage with the new camera, and transferred the images onto film to see how it'd look when projected. At Skywalker Ranch, "George had everybody there – anyone who was involved in the decision-making about whether to use the camera," Thorpe remembered. Lucas was proposing to use the camera for the entirety of the new movie. "We watched those films, and George said, 'I think this'll fly. Anyone got a problem? If anyone has concerns, now's the time.' And there was silence. Then George said, 'We're gonna do it.'"

Sony raced to get six cameras and videotape recorders ready to ship to Australia, and make sure that a new set of lenses being designed by Panavision – the fruit of another lobbying initiative by Lucas and McCallum – would work well with the cameras.

"We got the cameras about two weeks before the shoot started," McCallum said. "They were the most perilous weeks in our lives. We were doing some wardrobe tests, and I remember coming back three hours after the gear came in, and all of the guys were standing around looking at manuals, trying to figure out which [cable] went to which monitor." Sony gave the new 24P cameras the CineAlta brand name, but they were also known by a number: the F900.

"We thought there was a 50-50 chance that we'd be the laughingstock of the industry," said Michael Blanchard of Lucasfilm. McCallum had suggested that they shouldn't bring along a film camera as a back-up, Blanchard explained, "because then people might think that failure was an option, and just go back to shooting film."

There were some minor wrinkles. Whenever someone pulled out the power supply from a camera or removed its battery, the camera rebooted itself, and all the settings had to be verified again. The camera also had to be checked several times over the course of the day, he added, to make sure the heat it generated hadn't caused the background to drift out of focus.

But the rumor mill insisted that the *Attack of the Clones* shoot was a disaster. "When I was down in Sydney," said Fred Meyers of Lucasfilm, "I read online about how our cameras had blown up and how we'd switched back to film." McCallum's grapevine informed him that Lucas had only shot two days on digital, and that the tapes weren't usable. "It was so outrageous," McCallum said. "It was unbelievably depressing. I though we'd be picked up on everyone's shoulders, and given a ticker-tape parade down Hollywood Boulevard."

With *The Phantom Menace*, shooting on film, Lucas had averaged 26 set-ups per day. (A set-up is defined as a discrete shot from a particular camera position; multiple takes are usually done from each set-up.) On *Attack of the Clones*, that accelerated to 37 set-ups a day. And the latter film had taken 61 days to shoot, not the 65 Lucas had allocated. McCallum estimated that with *Clones*, the digital cameras helped save $3 million.

Lucas and McCallum knew that the digital cameras would only continue to get better. By the time *Attack of the Clones* was in post-production Sony had already developed a camera with improved resolution and more nuanced color, the F950.

Lucas and McCallum helped publicize the Sony camera and the Panavision lenses when *Attack of the Clones* was released, but they weren't advocating that everyone in the movie industry simply abandon film and take up digital (though many assumed that was Lucas' crusade, since he was one of the most prominent directors talking about the potential of digital cinematography).

Lucas said that some of his friends, such as Francis Ford Coppola, James Cameron, and Robert Rodriguez, were already shooting digitally, or getting ready to. Others, such as Steven Spielberg and Martin Scorsese, were staying with film.

"It's true that HD has certain unique characteristics that a lot of people complain about," Lucas said. "But film has them too — it has always had them, and they aren't necessarily that flattering to look at. It's just that film's flaws are built into the system — everyone has been using it for so long that no one recognizes the flaws anymore. No one wants to talk about them. People just maneuver around them silently, pretending they are not there, like big elephants that sit around the room. They pretend not to see the film elephant, but they point out the digital elephant."

After *Attack of the Clones* had been shot with the Sony digital camera, McCallum put out a standing invitation: anyone who wanted to see what the digital footage looked like once it'd been printed on 35-millimeter film, and how shooting digitally had changed the post-production process, was welcome to visit Skywalker Ranch.

Blanchard wasn't sure whether the open house created many new digital believers. "A lot of people came up for the curiosity factor, so they could say they had been to Lucas-land," he said. Most of the people who came were post-production staffers and executives from Fox, which was releasing the movie, and Warner Bros, though a few directors did tromp through.

As McCallum remembered it, "Not a single cameraman came up to the ranch during the 18 months that we were doing these demos."

•   •   •

Even before the release of *Attack of the Clones*, cinematographers seemed to realize that a digital revolution was in the offing – and they'd begun to debate its implications.

John Bailey was one of the first cinematographers to leap into the debate, writing an eloquent piece for the Sunday New York *Times* in early 2001.

Bailey had been the camera operator, in 1976, for director Terrence Malick's *Days of Heaven*, which won an Academy Award for cinematography. He later became a director of photography, responsible for movies such as *Ordinary People*, *The Big Chill*, *The Accidental Tourist*, and *As Good As It Gets*. (Camera operators are the crew members actually responsible for running the cameras; directors of photography, also called cinematographers, oversee not just the camera crew but also the lighting of the set.)

Bailey wasn't someone who refused to try out the latest digital cameras; in the summer of 2000, he collaborated on *The Anniversary Party* with actor-directors Alan Cumming and Jennifer Jason Leigh, using a digital camera. (Cumming and Leigh had suggested it, because of the project's tiny budget and tight schedule.) When the digitally-captured footage was printed to film in advance of the movie's release in 2001, Bailey acknowledged that it looked "much better than I had expected."

But Bailey was worried about big corporations like Sony and Panavision pushing the technology at cinematographers. "...It is the manufacturers and studio marketers who seem most invested in getting rid of film and who stand to rake in the most profits," he wrote. "For them, it is not an issue of creative expression, aesthetics or improved picture quality. It is an issue of bottom-line economics."

Bailey hoped that film and digital video might be able to coexist peacefully in the 21st century – rather than one replacing the other – just as painting and photography cross-fertilized each other in the 20th century.

Other cinematographers had dozens of other reasons for not picking up digital cameras, and they shared those reasons whenever they had the opportunity.

One of the most vocal was cinematographer Steven Poster, who served for one year as president of the American Society of Cinematographers. In June, 2000, he participated in an online chat organized by the International Cinematographers Guild. He commented on a Sony ad suggested that film was dead ("I can assure you film is not dead") and dismissed the notion that digital cinematography would supplant film cameras ("Remember the paperless office?")

"Don't be too quick to embrace new technologies that you've never seen. I like to call this techno-lust," he wrote.

And in an e-mail to a group of cinematographers shortly afterwards, Poster wrote about *Attack of the Clones* that director George Lucas was "shooting at least 30% of the movie (so far) on FILM. And it's just the beginning." (The statement wasn't true, though some backgrounds that had been shot on film for *The Phantom Menace* were recycled in *Attack of the Clones*.)

Poster, like Bailey, felt that the camera makers – and especially Sony – were trying to do an end-run around cinematographers, by selling producers on digital cinematography as a way to save money. "There was a lot of hype and over-promising," said Poster. "They'd say, 'You don't need lights, you don't need crews, this is just as good as film, if not better.'"

But Larry Thorpe of Sony wasn't avoiding the debate with cinematographers; he recalled visiting the American Society of Cinematographers clubhouse to discuss the differences between film and digital with ASC members. "I took some arrows," he said. "One of them called me the Great White Satan of Digital. It was said jokingly, but there was a little barb in there. Other times, it became quite heated," as when Thorpe sat on panel discussions with cinematographers. (In retrospect, Thorpe said that if he was able to do things over, he would've "spent a lot more time with folks like the ASC, and done workshops. But at the time, we were terribly busy.")

Cinematographers viewed themselves as the defenders of the purity of the image, and they had their allies.

Film critic Stephanie Zacharek of Salon.com wrote that "it probably hasn't occurred to most moviegoers that the 'Film is dead' movement may be more strongly driven by forces in the marketplace than by artistic considerations. ...[C]inematographers may be the last line of defense between those massive marketing forces and the rich visual heritage of movies."

•   •   •

The cinematographers and critics were joined by Kodak, the company that had been supplying the movie industry with film since the days of Edison. Kodak film fed just nearly every movie camera and projector in the world. Most years, the company could brag that all of the movies nominated for a Best Picture Oscar had been shot on Kodak film.

"There is no comparison between film and digital technology," said Colette Scott, a Kodak executive in Canada. The notion that film was on its way out was "ridiculous" and "laughable." She was speaking to a reporter from the Canadian film magazine *Take One* in 2001.

Kodak was one of the underwriters of a gathering in China, held in 2000, called the Beijing Motion Picture & Television Conference. That event gave Victor Kemper, then president of the American Society of Cinematographers, and Don Rogers, vice chairman of the Academy's Scientific Achievement Committee, a chance to express their opinions about digital. Rogers said that the technology available at the time (like the CineAlta cameras from Sony and Panavision being used on *Attack of the Clones*) still weren't good enough to be compared to film. Kemper knocked George Lucas as "dangerous to all of us in this business" for his use of new cameras that might not require as large a camera crew as film cameras did, and for his experimentation with digitally-created characters that might jeopardize the jobs of actors.

Endlessly, cinematographers debated how many pixels a digital camera would need to capture in order to match film. How many pixels could the human eye perceive? Was it equivalent to 4K (4,000 pixels per line)? 6K? (Kodak weighed in, saying that its best film stocks could capture details up to about 5.5K, or the equivalent of 5,500 pixels strung across the frame horizontally.)

Others held tight to film because of an aesthetic *je ne sais quoi*. The word "magic" was frequently employed. Lance Acord, the director of photography for *Being John Malkovich* and *Lost in Translation*, said, "There's an element of magic in the photographic process, and because of that, film will always be more interesting to me."

"Film is rather like the magic lantern," said Roger Deakins, who'd been the director of photography for *A Beautiful Mind*, which won the 2002 Oscars for Best Picture and Best Director, among others. "There's a sense of mystery, because you don't know what's going into the magic black box camera until you send the film to the lab. With digital, it's all very businesslike. We're not businessmen. We're artists and magicians."

Deakins also felt that the restrictions imposed by shooting on film were an important part of the filmmaking process. "You've got a certain length of film in the camera, and when you come to do a take, it's an important moment," he said. "People have to focus, because it's expensive to shoot that film. Whereas with video, you can keep it running forever." (A typical cartridge of 35-millimeter film might allow for ten minutes of shooting, before needing to be swapped out.)

Caleb Deschanel had some experience using a digital camera for TV shows. But most of Deschanel's work was in feature films: he'd shot movies like *The Patriot, Being There, The Right Stuff,* and the surprise blockbuster of 2004, Mel Gibson's *The Passion of the Christ.* And he still had concerns about shooting digitally.

Deschanel described the first decade of the 21st century as "this terrible transitional period" in cinema, for two reasons. The first was the bulkiness of the cameras, and their need to be connected to an external recording device. "It felt like taking one step forward, and two steps back," he said. "If you're going to give up film, you want something light and flexible." Deschanel compared it to the early days of Technicolor's three-strip process, when cameramen wrestled with big cameras that held three separate rolls of film.

The second reason was the possibility that some films shot digitally wouldn't be archived in a lasting way. Deschanel felt that the most commercially-successful movies would probably be printed onto stable polyester film stock, and stored in refrigerated warehouses. But he thought that many other movies might exist only as digital files. From a black bookcase in his office, Deschanel pulled out a square white plastic case, and dropped it onto his cluttered desk. It was a 45-megabyte removable disk made by the company Syquest. "I have no idea how to get the information that's on here, and that's going to be true of a lot of digital media," he said. "I'm not sure that digital movies will be truly archival, in the same way that you can take the film that the Lumière brothers shot in 1898 and put it onto a projector today."

"You look at *It's a Wonderful Life,* or a movie I worked on, *The Natural.* They were not big hits in their day, but both, I think, were worth preserving," Deschanel said.

Cinematographers also seemed worried that digital cameras would raise the portcullis that protected their craft from outsiders, just as editors worried that non-linear editing would do in their field. In an online chat sponsored by the International Cinematographers Guild in 1999, Richard Crudo (who would later become president of the American Society of Cinematographers) wrote, "As to whether or not [digital cameras] will make it easier for more people to become cinematographers, I don't believe that's true. This trend today that we're seeing towards the 'democratization' of filmmaking is the biggest fraud perpetuated by manufacturers and know-nothing individuals. It's almost akin to handing out typewriters to a bunch of chimpanzees and telling them they're novelists. It takes a long, long time to become a true cinematographer."

Changes in status on the set were also a concern for some. Victor Kemper had begun his career as a television engineer in the late 1950s, and gone on to shoot a range of movies from John Cassavetes' *Husbands* to *Dog Day Afternoon* with Al Pacino to *The Candidate*, starring Robert Redford. He'd also worked on comedies such as *The Jerk*, *National Lampoon's Vacation*, and *Pee-Wee's Big Adventure*.

Kemper said he hadn't yet shot a movie with a digital camera, although he wasn't opposed to the idea. ("The only concern I'd have would be my inexperience and unfamiliarity with digital," he said. "I've worked with film for so long.")

He felt that having monitors on the set, linked to the cameras, bogged down the process of making a movie, and disrupted the power structure. When it first became possible to attach a video "tap" to a film camera, capturing on videotape the images the camera saw and playing them back on a monitor, Kemper tried to fight it.

"Video tap was the bane of my existence," he said. "I come from the school where the camera operator ruled. The director would turn to the operator after a take and say, 'How was it for camera?' The camera operator would give him a thumbs-up or thumbs-down. There was always that wonderful relationship between the camera operator and the director."

Being able to see the take on a monitor was "a terrible interruption," to Kemper's mind. "You've got the producer and his daughter-in-law staring at the monitor. Then they want to play it back." He compared this on-set video review to the use of instant-replay in professional football: it slowed the pace. After Kemper consented to use a video tap on one project in the 1980s, he tried to talk directors out of it – but eventually gave in, once video taps started to be integrated into most 35-millimeter cameras. Digital cameras produced a better-quality image than video taps, which was often displayed on high-definition flat screens on the set.

Kemper also worried that new technologies would mean fewer jobs. "I think that what we as a team do is such a wonderful job – and has created so much entertainment over the years – I'd hate to see that disappear [and be replaced by] a machine."

Kemper also didn't feel that digital could match the picture quality of film. "If video came first, and then we invented film, anyone would look at film and say, 'Wow, that's a good picture,'" he said.

He didn't mind being cast as a defender of film against the digital onslaught, especially during his tenure as president of the American Society of Cinematographers. "No question. I certainly was," he said.

•   •   •

Lucas and McCallum wanted to share the results of their experiment with the new Sony digital camera, and so in April 2002, just before *Attack of the Clones* was released, they organized a digital cinema summit at Skywalker Ranch. The guest list was something out of a film student's fondest dreams: the directors in attendance included Steven Spielberg, Oliver Stone, Francis Ford Coppola, Martin Scorsese, John Lasseter, Michael Mann, Robert Rodriguez, and Bryan Singer.

It was an extended show-and-tell session, leavened by some friendly needling, as when Lucas observed that Scorsese had just built one of the biggest sets since 1961's *Cleopatra* at Cinecitta Studios in Rome for his epic *Gangs of New York*. Lucas, who was predominantly relying on virtual sets constructed inside computers, teased, "Marty's sets are getting more expensive. Mine are getting cheaper."

Lucas opened the summit by expressing his sense that getting digital cinematography and projection accepted was "still a very tough uphill climb, because the industry is against it." Throughout the day, he highlighted the advantages he'd been enjoying, while emphasizing that it was still early, and the tools would get better. "We're looking at 1902 technology here – this is the hand-cranked era," he said.

Rodriguez picked up on the historical theme, declaring, "I really believe that film peaked with Technicolor, and went downhill from there."

After Rodriguez talked about using his high-definition monitors on the set to adjust the camera and lighting, and see exactly what he'd be getting in each take, Oliver Stone piped up in protest. "Aren't you destroying the art of cinematography?" he asked. "There's no risk." Stone was suggesting that the iffiness of shooting on film – who knew what it'd look like when developed? – was a vital part of moviemaking.

"You can turn the monitor off," Rodriguez said, getting a laugh.

"What you're saying," Lucas said to Stone, jumping in, "is that we're going to lose the art of fresco because we have oil paints now. Nobody is saying fresco is bad. Artists can think differently, though, in a more malleable medium."

(Later, Stone said, "I don't think it was so much a protest on my part, as much as I was trying to ask out loud the questions I had. What is the nature of film? What are we losing?")

Michael Mann showed footage he'd shot digitally for *Ali*, and Coppola brought a montage of New York scenes that cinematographer Ron Fricke had shot digitally for a movie-in-progress called *Megalopolis*. Coppola had visited the set of *Clones* in Australia, and decided to try the Sony CineAlta camera.

Before showing the seven minutes of footage, Coppola spoke to his peers extemporaneously for a long while, talking about how he had tried to encourage the development of electronic cameras and editing systems since the 1960s.

"The mechanical genie, film, seemed to be at the apogee of its beauty," Coppola said. "And this electronic genie could do anything. It had no material body. It could be just magical.

"I thought that one day, with time, the electronic genie would get the beauty and luster of film, and then you'd have all the advantages of the quicksilver nature of electronics," he said. "You could play with [the image] and change it – it's malleable." Coppola believed the electronic genie was nearly there.

"I'm pretty much technology agnostic," Coppola said. "I'll work on a Macintosh, I'll work on a PC. I'll shoot on film, I'll shoot on video. It doesn't make any difference to me, other than how it can serve the theme of the movie."

"The art of any time," he concluded, "is usually made with the technology of that time."

•   •   •

Still, studio executives and producers didn't feel they could pressure the directors and cinematographers they hired to use the technology of their time; like film editors, they had been independent contractors, not employees of the studios, for decades now.

At Sony Pictures, even though the camera division of the company organized workshops to familiarize people with the new CineAlta, several years passed without any directors or cinematographers opting to use a digital camera.

"We encouraged them [to shoot digitally]," said Sony Pictures chairman Michael Lynton, "but you couldn't force the issue."

"There's no question that every 60-year-old cinematographer doesn't want to shoot with a digital camera," said Tom Pollack, a producer who'd formerly run Universal Pictures. "If the economics become really huge, people will force them to do it. But right now, the impression is it might save you a few hundred thousand dollars, which is not a lot of money, the way studios make movies."

> "If film versus digital is warring religions, I'm agnostic. I like the cafeteria-style religion, pulling from all of them. I don't have any absolutes, and I don't think film is dead. I might want that grain. For day exteriors, I still think 35-millimeter looks better. But check back with me in a year."
>
> — director Richard Linklater, 2006

Disney was one of the few studios that actually commissioned a cinematographer, Daryn Okada, to take the latest digital cameras and put them through a simulated day of production, and then report back on their strengths and weaknesses. "Except for Disney, not a lot of studios are actively taking the stuff out for a test run, which is what they really need to do to be better informed," said Okada. "If you wait for a director to tell you they want to shoot digitally, it's usually too late, because the project is already green-lit and they have a production schedule."

Indeed, when Peter Jackson was in pre-production for his re-make of *King Kong*, he investigated using a digital 3-D camera system, the Fusion, that James Cameron had helped develop, based on the design of Sony's CineAlta cameras. "Unfortunately, we started too late, in our last three or four months of pre-production, and so there was not enough time to really get our hands on the equipment," Jackson said. "The complexity of *Kong*, with all its miniatures and computer-generated characters, made us think that we might be biting off more than we could chew."

Jackson was a technophile who hadn't yet chosen to shoot a feature with a digital camera. He'd posted video updates from the set of *King Kong* on the Internet, and supervised the creation of more than 1600 computer-generated shots for the movie – more than half of its 2200 total shots. But, he said in 2006, "with what I've seen so far, I'm not that in love with digital cameras. We did tests with the Sony [CineAlta] camera in between the *Rings* trilogy and *Kong*, and we shot some digital footage side-by-side with film during *Rings*, but I just couldn't get it to look the way I wanted. The amount of detail that the whites and blacks could hold wasn't sufficient."

> "Being a movie director, you get to be a king. It's a seductive process, this crew of 300 people doing whatever you say. But it tends to be counter-productive if you want to explore something new, and break out of the mold."
>
> – Visual effects pioneer and director Doug Trumbull

Jackson was holding out, it seemed, for a digital camera that would surpass what film could do. "I'm waiting for the camera that gives you something like 65-millimeter – like what David Lean had with *Lawrence of Arabia*," he said. "I think we'll soon have digital cameras and projectors that can approximate the Imax experience, not just duplicate what we see with 35-millimeter." Finally, in 2007, he made a short film as a test, using a pair of new cameras from the start-up company Red Digital Cinema.

"The artist has to be driven by artistic opportunities, not just by economics," said Peter Guber, a producer and former head of Columbia Pictures and Sony Pictures. "If a filmmaker decides he can get a better texture or feeling or flavor by shooting on film, you can't just dictate that he should shoot on digital. The studio has to work with the artist." Guber said that if a director he was working with wanted to shoot digitally, "we're open to that. But the technology needs to be advanced in the hands of an artist."

And with few exceptions, most directors weren't convinced that their cinematographers should be wielding a digital camera.

Director John Landis, who said he'd been "very resistant" to using the Avid digital editing system, echoed the feelings of many of his peers when he said, "I like film. I like the feel of film. I like the smell of it."

Oliver Stone seemed troubled by how close digital images were getting to the quality of film, without precisely matching it. (He'd used a video camera for portions of 1994's *Natural Born Killers*, to produce a TV news camera look.) "The digital is so close, it's like a clone of film. We've fought so hard to make the clone seamless. But if you truly appreciate a painting, this is like a replication of it," he said. For science fiction movies, Stone thought it was appropriate – "it has a new feel"– but Stone couldn't imagine using a digital camera for an epic movie such as *Alexander*.

Not all directors reluctant to start working digitally were grizzled veterans. Andrew Bujalski made two low-budget features before he turned 30 (*Funny Ha-Ha* and *Mutual Appreciation*). Both were shot and edited on celluloid. M. Night Shyamalan's break-out hit, *The Sixth Sense*, was released when he was just 29. Before his 33rd birthday, Ben Younger had written and directed two features, the independent hit *Boiler Room*, starring Ben Affleck, Vin Diesel, and Giovanni Ribisi, and the Universal release *Prime*, starring Meryl Streep and Uma Thurman.

Bujalski, a Boston native, studied film at Harvard and graduated in 1998. As a low-budget filmmaker – his first two films were made for less than $100,000 each – Bujalski acknowledged that shooting and editing digitally can save money. But he decided to shoot on 16-millimeter film and edit on an old Steenbeck editing system that had been cast off by New York University's film school. The hulking piece of equipment sat in his living room and "sort of motivates me, in a way, to make another movie, because I need to take advantage of this machine," he said.

"For the films I've done so far, I felt pretty clear that they could only be done in this old-fashioned way that I'd been trained in and was used to," Bujalski said. (The results have earned critical accolades; New York Times critic A.O. Scott called *Funny Ha-Ha*, the story of a 23-year old woman in love with the wrong man, one of the ten best movies of 2005.) "They would feel completely different if they were done on video. To me, shooting and editing on film is a process, an aesthetic, and an end result that all tie together." Bujalksi was hopeful that digital cameras wouldn't render film cameras extinct. "I like to think that we'll always have choices, like riding the Amtrak train from Boston to New York versus flying versus taking the bus. There's plenty of great work being done on video, but it's a very different medium."

M. Night Shyamalan was of the same opinion. "Shooting digitally would bother me," Shyamalan said, adding that he still occasionally edited on film. "If it were up to me, I would keep the [film] stock from the 1970s that they shot *Dog Day Afternoon* with. That's more real to me. Instead, I have this very slick movie film now. You can shoot in any light. It looks very clean. And everyone has that glossy quality." Shyamalan said he wasn't itching to start experimenting with the latest digital cameras. "It's not my thing. I'm a little farm boy."

Ben Younger didn't live on a farm, and he explained that he wasn't anti-technology: "I love gadgets," he said. He was surrounded by them in his Tudor-style Laurel Canyon home. Parked outside the front door was a racing motorcycle; above the fireplace was a large-screen plasma TV, and in another room, there was a consumer version of Texas Instruments' DLP digital projector. Even the phones were high-tech.

But Younger had shot his two movies on film, and he was planning to do the same for his third production in 2006. "This is more of a litmus test about feeling and mood and emotion," he said. He remembered going to the movies in Flatbush, Brooklyn, with his father and grandfather and hearing the faint purr of the projector in the booth.

Younger wasn't fond of the movies he'd seen that had been shot digitally, including *Collateral* and *Attack of the Clones*. "It's too vivid. Maybe it resembles the home videos we've all taken – of bar mitzvahs or family vacations. To go and see a piece of fiction that has a similar look, we make that connection, and it ruins it."

Younger said he was conscious of not allowing the budgets of his films to balloon. *Prime* had cost $19 million to make, and earned a profit, and he was planning to make his next film for $8 million or $10 million. But he didn't want to economize by giving up film.

"I'm not sure that the general public notices the difference between film and digital, or at least not enough to protest," he said. "That's where my fear comes in. If it's cheaper to shoot digital, and people don't notice it to the point where they're willing to complain, we'll be forced to shoot it. That's something that makes me nervous."

He added, "I hear myself saying that, and I wonder, is this what directors said before *The Jazz Singer*? 'We don't want to have dialogue, because that will ruin our movies.' I know I sound like a dinosaur…"

•   •   •

Sony had made an aggressive incursion into Hollywood with its CineAlta camera; the message that cinematographers heard was that film's obituary was being drafted.

Panavision, the company that made the lenses for the CineAlta camera, took a different approach. The company had a long history in film – and close connections to innumerable top cinematographers – that it didn't want to jeopardize. While Panavision executives may not have wanted to push change to happen overnight, they realized they needed to offer a new set of digital tools to their customers.

The halls of the company's headquarters in the San Fernando Valley are lined with glamorous, soft-focus black-and-white photos by George Hurrell, taken in the 1930s and 1940s: Veronica Lake, Gary Cooper, Marlene Dietrich, Rita Hayworth. In the company's lobby is a mural of the iconic shot from *Lawrence of Arabia* of Omar Sharif riding on a camel toward the camera, slowly closing the distance. In the CEO's office, sitting on a credenza, is the famous Sphero Panatar lens that was used for that shot, now known as the "David Lean lens," for the film's director. It is a glistening chrome cylinder a-foot-and-a-half long that looks like a navigational device that might have aided 19th century explorers. It was used just once, for *Lawrence of Arabia*, which earned Freddie Young an Oscar for cinematography.

The company was founded in 1953, and since then, its name has become well-known among film buffs for one reason: any major movie production that uses Panavision cameras or lenses is contractually required to include a credit that says either "Filmed with Panavision Cameras and Lenses" or "Filmed in Panavision."

Panavision founder Robert Gottschalk had owned the Campus Camera Shop in Westwood Village, near UCLA. By talking to customers and vendors who did business with his camera shop, Gottschalk learned that Bausch & Lomb was having trouble filling the orders for the special anamorphic projector lenses that'd be required to show *The Robe*, the 1953 biblical epic starring Richard Burton, which was Fox's first picture in the CinemaScope wide-screen format.

Gottschalk and one of his acquaintances, an optical engineer named Walter Wallin, tinkered together to come up with a prism-type lens that turned out to be better at producing widescreen imagery and more flexible than the existing CinemaScope cylindrical lenses of the time. They were less expensive to make, and the prisms could be swiveled, with the twist of a knob, to go from a 1:1 image ratio to 2:1 widescreen. They sold for $1,100 a pair (two were necessary, since most projection booths of the time still switched back and forth between two projectors.) Eventually, Panavision's prism-based Super Panatar lens for projectors prevailed over its rivals, and the company sold about 35,000 prism attachments for movie projectors, until they saturated the market.

After that, Panavision shifted its business from selling equipment to renting it. That way, there'd be consistent demand for its products, and the responsibility for maintaining the gear would fall to Panavision, not the user. (Customers also wouldn't have to depreciate the cost of cameras or lenses they'd purchased.) But the shift also meant that Panavision started building up a large inventory of equipment, and its motivation became making sure it didn't become obsolete – not coming up with a "next big thing" that might render its rental inventory worthless overnight.

Panavision moved on to developing lenses for cameras. In 1959, *Ben Hur* was the first film shot with Panavision lenses to win the Oscar for cinematography. The company's camera lenses were used on *West Side Story*, *My Fair Lady*, *Exodus*, *Fiddler on the Roof*, *Superman*, and the original *Star Wars*. The company also designed soundproof housings to quiet the sound of a camera's motors, called "blimps," and a more portable, compact camera called the Panaflex, used for the first time on Steven Spielberg's *Sugarland Express* in 1973. (The movie was a flop that would've ended the young director's career, had he not already contracted to make his next movie, starring Roy Scheider and a shark.) For its technical achievements, Panavision collected three Oscars.

The company's maintenance technicians regard old cameras in much the same way airline mechanics regard superannuated planes: replace a part, refurbish a mechanism, oil it up, and it'll run forever. The second and third Panaflex camera ever made in the 1970s were still being rented out in 2005, as were Mitchells andArriflexes from the 1940s, which weren't capable of recording synchronized sound, and wind-up Bell & Howell Eymos, which were practically indestructible. "We still have some hand-cranked cameras from the 1920s," said Eric Erb, the director of operations finance at Panavision, walking through vast concrete-floored warehouses filled with camera gear and lenses, all packed in rugged boxes full of foam.

The company also had two types of digital cameras, both developed in partnership with Sony, starting in the late 1990s. The first of the two was the CineAlta High-Definition Camera System (also known as the F900), a version of the Sony camera first used during the production of *Attack of the Clones*. Panavision made the F900 more rugged, and capable of using the company's heavier, custom-designed digital lenses.

But Panavision discovered that digital cameras didn't necessarily improve its business; instead of renting high-end film cameras, production companies simply rented digital cameras (mostly for TV shoots). Though Panavision initially commanded a higher price for the digital cameras, as other rental houses started offering F900s – Panavision didn't have an exclusive – the price to rent one drifted down to about what Panavision charged for a top-of-the-line film camera.

When Bob Beitcher joined the company in 2003 as its CEO, Panavision was finding that most cinematographers weren't ready to jump to digital yet, and so it needed to figure out how to balance the old technology along with the new. "We'd starved our film research-and-development spending to invest in digital," Beitcher said. So Beitcher gave the go-ahead for work on a new version of Panavision's flagship film camera, the Millennium XL2, making about fifty small improvements to the camera.

But he also knew that it was important to come up with new digital cameras. "We had no choice but to stay in front of the big rolling ball behind us," he said. Working with Sony, Panavision started to develop its second-generation digital camera, the Genesis, which would assuage cinematographers by closely mimicking film cameras, and capturing pictures on a single electronic sensor (or chip) that was exactly the size of a 35-millimeter frame of film, rather than the CineAlta's three smaller chips. "The Genesis was designed to be a film camera that just happened to shoot on tape," said Panavision sales and marketing vice president Bob Harvey. "The ergonomics of it made it familiar to cinematographers. It could accommodate all 6000 of our lenses, and the kind of follow-focus that camera operators were used to." (Follow-focus is an attachment that allows the camera's focal distance to be adjusted precisely, often by a special assistant called a "focus puller.)

"We introduced the Genesis in such a way that there were no blinking lights on it, no one saying that 'film is dead, it's over," Beitcher said. "We just said, 'We think this is an interesting new alternative.'" Panavision found – to its relief – that it could charge almost double the rental price of a high-end film camera, making the case that the Genesis produced film-quality images while saving the cost of buying and processing camera negative.

•   •   •

Director and cinematographer Dean Semler had seen some sample footage shot with the Genesis camera, and when Mel Gibson asked his opinion about using a digital camera for the next movie the two were planning to work on, Semler set up a visit to Panavision.

"Mel is really curious about new technology, and as a producer, he's very much aware of the costs," said Semler. After their visit, "we sat on the grass outside of Panavision, and Mel acted out the *Apocalypto* story for me." After an initial scouting trip together to Veracruz, Mexico, Gibson decided to push production back by a year to try to avoid the worst of the rainy season there.

In the meantime, though, Semler suggested using the Genesis camera for an Adam Sandler comedy he was hired to shoot. *Click*, about a man who discovers a remote control that can impact the world around him, was made on the Sony Pictures lot. "We were able to shoot for 20 or 30 minutes at a time on *Click*," Semler said, "which allows the actors to keep in the moment, and allows directors to try alternatives. I think we'd change tapes maybe twice a day," as opposed to reloading a camera every ten minutes or so.

A tipping point for digital cinematography seemed tantalizingly near in 2005 and 2006. The first major feature to use the Genesis camera was *Superman Returns*, shot by Newton Thomas Sigel in 2005, a year after the camera was introduced. Sigel and director Bryan Singer considered shooting with a 65-millimeter film camera, before testing the Genesis. They "bulldozed and blitzed their way through Warner Bros.," Beitcher said, "and they got the OK a few days before production was going to start. Initially, we had film cameras on the set, and Genesis on standby."

With that lengthy shoot in Australia, rumors swirled, as they had when Lucas shot *Attack of the Clones* there, that the production would revert to the old way at any minute. One morsel making its way around the grapevine had it that the production had ordered a million feet of camera negative – which proved false. In the end, eight Genesis cameras were used on *Superman Returns*. A small amount of film was used when Singer and Sigel needed to shoot sequences at higher frame rates that weren't yet supported by the Genesis. (Faster camera speeds are often used for slow motion or visual effects sequences.)

Theaters began to fill, beginning in the summer of 2006, with other films shot digitally: the parody *Scary Movie 4*, the World War I action movie *Flyboys*, and the Mayan adventure *Apocalypto*, all shot with the Genesis. *Miami Vice* was shot using the Viper FilmStream digital camera from Thomson Grass Valley, along with other digital cameras and a few film cameras; cinematographer Dion Beebe complained about trying to shoot with digital cameras on a boat, since they had to be tethered to recording decks that were stashed away in the vessel's hull. David Fincher's *Zodiac*, released in February 2007, also used the FilmStream camera, recording this time to hard drives rather than tape – a first for that approach. *Variety* film critic Todd McCarthy liked the results, writing that the "Due to the...precise yet fluid HD camerawork, the pic possesses a kind of seedy dreaminess that most strongly recalls another indelible epic of '70s California, *Boogie Nights*."

Suddenly, demand for the Genesis started to spike, for both movie and TV shoots. Panavision and Sony couldn't make Genesis cameras fast enough. In the fall of 2005, the company had just 27 of them (compared to several hundred film cameras), and was expecting to be up to 34 by the end of the year. "We could use about 100," said Harvey.

Digital cameras also posed a problem to Panavision because no one expected them to have as long of a useful lifetime as film cameras; it was hard to conceive that a CineAlta from 1999 would still be renting out seventy years later, as some of Panavision's film cameras did. "We plan for much faster obsolescence with digital cameras – you have higher maintenance costs, and a faster upgrade cycle than film cameras," Beitcher said. "That's one of our justifications for a higher rental price than a film camera."

But Beitcher admitted that he didn't want the transition from film to digital to happen overnight. When asked in an interview how he'd react if someone flipped a switch on January 1, 2006, and made all movie production digital, Beitcher said, "We'd have a lot of stranded assets, and a lot of unhappy customers – there are great cinematographers who'll shoot on film for the next twenty years."

"We have this strange tension," he continued. "We've got a lot of film assets here, and a lot of lending [to finance Panavision as a company is] based on the value of those. So we need to invest in digital, but assure our lenders and investors that our film assets are going to be valuable for a long time."

Beitcher knew he was in a difficult spot: unable to push full-speed-ahead toward digital, and trying to listen to what his customers wanted today — film cameras, mostly — but realizing that their demands might change overnight. "We want to control the transition [from film to digital] as best we can, but at some point it's not controllable," he acknowledged.

In 2006, Panavision had quietly begun early research and development on the camera that'd succeed the Genesis, trying to ratchet up the image quality further, offering enhanced resolution and greater dynamic range.

By 2025, Beitcher expected that there'd be a "limited" number of movies still being shot on film. "Camera negative will certainly be more expensive," he said, since it'd be produced at lower volumes. But Beitcher said he could imagine that some projects would still shoot on film "primarily for aesthetic reasons."

In Erb's cluttered office, along with some battered, boxy gray Super Panatar lenses from the 1950s, he had a bulletin board of still photographs, all of them shot with a film camera. "The silver in film captures an image differently from a CCD [charge-coupled device imager, which was the basic light sensor chip used in every kind of digital camera]," he said. "I'd hate to try to add up the number of film cameras in the world — maybe 100,000? It's hard to conceive of how long it'll take digital to replace all of that technology."

"I don't think in my career that we'll see film cameras go away," said Erb, who was 37 at the time.

•   •   •

Since the arrival of sound, the cinematographer's job changed with nearly every new wave of technology: first they were trapped in the stuffy, soundproof iceboxes, then given responsibility for the gargantuan Technicolor cameras, then asked to share their images with the rest of the crew via the video tap.

But cinematographers tended to adapt, and find ways of making the new technology as flexible and expressive — or even more — than the old.

"I have no agenda where I want to see [film] disappear," said Tom Ackerman, who'd been among the first to shoot with the Genesis. "I like the photochemical process, and I've spent plenty of hours developing still film in the darkroom. But a lot of my colleagues have been too hidebound, in my opinion. We wax poetic about this stuff, and we allow it to become mythical, when we need to be talking about it as a tool."

Cinematographer Emmanuel Lubezki had first used a digital camera when he was scouting locations for the Michael Mann movie *Ali*. The footage "was so different and interesting," Lubezki said, that Mann asked him to try to recreate the surreal feeling with a film camera. Lubezki tinkered for weeks, but he couldn't do it. The only way to produce the same visuals was to use a digital camera.

Lubezki said, "I'd spent 20 years learning how to use a film camera. Now, I had to pick up something new, and there were all these other people who were far better at using this new technology than I was. You become afraid." Lubezki's resume included *The Birdcage*, *Sleepy Hollow*, and *Y tu mama tambien*.

"I took classes. I made mistakes," Lubezki said. "I was afraid. I didn't know if I could make it work. But I did, and it was worth it. This is different from film. Not better or worse, but different. You can't let fear of the unknown prevent you from taking that chance."

Allen Daviau was the rare cinematographer who'd been testing most of the new digital cameras as they became available: "I want to know what they can do," he said. (The cinematographer of *E.T.* and *Top Gun* had produced the test footage that helped convince Dean Semler and Mel Gibson to use the Genesis for *Apocalypto*, but he had yet to shoot a feature digitally himself.) Daviau felt that in the near future, he and his colleagues would be using film cameras for some projects, digital for others. "It's horses for courses," he said. "Which horse do you want for this course? If I was shooting *Top Gun 2*, you can bet I'd have a digital camera in the back of the fighter jet." But further out, Daviau believed that digital "will continue to get better and eventually, it will displace film – as much as it hurts me to say it."

Steven Spielberg liked to say that he planned to be the last director buying the last foot of film available. "The greatest films ever made were shot and edited on film, and that's very important to me," he said. "If it was good enough for Hitchcock, David Lean, Stanley Kubrick, John Ford, and Akira Kurosawa, it's good enough for me." Spielberg even liked the limitations imposed by the length of film that could fit in a cartridge. "I'm nostalgic about having a camera operator turn to me and whisper, 'we're about to roll out.' I do love having to reload. It reminds me of the days when I had to reload my little eight millimeter Bell and Howell camera." (George Lucas had tried to persuade Spielberg to switch to a digital camera with

Indiana Jones and the Kingdom of the Crystal Skull, which Lucas produced and Spielberg directed – but Lucas' argument didn't sway Spielberg.)

With the use of video taps and monitors, Spielberg said the impulse was to watch the actors' performances from the "video village," usually a tent set up with large monitors. "I am seduced even on my own movie sets to watch the monitor, as opposed to standing next to the camera and directing the actors the way [George] Cukor and John Ford and Howard Hawks directed them."

But as one of the founders of the DreamWorks SKG studio, Spielberg said he'd "never get in the way of a filmmaker wanting to shoot his film 100 percent digitally" (though none had chosen to do that).

Quoting his friend Francis Ford Coppola, he said, "I love the smell of film in the morning. It smells like victory."

Coppola, in fact, had begun using video cameras in 1965, shooting the rehearsals for one of his first films, *You're a Big Boy Now.* (This was even before *Why* and *Santee.*) "We used those tapes as a guide to making the film," he said. His strategy, throughout his career, was always "to use the most modern technology we could get our hands on," he explained. Coppola had used a digital camera on the set of *Youth Without Youth* in 2005, but he had already moved beyond making a distinction between film and digital.

"The technology is irrelevant," he said. "'Use the weapons at hand,' as Napoleon said. The important thing is that you're making cinema. I don't like to say how I'm shooting – film or [digital]. I shoot both. I don't even like anyone to know which it is."

10: Coming to Terms with the Net

I n a suburb south of Los Angeles, it looked as though a band of cell-phone-obsessed nomads had set up camp in the parking lot surrounding an office complex: a small village of tents had sprung up overnight, and white trailers were parked in neat rows.

A yellow AMC Gremlin was being towed slowly around the neighborhood by a truck; inside the car were the actors Morgan Freeman and Paz Vega, and a movie camera was mounted on the bed of the truck to capture their conversation.

The movie they were making, *10 Items or Less*, tells the story of a famous actor (Freeman) who enters and then alters the life of a convenience store cashier (Vega). It was fairly typical for a low-budget movie made without studio support: costs were being kept under $10 million, the shoot would be completed in just fifteen days, and the script didn't call for any flashy visual effects or elaborate sets. (In 2006, when *10 Items* was made, the average cost of producing a studio movie was $65 million.) It was also being shot on 35-millimeter film, like most movies of its vintage.

What made this particular production unique was that it would be the first movie with recognizable stars, and made by an established director, Brad Silberling, to be offered as a legal Internet download only a few days after it debuted in movie theaters. (Silberling's last movie, *Lemony Snicket's A Series of Unfortunate Events*, starred Jim Carrey and had earned more than $200 million at the box office.)

Relaxing in his trailer, Freeman was sprawled out on a leather couch. Freeman and his producing partner, Lori McCreary, had created a partnership with the microchip company Intel to set up a Web site called ClickStar, which would offer the downloadable version of the movie, along with a selection of others. Freeman was convinced that new approaches to distributing movies – especially making them available in whatever form the viewer wanted, at whatever time – were "going to change the whole nature of filmmaking." The big unknown, he continued, was how soon it'd happen.

•   •   •

10 Items wasn't the first movie to devise a strategy to make the most of consumers' intense interest in newly-released movies.

Just one month before the *10 Items* shoot began, an even lower-budget movie, *Bubble*, had surfaced briefly in theaters. Like *10 Items*, it was made by a well-known director – Steven Soderbergh, who'd begun his career with *Sex, Lies and Videotape*, and had most recently made the sequel *Ocean's Twelve*, starring George Clooney, Julia Roberts, and Brad Pitt. But unlike *10 Items*, *Bubble*'s cast was made up of people who'd never acted before, and Soderbergh shot it with a digital camera. (It relied on a rig similar to what had been used for Lucas' *Attack of the Clones*, with a CineAlta camera from Sony and lenses from Panavision.)

The movie, about the tense relationship among workers in a doll factory in the aftermath of a murder, was financed by 2929 Entertainment, a production company founded by the technology entrepreneurs Mark Cuban and Todd Wagner. With Soderbergh's OK, their plan was to put *Bubble* in theaters on the same day that they aired it on a cable channel they owned, HDNet Movies. The DVD would show up in stores the following week, distributed by a new company that Cuban and Wagner had started.

> In 1955, NBC bought the rights to broadcast *Richard III* on the same day it premiered in theaters, paying $500,000. The movie was directed by Laurence Olivier, who also played the lead. While the television audience may have been as large as 40 million, *Richard III* tanked at the box office. And Olivier was disappointed by the broadcast: most of the blood and gore had been snipped by censors, and he was bothered by the commercial interruptions.

Their experiment in releasing the movie through several avenues simultaneously – rather than sequentially, as was the standard practice – was motivated by three things.

One was a desire to promote their inter-connected businesses (Cuban and Wagner also owned the largest chain of independent theaters in the U.S., Landmark Theatres, which would show *Bubble*.) The second motivation was advertising-related: they felt it was illogical to spend money on two separate ad campaigns for a new movie, first to get people to see it in theaters, and then again several months later to get them to buy or rent it on DVD. The third reason was the tendency for Internet users, especially young men, to hunt down movies they wanted to see online, and download an illicit copy from file-sharing networks. More profit-driven rings of movie pirates produced DVDs and peddled them on the sidewalks of Manhattan and Beijing.

"Name any big-title movie that's come out in the last four years," Soderbergh said. "It has been available in all formats on the day of release. It's called piracy. Peter Jackson's *Lord of the Rings*, *Ocean's Eleven*, and *Oceans's Twelve* – I saw them on Canal Street on opening day. Simultaneous release is already here. We're just trying to gain control over it." Soderbergh predicted that within five years, all movies would be available on the day of their release in any format.

But while a few innovators such as Soderbergh and Cuban, or Silberling and Freeman, were trying to prepare for that eventuality and exploring the implications for their bottom lines, the major studios were sticking to their traditional releasing practices. Movies played in theaters first; four months later, on average, they were offered as DVDs, and after that, on cable; years later, they'd be shown on free television.

Studios continued sailing that course, despite evidence that hundreds of thousands of consumers were ignoring the law and using high-speed Internet connections to download movies before they were released on DVD. In the fall of 2005, a research firm called BigChampagne released an unusual Top Ten list: the most popular movies that were being downloaded illegally from the Internet. In position #1 was *The Wedding Crashers*, with an estimated 821,390 downloads in a single week; occupying the #10 slot was *Star Wars: Episode III – Revenge of the Sith*, with an estimated 687,477 downloads. Neither was yet available on DVD.

It wasn't only pirated movies that Internet users were watching, however. They'd begun to develop a taste for short, homemade videos posted on the Internet. Hollywood directors tended to dismiss these videos as "dogs on skateboards," since most were mildly amusing clips that lacked any sort of narrative. The camerawork was shaky, and the editing non-existent. (Many of the videos resembled the short films that had been made a century earlier by Edison's engineers: a single, unedited take of someone dancing for the camera, or doing a trick.) A Web site called YouTube launched in 2005, allowing Internet users to upload and store their videos for free, or watch videos that the site's editors spotlighted. It became a magnet for clips of the "dogs on skateboards" variety (as well as clips from TV shows posted without permission), and before long YouTube was the fastest-growing site on the Web.

The Internet wasn't a new technology; its roots dated back to 1969, as a project of the Department of Defense. In the mid-1990s, when companies like Apple and Progressive Networks began making it possible to deliver video files over the Internet, movie studios started to employ it as a promotional mechanism, offering trailers and clips from upcoming releases – just as they'd done with television 40 years earlier. But they were slower to explore the opportunity to deliver full-length features to Internet users, since that had the potential to disrupt the studios' existing businesses. How would it affect sales of videotapes and DVDs, they wondered, or change the value of their licensing deals with cable and broadcast networks?

> One of the first movies to be offered online in its entirety was Lance Weiler and Stefan Avalos' *The Last Broadcast.* Shortly after the movie was distributed to make-shift digital cinemas via satellite, the Independent Film Channel made a streaming video version available on its Web site, on November 15th, 1998.

Using the Internet to check e-mail and visit Web sites was becoming a daily habit, and a growing number of people had access to high-speed connections, which provided a better experience for viewing video (even if it still didn't equal TV's quality). Still, studios and the operators of theater chains didn't want to tinker with the established "theatrical release window" – the exclusive exhibition period guaranteed to theaters, before movies were available elsewhere. Even some directors spoke out against making movies available online, on television, or on DVD while they played in theaters. (The verb "preserve" popped up an awful lot in their comments.)

Universal vice chairman Marc Shmuger told *Variety*, "We would like to preserve the windows where they're at now. We're not eager to push them forward any closer. We want to preserve the uniqueness of the theatrical experience." Dan Fellman, the president of domestic distribution at Warner Bros., drew an even sharper line in the sand: simultaneous release of a film in theaters and on DVD was simply "not going to happen at Warner Bros.," he told the *Hollywood Reporter*.

Major theater chains snubbed the notion of simultaneous releasing, too. AMC Theatres, Loews Cineplex, Cinemark USA, National Amusements, Regal Entertainment Group, and Pacific Theatres all declared that they wouldn't show movies that were available in the home market. "I just think it's a wrong-headed approach," said Tony Karasotes, chairman and CEO of Karasotes Showplace Theatres in Chicago, in the *Hollywood Reporter*. The release strategy for *Bubble*, he continued, "is ass-backwards, and I don't want to encourage that kind of approach, because I own motion picture theaters."

Disney chairman Bob Iger was the only studio chief to publicly express interest in tinkering with movie release timing in the Internet era. "I think windows in general need to change," Iger told Wall Street analysts in mid-2005. "They need to compress. I don't think it's out of the question that a DVD can be released, in effect, in the same window as a theatrical release, although I'm sure we will get a fair amount of pushback on this from the industry." Within days, John Fithian, president of the National Association of Theater Owners, labeled Iger's comments a "death threat" against his members.

Among directors, M. Night Shyamalan, was the first to speak out against altering the windows. In the fall of 2005, Shyamalan gave a speech to theater owners at the ShowEast trade show in Orlando. (He was at the event to promote *The Lady in the Water*, his seventh film as a director.) He told the audience that he believed there was a "collective soul" that existed among the people in a theater. "The ideal form is the movie theatrical experience," he said. "If they try to convince us otherwise, they are lying."

"I don't believe this is inevitable," Shyamalan told the ShowEast attendees. "If this goes through, you know theaters are closing down. It's going to crush you guys." He'd earlier told the *Reporter*, "If there's a last film that's released only theatrically, it'll have my name on it. This is life or death to me."

Another speaker at ShowEast that year was John Fithian. He openly referred to the idea of eliminating release windows as a "death threat" against the exhibition industry. The traditional theatrical release, Fithian said, served as a promotional platform for new films, building awareness and helping studios sell DVDs.

Fithian acknowledged that if consumers were asked whether they wanted a new movie to be available in all kinds of formats on the day of its release, "their answer is 'yes.' But what if some of your local theaters go out of business, and you don't have the choice to see movies that way? Their answer changes."

But Cuban and Wagner felt simultaneous releasing could benefit theater owners. One idea they proposed: sharing one percent of a movie's eventual DVD revenues with theater owners who showed movies like *Bubble*, since by showing the movie they were helping market it (as Fithian rightly observed.) But when asked if he thought a simultaneous release could help exhibitors in any way, Fithian didn't need much time to consider the question. "No, I don't," he said curtly.

Cuban had five defiant words for the skeptics: "I don't give a shit." At every moment of transition, innovators have encountered doubters, he said. "You can't find a great business where somebody didn't say the exact same things at the beginning," Cuban said.

After all of the rhetoric had been thrown down, only 32 theaters agreed to show *Bubble* when it was released in January 2006 – and 19 of those were part of the Landmark Theatres chain that Cuban and Wagner controlled. With a budget of $1.6 million, the movie earned just $145,000 at the box office during its U.S. release, prompting snarky headlines like "*Bubble* Bursts." But Wagner later declared victory, claiming that DVD revenues and sales of foreign rights had helped the movie turn a respectable profit.

•   •   •

Around the time that the studios were laying the groundwork for Digital Cinema Initiatives, they were starting another joint venture to determine the best way to make full-length movies available online.

The venture, which was named Movielink, was in development for almost two years before it launched a Web site in November 2002. The studios, with Sony as the prime mover, selected as Movielink's CEO Jim Ramo, a careful and conservative executive who'd been part of the founding team at DIRECTV, the satellite television service. (Another site for legally-downloaded movies, CinemaNow, began offering full-length features in 2000 – mostly in the martial arts and horror genres. It had been funded by the independent film company Lions Gate Entertainment and Microsoft.)

While Movielink was in the works, the studios decided to start battling underground file-sharing networks where users could search for and download digital copies of movies for free. The Motion Picture Association of America, the lobbying group backed by the six major studios, joined forces with the music industry's lobbying group to try to shut down several file-sharing services that both viewed as major copyright-infringers. They targeted services like Grokster, based in the West Indies, KaZaA, based in Amsterdam, and Morpheus, based in Tennessee. One suit called the services a "21st century piratical bazaar where the unlawful exchange of protected materials takes place across the vast expanses of the Internet."

A month before the Movielink service was launched, the MPAA also sent letters to more than 2,000 colleges, alerting them that their students had been using school networks to swap illegal copies of movies; while the letters didn't threaten a lawsuit, they asked school administrators to do their best to stop the illegal activity.

At the outset, Movielink was more notable for what users couldn't do than what they could. The site offered "more than 170" titles, including *Harry Potter and the Sorcerer's Stone, Psycho*, and *A Beautiful Mind*. (There were no titles from Disney or Fox, which were exploring whether to create a download service of their own. That never happened, and Disney and Fox titles showed up on Movielink in 2003 and 2005, respectively.) Only users in the United States could access the site, and then only if they had a computer running Microsoft's Windows operating system. Once a user began playing a movie, she had to finish watching it within 24 hours, or else the movie would expire. There was no way to download a movie in digital form and keep it in a collection for repeated viewing.

The number of movies in the inventory grew slowly, too, since the studios couldn't just hand movies to Movielink; making a movie available required the attention of attorneys who needed to make sure the studio had the rights to deliver the movie online. Getting those clearances, Ramo complained, was expensive and time-consuming.

The studios "almost certainly know that Movielink won't make them any money," Hollywood journalist Ben Fritz wrote in 2002. The site, he said, was "pure PR." "Movielink's primary purpose...is to demonstrate that the studios are providing a legal alternative for Internet movie pirates."

Meanwhile, in Silicon Valley, a start-up company had just raised $82 million by going public, and its plan definitely did involve making money.

The company had chosen the name Netflix because its founder, Reed Hastings, knew that movie delivery would eventually take place over the Internet. But for the time being, Hastings believed that delivering DVDs through the mail was less expensive, and would give him access to a vast audience: the 110 million homes served by employees of the U.S. Postal Service. For a monthly subscription fee of about $20, Netflix members could rent and return as many DVDs as they wanted each month – and hold onto a disc until they got around to watching it, without incurring any late fees.

Netflix also offered more than 11,000 different movies – far more than Movielink, CinemaNow, or other movie download services. Netflix didn't have to secure special rights or guarantee the studios a minimum amount of revenue from each title, as the download services did – all it needed to do was purchase copies of the DVDs it wanted. (With most studios, though, Netflix signed revenue-sharing agreements that gave the company access to large numbers of discs when a popular movie was released, and gave the studios a percentage of the rental revenues in return – a very symbiotic relationship.)

"We see our future as the downloadable DVD," Hastings said in 2001. "Our ten-year plan is to be the world's leader in that. But the way to win is not to focus on the technology. It's to get the customers – a couple million subscribers, who are addicted to the Internet for choosing their movies. Those are exactly the people who will do downloading. It's the customer relationship that will be valuable."

Hastings said he was happy to see the other downloading sites getting started, but that Netflix wasn't in a rush to deliver movies that way. "They're going to spend the bucks necessary to create a market in downloading," he said. "But we have no fear. Video rental is a $10 billion market today. We may wait for downloading to be a $1 billion market, and someone has to go and create that market. Those are expensive investments." He didn't plan to be the technological innovator, but instead intended to poach customers from traditional video rental stores. Netflix started 2002 with half a million subscribers, and had hit the one million mark by 2003.

·   ·   ·

To the studios, Internet services like Grokster, KaZaA and Morpheus were starting to resemble a threat from 20 years ago: the VCR. And Jack Valenti, on the verge of retiring as the CEO of the MPAA, was once again mounting a vigorous defense.

"There are more than nine and a half million broadband subscribers now," Valenti said in 2002. "Once those large pipes and high-speed access subscribers begin to increase, we can be terrorized by what's going on."

"In a digital world, who on earth is going to invest large sums of venture capital in a movie if they believe it is going to be ambushed early? The value of that movie is going to be diminished. You don't have to be a Nobel Prize winner to figure that out."

Valenti frequently quoted a statistic about how much money the U.S. movie industry lost to piracy. In 2004, the number was $3.5 billion a year, and that, he noted, didn't include Internet piracy – only illicit sales of bootleg DVDs and tapes. When the numbers were revised to include digital trafficking, they rose to an estimated $6.1 billion in annual losses.

Sid Sheinberg, Valenti's old ally from the Betamax battles, was now a producer, real estate developer, and philantropist. But he couldn't help noticing what was happening. "Somebody told me that Universal's remake of *King Kong* was lousy," Sheinberg said. "I said, 'Did you go to the premiere, a sneak preview?' They said they'd downloaded it. So you not only have the prospect of people seeing a movie before it's released, but they can also bad-mouth it before it comes out."

By some estimates, on file-sharing networks like Grokster, as much as 90 percent of the material being sent from one computer to another was protected by copyright. (The networks could also be used, of course, to send a home movie or a batch of high-resolution vacation photos – which would've been perfectly legal.) Some of the movies had been "ripped" from already-released DVDs and converted into digital files, but others came from videotapes made by someone operating a camcorder in the back of a theater. Valenti and the MPAA were on a mission to shut down the file-sharing networks. But several courts, referring back to the 1984 Supreme Court decision that allowed Sony to continue selling the Betamax recorder, ruled that the networks couldn't be held responsible for what users did with their software.

The MPAA didn't give up, and eventually, the case against Grokster and Morpheus, two of the most popular file-sharing networks, wound up in front of the U.S. Supreme Court. This time around, Sony (which now controlled a movie studio of its own, having purchased Columbia Pictures in 1989) had allied with studios like Disney, Fox, Universal, and Warner Bros. in branding a new technology as a threat to the business. And helping to finance the defense of Grokster and Morpheus was Mark Cuban, who worried that a victory for the studios would squelch innovation. As the majority of people's photos, music, documents, and video were stored in digital form, new networks would be needed to get them from place to place, Cuban thought.

"What innovations will be condemned by law before they have a chance to come to market because they could have an impact on Hollywood and the music industry?" Cuban asked on his blog. "We have no idea, and that is a very scary prospect."

In June 2005, the Supreme Court issued a unanimous decision that diverged from its ruling on the Betamax case two decades earlier. A company that created a new technology "with the object of promoting its use to infringe copyright...is liable for the resulting acts of infringment," Justice David Souter wrote. The court didn't provide any sort of litmus test that would indicate whether the developer of a new technology was actively encouraging its users to infringe copyright, however. The Grokster decision didn't undermine the Sony ruling from 1984, but it made the waters much murkier.

> On the steps of the Supreme Court during the Grokster case, a Grokster supporter with a sense of historical precedent handed Jack Valenti an old Sony Betamax tape, asking him to autograph the label. Valenti agreed, and within hours, photos of the signed tape were posted all over the Internet. (The tape contained a recording of Woody Allen's *Sleeper*, taped from a television broadcast.)

Dan Glickman, who had taken over Valenti's post in 2004, rejoiced, calling the ruling "a historic victory for intellectual property in the digital age. The Supreme Court sent a strong and clear message that businesses based on theft should not and will not be allowed to flourish," he said.

Morpheus vowed to keep pressing its case in the courts, but Grokster shut down its file-sharing service in November 2005, and paid $50 million to the movie and record industries in a settlement. The company posted a message on its home page that read, "There are legal services for downloading music and movies. This service is not one of them."

•   •   •

Around that time, Apple Computer mailed out a cryptic invitation to journalists. On the front were red curtains, and the words "One more thing..." Apple's CEO, Steve Jobs, habitually used that phrase to introduce a surprising new product at the end of his speeches.

With the media assembled in a San Jose theater, Jobs unveiled a new Macintosh computer, before discussing the company's portable music player, the iPod. Jobs said Apple had shipped almost 30 million of the pristine white devices. "It has been a huge success for us," he said, a wry smile on his lips. "And therefore, we're going to replace it." A new version of the iPod would store up to 150 hours of video, which could be played back on a screen the size of a Saltine cracker. (The solitary viewing experience harkened back to the days of Edison's Kinetoscope.) The price was $399 for the most capacious model. Apple also added television shows and music videos to its online marketplace, the iTunes Store, along with six short films from Pixar Animation Studios. (Jobs still served as CEO of that company.) The videos cost $1.99 – but unlike the rental movies on CinemaNow or Movielink, they belonged to the customer once the purchase was complete. Within 30 days, Apple announced that it had sold more than a million videos.

iTunes, Movielink, and CinemaNow began vying with one another to be the first to introduce various features. In 2006, Movielink and CinemaNow began offering full-length films for purchase, rather than rental; consumers griped that the downloads often cost more than buying a DVD at Amazon.com or Wal-Mart. CinemaNow was the first to allow its customers to burn a downloaded movie onto a DVD, so that it could be more easily viewed on the living room TV set. Amazon launched its own download service, called Unbox, in September 2006, and shortly after, Apple added full-length movies from just one studio, Disney, to its iTunes Store.

Other studios withheld their movies from Apple, both because they worried that the anti-copying "locks" integrated into iTunes' digital files weren't tough enough, and because they didn't want Apple to become the sort of dominant digital retailer with movies that it had become with music – a kind of Wal-Mart of the Internet. (In 2006, Apple sold about 67 percent of all digital music downloads.)

Quickly, that started to look like a mistake. After the first week of movie sales on iTunes, Bob Iger, Disney's CEO, announced that the studio had sold 125,000 downloads, generating $1 million in revenue. He said he expected iTunes to generate about $50 million for Disney over the coming year.

Andre Blay, the first videotape dealer, was semi-retired, but he saw most of the studios fretting once again that "their golden goose is going to be hurt, that the Internet is going to be disruptive rather than supportive. But my instincts tell me that sometime in the next ten years, the Internet will be a major source of revenue for the studios."

None of the other download services released information about how many movies they were selling or renting. Four months after it started offering full-length films, Apple said it had sold more than 1.3 million of them, knighting itself "the world's most popular online music, TV, and movie store" in a press release. Slowly, other studios began to put their wares on the shelves of the iTunes Store, starting with MGM and Paramount.

Jobs had a clear vision for making entertainment products, whether movies, songs, or TV shows, easier to buy in digital form than they were to obtain from one of the illegal file-sharing sites. He simplified pricing: TV shows cost $1.99, older movies were $9.99, and new releases were $14.99. All the content was fluid: it moved easily from a computer to an iPod. (There were even rumors that Apple was developing a new device that would sit atop a television, and allow consumers to watch iTunes content in the living room.) The studios didn't want to let Apple develop into a gatekeeper, but that seemed to be happening anyway, by virtue of the new approach to buying and consuming digital entertainment the company had pioneered. Jobs' influence in Hollywood seemed like it would only grow. In 2006, he joined Disney's board of directors, once Disney's acquisition of Pixar was finalized.

> 2006: Hollywood studios announce they will no longer release new movies on VHS tapes, slightly less than ten years after the DVD format was first introduced.

Movielink, meanwhile, was lagging behind, renting or selling only about 75,000 movies a month.

The studios hired an investment bank to try to sell the joint venture, but discussions with prospective buyers like Blockbuster, Comcast, and AT&T went nowhere. Ramo's allowance was running out: he had spent most of the $150 million in start-up funding that Movielink had been given by the studios. When Blockbuster sniffed around Movielink a second time, the price tag mentioned was $50 million. And when the video rental chain finally bought Movielink, to make digital movie rentals available to its customers, the *Wall Street Journal* reported that the deal was a fire-sale, valuing Movielink at just $20 million.

As the download services were trying to win over consumers, Hollywood was also introducing two new physical media products: high-definition DVDs called Blu-ray and HD DVD. By packing more digital data onto the surface of the disc, both offered crisper images than a standard DVD (and certainly better resolution than the Internet sites offered – legal or otherwise.) The studios' hope was that as consumers' purchasing of DVDs started to level off, the high-definition discs (priced as much as $10 higher than regular DVDs) would encourage them to keep buying – and perhaps even replace some of their existing DVD library.

> Just as some actresses had expressed their reluctance to appear in a Technicolor production in the 1930s, as television switched to high-definition broadcasting in the early part of the 21st century, actresses were once again speaking out – and taking action. Blythe Danner said she was "appalled" by how she looked on a cable TV show broadcast in high-def. "I don't think I am terribly narcissistic, but you don't want to look your worst." Danner admitted to seeking "a little [cosmetic] help" after seeing the broadcast.
>
> A Canadian company even introduced a line of make-up called "blu_ray," intended to help women look better in front of the all-seeing digital lenses.

But despite the fact that both formats relied on the same technological advance – a blue-violet laser that could read more information from the surface of the disc than the red lasers built into older DVD players – the Blu-ray discs wouldn't work in HD DVD players, and vice versa.

Sony Electronics led the group promoting Blu-ray, and Toshiba the HD DVD camp. HD DVD hit the market in the US first, in the spring of 2006, and the HD DVD players were about half as expensive as the Blu-ray players that arrived later in the year. Disney, Sony Pictures, Fox, and MGM decided to release their movies on Blu-ray discs, and Universal Pictures supported HD DVD. Paramount and Warner Bros. opted to release movies in both formats.

To help the Blu-ray format find its way into consumers' homes, Sony decided to integrate a Blu-ray player into its PlayStation 3 gaming console, which went on sale before the 2006 holiday season – even though the high-definition capability would bump up the price of the console.

Numerous attempts to combine the two formats failed. Warner Bros.' home video division developed a disc called Total HD that contained a single movie in both formats, one on each side; LG Electronics announced a player that could play both kinds of discs.

But as they'd done when they were offered a choice between the incompatible Betamax and VHS formats thirty years earlier, consumers largely decided to postpone their purchases of a high-definition DVD player. "One would hope that we'd learn from history, but sadly, sometimes we don't," said Pat Wyatt, a former president of Fox's home video division. Forcing retailers to decide which format to carry, and forcing consumers to guess which format would prevail – or risk being stuck with an obsolete high-def DVD player – quickly started to look like a losing proposition.

•   •   •

Consumers seemed to be falling out of the habit of going to see movies in actual movie theaters. The reasons were debated endlessly over lunches in studio commissaries. In 2005, 1.4 billion movie tickets were sold – the lowest total since 1997. One possibility was that Americans were spending more time on the Internet (perhaps surfing the Web, playing games, downloading free videos to watch, or tracking down pirated movies from the file-sharing sites.)

But another possibility was that people were setting up home theaters that were becoming their first-choice venue for movie-viewing, liberating them from sticky floors and fellow patrons who answered cell phones during climactic moments. They were popping in DVDs from Netflix, or ordering movies through their cable or satellite provider's pay-per-view service.

An Associated Press-AOL poll found that 73 percent of adults preferred watching movies at home. Newspaper stories profiled consumers who were investing more than $10,000 in their home theater systems – which inevitably led to fewer visits to the local multiplex.

In a front page story headlined "Why movie fans are staying home," the San Jose *Mercury News* profiled a California family that had purchased a $13,000 home theater system. They'd once gone to the movies almost every weekend, but now, they preferred to watch DVDs with their new surround-sound speakers turned up high.

One response to the increasing quality and plummeting costs of home theater technology was the second coming of 3-D. Dimensionality wasn't something that a home theater system could offer (yet), and the new digital projectors could offer a crisper 3-D image than what had been possible before.

For *Chicken Little*, a Disney cartoon released in late 2005, Dolby Laboratories and Real D, a California start-up company, outfitted 84 theaters in the U.S. to show the movie in digital 3-D.

They used a single digital projector showing 144 frames each second – half of them intended to be seen by an audience member's left eye, and half by the right. Dolby spent $7 million installing servers and projectors in the 84 theaters, and theater owners spent about $25,000, on average, for each auditorium that received the upgrade. That money paid for modifications to the projection booth, new silver screens, and special 3-D gear from Real D that polarized the images coming out of the projector. Audience members received a pair of green plastic 3-D glasses that resembled those worn in the movie by the lead character, and the glasses' polarized lenses ensured that each eye saw only the frames intended for it – which produced the illusion of depth.

Disney and Dolby branded the *Chicken Little* release a success, though the reality was a bit hazier. The movie earned $40 million in its opening weekend, and more importantly, the version shown in digital 3-D generated more revenue than the 2-D version. During the opening weekend, *Chicken Little* grossed about $11,000 per theater in 2-D, but $25,000 per theater where it was being shown in 3-D. (And the difference wasn't just due to the fact that some theater owners were charging $1 or $1.50 more for tickets to the 3-D screenings.) But the *Hollywood Reporter* said that it had cost Disney about $8 million to have the 3-D version of *Chicken Little* produced by Industrial Light & Magic.

"This chicken has legs," Disney distribution chief Chuck Viane boasted after the movie's opening. He had committed Disney to producing a string of movies in digital 3-D, just as the studio had promised several years earlier to provide a consistent supply of digital cinema releases.

One person who viewed the *Chicken Little* results as a half-empty glass was John Fithian. He observed that theatre owners would have to bear the cost of the Real D equipment necessary for 3-D screenings (not including the cost of the digital projector or servers). "As a technical proposition it is way cool," he told the Los Angeles *Times*. "As an economic proposition it clearly doesn't work everywhere."

But some directors and producers were getting excited about digital 3-D.

Producer Jon Landau compared the transition from 2-D to 3-D to the shift from mono to stereo in the recording business. "We think of movies as a great visual presentation, and there has been no quantifiable advancement in the visual presentation of the movies since the late 1950s," he said. "With music, why did we go to stereo? It heightened the experience. 3-D is like visual stereo. It'll heighten the experience that much more, whether you're making a drama, a tragedy, or an action movie. It's not about gags coming off the screen. It's about creating a window into the world, so that the screen goes away."

Landau was working with director James Cameron to make the science fiction movie *Avatar* in digital 3-D. They were shooting with a new camera system, called the Fusion and based on a pair of digital cameras from Sony. Cameron had designed it, in collaboration with Vince Pace. At DreamWorks Animation, Jeffrey Katzenberg announced plans to release its future movies in digital 3-D, starting with 2009's *Monsters vs. Aliens*. Other directors, including George Lucas and Randal Kleiser, had allowed a start-up company called In-Three to convert portions

> 2007: More than 10 percent of the 35,000 movie screens in the U.S. can now show digital releases, due in large part to the aggressive conversion campaign of a New Jersey company called Access Integrated Technologies. Access predominantly uses projectors made by Christie Digital.

of their older movies (including *Star Wars: Episode IV* and *Grease*) into digital 3-D, with an eye toward eventually re-releasing the movies.

•   •   •

Not long after YouTube launched, allowing anyone to publish video content to the Web, other video sites began to appear that allowed anyone to edit video online. These sites, which included JumpCut, EyeSpot, and Motionbox, offered fewer advanced features than systems like Final Cut Pro or Avid, but they had the advantage of being free – and users didn't even have to supply their own footage to edit; they could play with music and video footage that had been uploaded by others.

Bands began inviting their fans to use the sites to assemble music videos, supplying the soundtrack and some generic video clips. One independent producer/director, Leone Marucci, used one of the sites to solicit audition videos for a bit part in one of his upcoming movies. Would-be supporting actors and actresses could edit their audition videos together with footage that Marucci had supplied of the movie's stars reading their lines, in a scene set in a pizza shop.

One well-known independent director, Richard Linklater, agreed to allow his fans to use JumpCut to edit together their own version of a movie trailer for *A Scanner Darkly*, a dystopian animated movie scheduled for release in the summer of 2006. The editor of the best trailer would win a trip to the movie's premiere. The contest generated hundreds of trailers promoting the movie, at little cost to the studio that released it, Warner Independent. Editors who created the trailers no doubt showed them to friends and family members, creating a grassroots marketing campaign for the movie.

2007: Netflix begins allowing its subscribers to view movies on its site in digital form, through a feature called "Watch Now." Movies can be viewed on the Netflix site, but not downloaded for later viewing. Because of difficulty securing download rights, Netflix starts the "Watch Now" service with just 1000 titles, at a time when its DVD library contains 70,000 titles.

But many directors and studios worried about the loss of control inherent in giving amateur editors footage to play with – even if the potential existed to help build a larger audience for a given movie. "That's one of the reasons the Director's Guild of America exists," said Randal Kleiser, a DGA officer who helped to organize the guild's annual new technology showcase. Kleiser, who'd been in the vanguard of using computer-generated effects, digital cameras, and virtual sets, was responding to the idea that someday, dozens of editors might create dozens of different cuts of a finished movie, giving the studio dozens of different products to sell rather than just one: a shorter cut, a funnier cut, a more serious cut. "The DGA is there to prevent people from editing our work without our approval," he said.

•   •   •

In advance of its December 1, 2006 opening, Morgan Freeman made the talk show rounds to promote *10 Items or Less*. He was on "Live with Regis and Kelly" and "The Tonight Show with Jay Leno," and his co-star, Paz Vega, appeared on several second-string talk shows.

At the age of 69, Freeman said he was enthusiastic about the experiment's potential to help independent movies find new ways to reach audiences. "I'm just a firm believer that things continue to grow, get better," he said.

But like *Bubble* before it, theater owners froze out *10 Items*, since it'd be available on the Web site ClickStar just two weeks after its theatrical debut. (Online, the movie was priced at $11.99 for a 72-hour rental.) Only Mark Cuban's Landmark Theatres chain was willing to show *10 Items* in the U.S. The movie earned less than $100,000 during its U.S. theatrical run. But the movie made five times as much overseas – where would-be viewers weren't able to access to the ClickStar version.

Neither ClickStar nor Freeman ever released figures about how many people had rented the digital version of the movie, or how well the DVD release had performed. *10 Items* earned the distinction of being the first movie available legally on the Internet while it was still in theaters. But it was the second movie, after *Bubble*, to be boycotted by cinema owners for using a new technology in a way that seemed to threaten the stability of their businesses.

Afterword:
Imagining the Future

Arriving early for several interviews on the Sony Pictures studio lot one day, I took the opportunity to wander around.

The lot is in Culver City, wedged between downtown Los Angeles and Santa Monica, and it has been occupied by filmmakers since 1915. For a while, it was home to directors D.W. Griffith and Mack Sennett (father of the Keystone Kops), but its longest run was as the headquarters of MGM Studios, which set up shop along Washington Boulevard in 1924. President Calvin Coolidge, star of one of the early Phonofilm talkies, was there for MGM's grand opening, as was Will Rogers.

Louis B. Mayer, who aimed to attract more stars to MGM than there were in the heavens, had his office here. A crop of child actors, including Mickey Rooney, Elizabeth Taylor, and Judy Garland, attended classes on the lot when they weren't in front of the camera. It was inside the cavernous Stage 27 that Dorothy's house plummeted into Munchkinland and she began her journey down the yellow brick road. The Marx Brothers made *Duck Soup* in Stage 15, and seven decades later, Tobey McGuire shot the *Spider-Man* trilogy there.

Now, the lot is anchored by a reconstituted Main Street "set," with a Loew's theater marquee, a bowling alley facade, and a faux dry cleaners. When MGM was busy releasing one movie every week, this was the sort of street scene that they'd have used over and over again, simply repainting the signs on the shop windows and changing an awning or two.

At the start of the 21st century, Sony Pictures not only owned the old MGM lot, but it owned a piece of MGM, too, which was still making movies like *Casino Royale* and *Rocky Balboa* – though far fewer than in its heyday. Sony also owned Columbia Pictures, founded in 1924 by Harry Cohn, as well as a computer animation and visual effects division called Sony Pictures ImageWorks, and several TV production companies. Its parent company, Sony Corporation, manufactured not just digital cameras for cinematographers and 4K digital projectors for cinema owners, but also high-definition televisions and Blu-ray disc players for consumers, the PlayStation videogame console, Vaio laptop computers, and portable digital audio and video players bearing the venerable Walkman brand name.

When I visited, Sony Pictures was in the midst of a hot streak; in 2006, Sony broke the all-time U.S. box office record for a studio, raking in more than $1.7 billion, and releasing a record thirteen films that occupied the #1 spot; the studio earned $3.3 billion worldwide at the box office (and that figure didn't include income from DVDs, Internet distribution, or television broadcasts.) Sony Pictures was the most successful maker of movies in an industry that had managed to survive for more than a century.

My interviews were in the Irving Thalberg Building, named after the wunderkind producer who oversaw MGM movies like *Grand Hotel* and *Mutiny on the Bounty* in the 1920s and 1930s. (Of course, it was also Thalberg who dismissed talkies as a "passing fancy.")

Michael Lynton was the studio's current chairman. Before coming to Sony, he'd attended Harvard Business School and worked in book publishing and at the online service

> 2006: Sony Pictures pays $65 million to purchase Grouper, an Internet video-sharing site, which it later uses to experiment with delivering officially-sanctioned clips from Sony movies. Internet users can 'embed' the clips into their own sites or blogs, expanding their distribution. (Sony hopes the clips will encourage viewers to buy the full-length movies on DVD.)

America Online. Sitting at a round table in Lynton's understated office, I asked him why Sony Pictures hadn't yet shot any movies using one of the digital cameras made by Sony Electronics, which had been available for five years, or announced any plans to release movies in the ultra-high-resolution 4K format that Sony Electronics' projectors were capable of showing.

"The fire under our butts is high," Lynton said. "It's an embarrassment that it hasn't happened until now."

He said that the studio was also aware that consumers were eager to purchase its products in digital form. The movie industry was undergoing a shift from "packaged goods" to movies distributed "over a wire," Lynton told me. But despite offering its movies on the underwhelming Movielink service, Sony titles weren't yet available for purchase on iTunes, the leading digital marketplace. In part, that was because Sony wouldn't sell the movies to Apple at a price lower than the DVD wholesale price, for fear of antagonizing big sellers of DVDs like Wal-Mart.

Internet distribution "looks on paper as though it's an easier way of delivering movies," Lynton said, "but we're very hamstrung by our existing DVD businesses and TV contracts." As the conversation went on, I heard echoes of MGM executive Dore Schary, complaining that in the early days of television, theaters were the studios' most important customers, and TV broadcasters simply couldn't pay enough for MGM's content.

> "The average tenure of a Hollywood executive is two years. Three if he doesn't make a decision."
>
> – Malcolm Ferris
> Chairman, Cinematica

Lynton was a successful executive at a successful company in a successful industry. Few places are less hospitable to the new idea, tool, or technology.

"When you become the incumbent, you're wary of change," said Peter Guber, a producer who'd run both Columbia Pictures and Sony Pictures. "You want to use the same formula all the time."

MGM, Columbia, and their brethren had been founded in the early 20th century by a risk-taker who saw potential in the new medium, like Louis B. Mayer, who'd begun his run in 1907 by transforming an old 600-seat burlesque house in Haverhill, Massachusetts into a movie theater.

One hundred years later, each studio was part of a much larger, publicly-traded conglomerate. Universal, for instance, was now part of General Electric, and the studio represented about two percent of the company's total earnings. Studios were subject to the immutable rules of Wall Street: continually increase profits, and don't serve up any surprises.

"The institutionalized lack of imagination is frustrating," said director Peter Jackson. "You go to a company like Microsoft, and they've got people thinking, 'How are we going to make the world a different place in five years?' At the studios, you've got executives who are terrified of risk, making a move, and losing their jobs. They're worried about getting through this year's slate of films, not changing the face of entertainment. They're part of a system that doesn't support innovation in any way, shape, or form."

Other industries, including high-tech, aren't much different: preserving the status quo takes precedence over exploring a new idea with the potential to shake things up. (Even Microsoft is accustomed to purchasing or investing in small start-ups that come up with important innovations that Microsoft missed.) Innovators need a strategy for sustaining themselves over the long stretches of time it takes to gain acceptance, and win over the preservationists and sideline-sitters.

•　　•　　•

The tension between innovation and preservation is present in every established, successful business and art form. It has been present in the movies ever since Thomas Edison dismissed the potential of projected movies, hoping to extend the dominance of his Kinetoscope machines in the 19th century. And it is still a force in the 21st.

The tension is manifesting itself in three areas.

First, new technologies are making it possible for movies to be watched on anywhere: on a mobile phone, an iPod, a laptop computer, or on the living room television, delivered over the Internet. (A group of drive-in revivalists, MobMov, are even using the Net to promote impromptu movie showings in vacant lots, using low-end digital projectors.) But many in Hollywood feel compelled to defend the shared experience of watching a movie in a dark theater full of fellow fans. Even if that is no longer the source of the bulk of their paychecks, it is still the place where they believe their work can be best appreciated – not the matchbook-sized screen of an iPod.

> "When confronted with something new, they come up with all of these reasons why it can go wrong, and they don't come up with any reasons why it's the right thing to do."
>
> – George Lucas on preservationists

At the Oscar ceremony in March 2006, Academy president Sid Ganis and actor Jake Gyllenhaal made impassioned speeches about seeing movies on the big screen, not on DVDs. Introducing a montage of scenes from movie epics, Gyllenhaal said, "You can't properly watch these [movies] on a television set, and good luck trying to enjoy them on a portable DVD." This, despite the fact that most Academy voters cast their ballots after watching the nominated films on studio-supplied DVDs, in the comfort of their own homes.

"I believe in the magic of the communal social experience of sitting in a movie theater, and letting someone's dreams wash over you," Spielberg said. "I don't think you can achieve that by watching a movie on an iPod, or a compressed, low-resolution version on your laptop."

George Lucas doesn't expect theaters to vanish, but he thinks they'll evolve into "the cultural center of the future, which means you go there to meet people, to hang out, to be entertained." Lucas also predicts that, despite the hostility engendered by *Bubble* and *10 Items or Less*, a new movie will eventually be available on television while it is playing in theaters. He compares it to a football game: fans can choose to go to the stadium to yell and cheer with a group of others, or watch the game at home. Either way, the National Football League and its teams make money.

Despite the early resistance to digital cinema, Lucas envisions that digital projectors and digital transmission of movies to cinemas will expand the theater-owners' choice of films. "If you can send out your trailer to 20,000 theater owners, and the theater owner says, 'This is interesting – send me a copy, I want to see it,' then he might book it for a week," Lucas said. (That'd be the polar opposite of the blind booking practices of old: call it "omniscient booking.")

Films that appeal to a niche audience might start off by being released on DVD or on the Internet, Lucas said, and then get picked up by theater owners once they prove their worth. "If people are buying a lot of DVDs, a theater owner will say, 'I bet people would like to come to the movies and see this.' The current state of things will probably reverse itself," he said. The idea is similar to the way new musicals often get to Broadway – by proving themselves first in out-of-town try-outs.

Peter Guber observed that the new terms of competition weren't how many DVDs, theater tickets, or downloads were sold, but that Hollywood was "competing for people's attention."

"There is a limited amount of time in a day, and they're not making any more," Guber said. "We have to be able to have the skills to move where the audience is, whether it's portable digital assistants or mobile phones or location-based entertainment." For most of the 20th century, consumers had fewer entertainment choices, and if studios put enough star power and promotional dollars behind a release, people would pay attention. "But that was the 'push economy,'" Guber said. "Now we're in a 'pull economy.' The audience is becoming more discerning about how they spend their time, even more so than how they spend their money."

Consumers have a panoply of entertainment choices, and they want their selections delivered instantly, on their own terms. Many preservationists choose to ignore that reality, trying to dictate what audiences can watch, where, and when; that forces them to wage difficult battles with pirates, who are only too happy to deliver instant gratification, either cheaply or totally free.

A second area where the chasm between innovators and preservationists is apparent is in the relationship between movies, the Internet, and videogames. As the 21st century began, the Internet was used predominantly for promotional purposes (making available movie trailers or deleted scenes), and videogames tended to be released alongside big budget movies (though occasionally games spawned movie projects of their own.)

But boundaries between the three mediums are dissolving. It seems possible that the Internet can be used in other, powerful ways: to maintain interest among a movie's fan base in between theatrical releases with a

> 2005: Steven Spielberg announces a partnership with the videogame company Electronic Arts. While other directors, such as Peter Jackson, also choose to be involved in the creation of games based on their movies, Francis Ford Coppola complains when a game based on *The Godfather* is released by Electronic Arts. Coppola says, "I had nothing to do with the game, and I disapprove." (Paramount had sold the game rights to EA.)

series of short videos, for example, or to create online environments where fans can interact with characters from the movie and one another. And what if popular avatars created by videogame players had a chance to be cast in the computer-animated movie version of the game?

A third area where innovations are spurring changes that rankle preservationists is the friction between the movie industry's endemic elitism and the forces of democratization.

Like most other industries, Hollywood has long been choosy about the people who could rise to the top – the actors, cinematographers, editors, producers, and directors deemed to be dependable money-makers. It is also selective about the products that get released; in 2006, about 600 movies had a theatrical release in the United States, according to the MPAA.

But inexpensive digital cameras, cheap (or free) editing software, and newly-accessible avenues of distribution (like digital cinemas and the Internet) are democratizing the art of cinema.

It is starting to seem that studios might one day act only as banks and marketing agencies for the biggest-budget releases with the best-known stars. Lance Weiler and Stefan Avalos had proven, with *The Last Broadcast*, that they could make a movie for less than $1,000 and send it to theaters via satellite. Jonathan Caouette, a first-time documentary filmmaker, made *Tarnation* on a Macintosh computer in his New York City apartment for less than $300; the movie played at the Sundance and Cannes film festivals, and earned a spot on several critics' "ten best" lists in 2004. Even independent filmmakers who'd already carved out a reputation, like Ed Burns, were trying new distribution strategies for films that didn't attract sufficient interest from mainstream distributors. In the fall of 2007, Burns released *Purple Violets*, his eighth feature film, on Apple's iTunes Store before it was available anywhere else.

> "The future of cinema lies in the power of the pixel. The injection of fresh ideas and methodologies will only serve to mix up the metaphorical gene pool and empower a new generation of filmmakers."
>
> – Roger Corman, director and producer

And sites with names like IndieGoGo and IndieMaverick are trying to make it possible for filmmakers to raise money for their projects on the Internet. Their hope is that hundreds or thousands of people will be willing to bankroll independent films that appeal to them with small $50 or $100 investments. Some sites promise a return on investors' money if a film proves profitable; others only guarantee that investors will receive a "limited edition DVD" of the finished product.

"The tectonic plates are rubbing," said Jeffrey Katzenberg, a founder of the DreamWorks SKG studio and chief executive of DreamWorks Animation. "You can feel the pressures." Katzenberg didn't think the day was far off when "five kids in their garage will be able to make *Shrek*." (Already, young animators are tinkering with the software used to render environments and characters in video games, employing it to tell their own stories, a new form of expression they've dubbed "machinima.")

Francis Ford Coppola observed that "cinema is escaping being controlled by the financier, and that's a wonderful thing. You don't have to go hat-in-hand to some film distributor and say, 'Please, will you let me make a movie?'" The new production technologies, he said, were allowing filmmakers "do pretty much anything. If you can see it, you can do it. You can use those tools to make the same films over and over again, [as the studios are doing,] or you can use them to make films that illuminate life, and discover the human soul. That's what the cinema is for."

"The tools are more accessible than they've ever been," said Spielberg. "The only thing stopping someone from letting us know who they are is the length and breadth of their imagination. It's giving so many more filmmakers a chance to be filmmakers, and share their work on sites like iFilm and iTunes."

Lucas thought back to the days when his movies were released on videotape, and they competed with several hundred other movies on the shelves of a rental store. But in the 21st century, new movies competed with tens of thousands of other titles in places like Amazon.com or NetFlix. That creates new marketing challenges.

With the democratization of filmmaking, Lucas thought that "the future of American cinema will be tiny personal movies made for $2 million or $3 million, not big extravagant Hollywood movies. Those will go by the wayside," he said.

"Filmmakers will be able to make their films less expensively, and have more freedom in what kind of material they make," he said. "But they will [succeed or fail based] on the whims of the marketplace, instead of the whims of the studios or the hierarchy of the corporations that own the studios."

Most of the technologies that will shape cinema over the coming decades, Lucas believes, are already present in fledgling form – they just aren't being used widely enough, or creatively enough. "Everything that will exist in the future exists right now," he said. But he likened the new technologies to the hand-cranked cameras of the 1890s – in need of continued investment. "We've got a hundred years of development ahead of us," he said. "If we use the technology, the medium will grow and be big. But if you don't, then you'll be hand-cranking it for the rest of your life."

·   ·   ·

Hollywood is hardly the only industry (or art form) dealing with wildfires sparked by new technologies. In fields as disparate as music, retail, banking, and publishing, technologies are allowing consumers to demand that products and services be delivered on their terms, in a way and at a price that is convenient. Boundaries that have long existed between different fields are crumbling. And technologies are making it easier for new competitors to get into the game with much less investment than was historically required, presenting consumers with an infinite buffet of choices. Established players can try to ignore these changes and preserve their position, or they can look to innovation as a way to stay in tune with their customers.

Luckily, every industry has its forward-thinking innovators (at least those industries that are still alive and kicking.) In Hollywood, the thread began in the 19th century with Thomas Edison and the Lumière brothers, continued with the Warner brothers and Walt Disney in the 20th century, and is still being spun in the 21st by people like George Lucas, Steve Jobs, and Mark Cuban.

When innovators see a change happening, or believe that a new technology is about to create a new opportunity, they're not dissuaded by the fact that no one has been through this particular door before. While preservationists and sideline-sitters tend to avoid the unknown (too little information to make a decision, they warn), innovators are motivated to explore it.

> 2008: After head-to-head battle in the marketplace, Sony's Blu-ray high-definition disc format prevails. Sony's early decision to integrate Blu-ray players into its PlayStation 3 videogame console is a key factor, but the final nail in HD DVD's coffin is Warner Bros.' eventual choice to support only the Blu-ray format.

And the most successful innovators understand that they'll have to counteract the doubts and defensive posturing of preservationists. They also understand the importance of what might be called "persistence of innovation": not every new idea succeeds the first time around, as Technicolor's Herb Kalmus learned over the 24 years it took to convince Hollywood to leave black-and-white behind. Sometimes, it's necessary to develop a technology and win over detractors in a series of what Kalmus called "progressive steps."

From the opening of the Holland Brothers' Kinetoscope Parlor, in April 1894, to the launches of YouTube and the iPod, nearly every new development in the movie industry has supplied an example of how innovators use new tools and business models to create something compelling for audiences and enable new kinds of stories to be told, overcoming the resistance of those who'd prefer to maintain the status quo.

Innovations are usually tempting to write off at first: just as the first Kinetoscope movies were mundane, shot from a single camera position with no cuts, so were some of the earliest YouTube videos. Why would anyone choose to watch this rudimentary junk instead of the sophisticated forms of entertainment that already exist?

But without the regular infusion of new ideas from businesspeople and artists, Hollywood would have had no chance of maintaining its hold on our imaginations and its place in the popular culture for more than a century. Resting only on its rich history, for instance, rather than pushing toward digital cinema, computer-generated animation, and Internet video (despite the friction these new initiatives can create), Sony Pictures' lot in Culver City would eventually molder and become a museum.

Innovators working within big organizations like Sony, at small start-ups, or as free agents, have one thing in common: their ideas are always regarded as insignificant or disruptive at first. But innovators are essential to any industry's continued vitality. Whether their ideas are embraced – or dismissed and derided – is an indicator of whether an industry has a future, and how quickly it will get there.

Appendix A

Preservationists...	Innovators...
Fear the unknown. They view change as a threat. Low tolerance for risk.	**Are motivated to explore and tame the unknown.** They view change as an opportunity. High tolerance for risk.
Think short-term: they're consumed with protecting the established hierarchy and existing revenue streams.	**Think long-term**: they invest time, money, and energy in research and development – potentially re-arranging the hierarchy, but also creating new revenue streams.
They tend to shoot down new ideas and technologies because they are "not ready for prime time."	They realize that most new ideas and technologies aren't perfect from the start – but that there's value in shaping them to suit one's needs and making them better.
Preservationist leaders talk about the status quo and the short-term future – this quarter's products, projects, and revenues.	Innovative leaders talk about the long term – where the industry is headed, and what new opportunities and challenges are emerging.
Are internally focused. They tend to overlook customer needs or changes in the rest of the marketplace, fixating instead on company priorities; put their own reputations and corporate pride first.	**Are externally focused.** They watch what customers are doing – or what changes are happening elsewhere in the marketplace – and try to understand and take advantage of new possibilities.

Appendix B

There are an endless number of reasons that preservationists resist change and sideline-sitters try to ignore it; some reasons are conscious, and others aren't. Here's just a sampling:

- Attachment to tradition or the tools a person has always used; "That's the way I learned to do it from my mentors"

- Desire to preserve corporate culture

- Concern that change is happening too fast

- Fear of not being as facile with a new tool or new process

- Hesitance about learning new tools from someone younger; sense of competitiveness; fear of being rendered irrelevant

- Reluctance to render current products or tools obsolete

- Procrastination; "I'll learn it after my next project," or "I'm retiring in two years, and this new technology won't be essential until well after that"

- Focus on the limitations of new tools, rather than their possibilities; "I'm using a superior tool already"

- Frugality: "The new equipment is too expensive...and not worth it"

- Belief that change is being pushed by someone for the sake of profit, or being introduced as part of a power grab

- Desire to protect current reputation and pricing in the marketplace; "People won't pay as much for that new generation of product/service," or "It seems cheap"

- Reluctance to be a "lone wolf," operating outside the community and adopting new technologies first; "Let's wait to see what happens to other people"

- Concern that new technologies may lower the barriers to entry for others, increasing competition in one's field (often called "democratization")

- Division into camps or movements; "those guys" are part of the new technological wave, and "we" have chosen not to be: innovators vs. preservationists

Acknowledgments

An earlier version of this project began as a collaboration with the director George Lucas and his colleagues at Lucasfilm Ltd., including Rick McCallum, and Lucy Wilson, and I'm grateful to them for their guidance and feedback. Thanks are also due to Alex Ben Block, long-time editor of *The Hollywood Reporter*, who read a nascent version of the manuscript and shared his insights on the inner workings of the entertainment industry.

Liz Gannes provided high-octane research help under a very tight deadline. Bob Lambert at Disney shared his recollections of the early days of digital cinema, as well as his extensive clippings file. Ian Calderon and Jeffrey Winter at the Sundance Film Festival were kind enough to let me moderate several of the festival's panels about the future of the film business, which let me tap into great insights from the Sundance community. I've done the same for several years now at the South by Southwest Film Festival, thanks to invitations from Matt Dentler and Jarod Neece.

Regular conversations with Peter Broderick of Paradigm Consulting helped keep me on the right course ever since our first chat at a Harvard Square coffee shop. Peter Bart, editor of *Variety*, invited me to start writing occasional articles for his paper after I interviewed him in San Francisco – and I've had great fun doing that.

I'm constantly surprised by the sharp ideas supplied by readers of my blog CinemaTech, and I owe a debt to the many film and tech bloggers whose postings I read avidly (usually when I should be doing something else.) My journo-mentors Ande Zellman, Bill Taylor, Caleb Solomon, and Lew McCreary also provided priceless advice and support.

Finally, there's no way to properly thank my wife Amy and my family, who've always been generous with their encouragement. I'll keep trying.

Scott Kirsner
Cambridge, Massachusetts
July 2008

A Note on Sources

I relied on many excellent books, articles, and online resources while writing *Inventing the Movies*. They are listed below, chapter by chapter. I've also listed the original interviews I conducted.

Chapter 1

Scott Eyman. *The Speed of Sound*. New York: Simon & Schuster, 1997.

Lillian Gish. *The Movies, Mr. Griffith and Me*. Engelwood, NJ: Prentice Hall, 1969.

Benjamin Bowles Hampton. *History of the American Film Industry From Its Beginnings to 1931*. New York: Dover Publications, 1970.

Paul Israel. *Edison: A Life of Invention*. New York: John Wiley and Sons, 1998.

Joseph Medill Patterson. "The Nickelodeons." *Saturday Evening Post*, November 23, 1907.

Terry Ramsaye. *A Million and One Nights: A History of Motion Pictures*. New York: Simon & Schuster, 1926.

David Robinson. *From Peep Show to Palace: The Birth of American Film*. New York: Columbia University Press, 1996.

Chapter 2

Eyman. *The Speed of Sound*.

Harry M. Geduld. *The Birth of the Talkies: From Edison to Jolson*. Bloomington, Indiana: Indiana University Press, 1975.

E.S. Gregg. *Shadow of Sound*. New York: Vantage Press, 1968.

Martin Hart. "The American Widescreen Museum." Web site: http://www.widescreenmuseum.com.

John Izod. *Hollywood and the Box Office, 1895-1986.* New York: Columbia University Press, 1988.

Chapter 3

Fred E. Basten. *Glorious Technicolor: The Movies' Magic Rainbow.* Cranbury, New Jersey: A.S. Barnes and Co., Inc., 1980.

John Culhane. *Walt Disney's Fantasia.* New York: Harry N. Abrams, 1983.

Raymond Fielding. *A Technological History of Motion Pictures and Television.* Berkeley, California: University of California Press, 1967.

Neal Gabler. *Walt Disney: The Triumph of the American Imagination.* New York: Alfred A. Knopf, 2006.

Douglas Gomery. *Shared Pleasures: A History of Movie Presentation in the United States.* Madison, Wisconsin: University of Wisconsin Press, 1992.

Hart. "The American Widescreen Museum." Web site: http://www.widescreenmuseum.com.

James Lardner. *Fast Forward: Hollywood, the Japanese, and the VCR Wars.* New York: W.W. Norton and Company, 1978.

Kerry Segrave. *Drive-In Theaters: A History from Their Inception in 1933.* Jefferson, North Carolina: McFarland & Company, 1992.

Kerry Segrave. *Movies at Home: How Hollywood Came to Television.* Jefferson, North Carolina: McFarland & Company, 1999.

"Becky Sharp." *Variety,* June, 1935. Available at http://www.variety.com/review/VE1117788944.html.

"What? Color in the Movies Again?" *Fortune,* October 1934.

Chapter 4

Edward J. Epstein. *The Big Picture: The New Logic of Money and Power in Hollywood.* New York: Random House, 2005.

Joshua M. Greenberg. *From Betamax to Blockbuster: Video Stores and the Invention of Movies on Video.* Cambridge, Mass.: MIT Press, 2008.

Lardner. *Fast Forward*.

Segrave. *Movies at Home*.

Author interviews: Andre Blay, Barry Diller, Sidney Sheinberg.

Chapter 5

Ty Burr. "'Home' Looks Like Last, Not Best, of Disney's Hand-Drawn Films." Boston *Globe*, April 2, 2004.

Gabler. *Walt Disney*.

Bill Kroyer gave a keynote address at the Ojai Animation Conference on July 22, 1995, in which he discussed *Tron*. He adapted that address into an article that is available at http://www.tron-sector.com/articles/article.aspx?ID=218.

Karen Paik. *To Infinity and Beyond: The Story of Pixar Animation Studios*. San Francisco: Chronicle Books, 2006.

Michael Rubin. *Droidmaker: George Lucas and the Digital Revolution*. Gainesville, Florida: Triad Publishing Company, 2006.

James B. Stewart. *Disney War*. New York: Simon & Schuster, 2005.

Kenneth Turan. "The Secret Life of Toys: A 'Story' for All Ages." Los Angeles *Times*, November 22, 1995.

"Computers Taking Big Byte Out of Filmmaking." *Variety*, January 18, 1993.

Author interviews: James Cameron, Ed Catmull, Richard Chuang, Rex Grignon, George Joblove, Jeffrey Katzenberg, Jeff Kleiser, John Lasseter, Ed Leonard, Steven Lisberger, George Lucas, Jeff Mann, Frank Marshall, Dennis Muren, Jim Rygiel, Steve Starkey, Douglas Trumbull.

Chapter 6

Rubin. *Droidmaker*.

Author interviews: Steven Cohen, Dean Goodhill, Mark Goldblatt, Seth Haberman, Michael Kahn, Bob Lambert, Richie Marks, Walter Murch, Eric Peters, Bill Warner.

Chapter 7

Albert Abramson. "A Motion-Picture Studio of 1968." *The Quarterly of Film, Radio, and Television,* Winter 1954.

Albert Abramson. *Electronic Motion Pictures.* New York: Arno Press, 1974.

Matthew Doman. "It's Now a Digital Jungle Out There for Dis 'Tarzan.' *The Hollywood Reporter.* July 23, 1999.

Matthew Doman. "Studios, Exhibs Begin Digital Cinemas Debate." *The Hollywood Reporter,* October 20, 1999.

Matthew Doman and David Finnigan. "ShoWest Opens to Exhib Woes." *The Hollywood Reporter,* March 6, 2000.

Mark Graser. "Hollywood (Finally) Goes Digital." *Daily Variety,* January 7, 2000.

Kirk Honeycutt. "ShoWesters Shown That the Digital Future is Now." *The Hollywood Reporter,* March 12, 1999.

Jennifer Parsons. "Technology a Draw for Film Fans." *Orange County Register.* July 30, 1999.

Peter Putman. "Digital Cinema: The Studio Perspective Part II." *Millimeter,* November 1, 1999.

Andrew Revkin. "Showing in Theaters: The Digital Revolution." New York *Times,* July 3, 1999.

Author interviews: Stefan Avalos, Phil Barlow, Curt Behlmer, Paul Breedlove, Gino Campagnola, Chris Carey, Dick Cook, Doug Darrow, Mark Gill, Rob Hummel, Bob Lambert, Rick McCallum, Loren Nielsen, George Scheckel, Dave Schnuelle, Garrett Smith, Charles Swartz, Lance Weiler, Russell Wintner.

Chapter 8

Sheigh Crabtree. "Differing Views From Tech Panel." *The Hollywood Reporter,* May 21, 2001.

Carl DiOrio. "'Clones' Shows Digital Heft." *Variety,* June 24, 2002.

Michael Goldman. "Exclusive: The Lucas POV." *Millimeter.com*, March 1, 2004. Available at http://digitalcontentproducer.com/hdhdv/depth/video_exclusive_lucas_pov.

Jon Healey and P.J. Huffstutter. "Filming Without Film." Los Angeles *Times*. July 11, 2002.

Todd McCarthy. "Zodiac." *Variety*, February 26, 2007.

"Producer's Perspective." *American Cinematographer*, October 1972.

"Beijing Motion Picture & Television Conference – Day 3." The Hot Button by David Poland, August 5-6, 2000. Available at http://www.thehotbutton.com/today/hot.button/2000_thb/20000805_weekend.html

Author interviews: Tom Ackerman, Dion Beebe, Bob Beitcher, Michael Blanchard, Andrew Bujalski, Francis Ford Coppola, Allen Daviau, Roger Deakins, Caleb Deschanel, Eric Erb, Peter Guber, Bob Harvey, Peter Jackson, Victor Kemper, Michael Lynton, Rick McCallum, Fred Meyers, Daryn Okada, Tom Pollack, Steven Poster, Robert Rodriguez, Dean Semler, M. Night Shymalan, Steven Spielberg, Oliver Stone, Vittorio Storaro, Larry Thorpe, Gareth Wigan, Ben Younger.

Chapter 10

John Borland. "An end to digital piracy?" CNET News.com, April 4, 2002. Available at http://news.com.com/2008-1082-875394.html.

Clint Boulton. "MPAA, RIAA Sue File-sharers." InternetNews.com, October 3, 2001. Available at http://www.internetnews.com/bus-news/article.php/897071.

Jake Coyle. "Actor releases new film '10 Items or Less' by digital download." *Arizona Republic*, December 2, 2006.

Mark Cuban. "Grokster and the financial future of America." Blog Maverick, January 31, 2005. Available at http://www.blogmaverick.com/2005/01/31/grokster-and-the-financial-future-of-america.

Ben Fritz. "HudsonHawk.com: Movielink Will Be Another Internet Flop." *Slate.com*, Monday, November 11, 2002. Available at http://www.slate.com/?id=2073743.

Xeni Jardin. "Thinking Outside the Box Office." *Wired Magazine*, December 2005. Available at http://www.wired.com/wired/archive/13.12/soderbergh.html.

Merissa Marr. "Debut of 'Chicken Little' Gives Disney Something to Crow Over." *Wall Street Journal*, November 7, 2005.

Sarah McBride and Geoffrey A Fowler. "Studios See Big Rise in Estimates of Losses to Movie Piracy." *Wall Street Journal*, May 3, 2006.

Bruce Newman. "Why movie fans are staying home." San Jose *Mercury News*, June 20, 2005.

Martin Peers and Marissa Marr. "Blockbuster Adds Film Downloading With Movielink Deal." *Wall Street Journal*, August 9, 2007.

William Triplett. "Grokster tuned out." *Variety*, June 28, 2005. Available at http://www.variety.com/article/VR1117925116.html.

Associated Press. "Hollywood has dismal year at box office." MSNBC.com, December 19, 2005. Available at http://www.msnbc.msn.com/ id/10479868.

"Movies File Share Top Ten." P2PNet.net, September 2005. Available at http://p2pnet.net/story/6179.

Author interviews: Andre Blay, Mark Cuban, John Fithian, Morgan Freeman, Reed Hastings, Randal Kleiser, Jon Landau, Jim Ramo, Sidney Sheinberg, Todd Wagner, Pat Wyatt.

Afterword

Tatiana Siegel. "Sony renews contract with Lynton." *Variety*, October 3, 2007.

Julia Ward. "Oscar to DVD: Drop Dead." Pan and Scan: The DVD Blog, March 6, 2006. Available at http://www.panandscan.com/news/show/Awards/Oscar_to_DVD:_Drop_Dead.

Author interviews: Peter Guber, Francis Ford Coppola, Peter Jackson, Jeffrey Katzenberg, George Lucas, Michael Lynton, Steven Spielberg.

About the Author

Scott Kirsner is a journalist and blogger who writes about new ideas and their impact on the world. He edits the blog CinemaTech (http://cinematech.blogspot.com), and is the author of *The Future of Web Video: New Opportunities for Producers, Entrepreneurs, Media Companies and Advertisers*, published in March 2007. He writes regularly for *Variety* and the Boston *Globe*. Scott's writing has also appeared in the New York *Times*, *The Hollywood Reporter*, *Wired*, *Fast Company*, the Los Angeles *Times*, the San Francisco *Chronicle*, *BusinessWeek*, and *Newsweek*, among other publications. Scott is one of the founders of the Nantucket Conference on Entrepreneurship and Innovation, held each May. He also speaks and moderates regularly at entertainment industry events, including the Sundance Film Festival, the Toronto International Film Festival, and the South by Southwest Film Festival. Scott is a graduate of Boston University's College of Communications and the New World School of the Arts, in Miami. He can be reached at kirsner@pobox.com.